SUPERTECH

How America Can Win the Technology Race

SUPERTECH

How America Can Win the Technology Race

Thomas G. Donlan

BUSINESS ONE IRWIN
Homewood, Illinois 60430

127829

We recognize that certain terms in this book are trademarks, and we have made every effort to print these throughout the text with the capitalization and punctuation used by the holder of the trademark.

This publication is designed to provide accurate and authoritative information in regard to the subject matter covered. It is sold with the understanding that neither the author nor the publisher is engaged in rendering legal, accounting, or other professional service. If legal advice or other expert assistance is required, the services of a competent professional person should be sought.

From a Declaration of Principles jointly adopted by a Committee of the American Bar Association and a Committee of Publishers.

Sponsoring editor: Jeffrey A. Krames
Project editor: Margaret Haywood
Production manager: Ann Cassady
Designer: Laurie Entringer
Compositor: Eastern Graphics
Typeface: 11/13 Palatino
Printer: Book Press, Inc.

Library of Congress Cataloging-in-Publication Data

Donlan, Thomas G.
    Supertech: how America can win the technology race / Thomas G. Donlan.
      p.   cm.
    Includes bibliographical references (p.   ) and index.
    ISBN 1-55623-371-X
    1. Technology and state—United States. 2. High technology
industries—United States. I. Title.
    T21.D66 1991
    338.97307—dc20   90–49773

Printed in the United States of America
1 2 3 4 5 6 7 8 9 0 BP 8 7 6 5 4 3 2 1

Dedicated to my mother,
Elizabeth M. Donlan

Preface

"Here are two situations that might occur:

Situation A: The U.S. economy grows at a high rate, but the Japanese economy grows even faster, and over a period of several years, Japan becomes the world's leading economic power.
Situation B: The U.S. economy grows at a slower rate than situation A but faster than the Japanese economy, and the United States continues to be the world's leading economic power.

Which would you prefer?"

Harvard economist Robert Reich uses this question to separate the sheep from the goats in his audiences. A Hart-Teeter poll in May 1990 for the NBC network and *The Wall Street Journal* picked up Reich's question and produced this estimate of the national opinion:

Situation A	9%
Situation B	86%
Not sure	5%

This is no way to win the technology race, or any other kind of business competition. An economic race is a different sort of race than a horse race. We must understand that the race is really with ourselves, to measure up to our full potential as individuals and as a nation. As employees, managers, shareholders, and lenders, we must understand that we invest our labor and capital to receive a return, earnings on our investment. We will be most successful—we will win the race—if we choose our investments with the intentions of receiving the highest possible return. If we are too concerned about who's ahead, we will lose.

Clyde Prestowitz, an aggressive trade negotiator who became frustrated with endless and fruitless negotiating with Japan, advises, "The U.S. should not envy Japan's successes, the U.S. should figure out how to be more successful." He comes to different policy conclusions, but the truth of this advice overwhelms the difference between his prescriptions for managed trade and the advice you will find in this book. That's why this book, which suggests how the United States can win the technology race, is not a book about trade or trade policy, nor a book about Japan or Japanese management. Foreigners appear in this book only as they participate in the American computer and communications industries. *Supertech* is a book about American industry and American government, as they operate in a crucial sector of the American economy.

That economy is far more open in the 90s than it has ever been before, though pressures are also higher to close it than they have been in many years. Needing competition to press corporations that stagnated during the 70s, we imported competitors in many industries during the past decade. Smokestack industries such as steel and autos, sweatshop industries such as textiles and televisions, even high-tech industries such as computers and communications have found that competitors around the world are stronger, smarter, and faster than they used to be. The healthy result has been more efficient steel mills, better cars, cheaper clothing, automated televisions, powerful computers, and rapid communications.

We will look at the powerful computers and rapid communications of the 90s—a layman's idea of how the technology works, a consumer's and investor's idea of how the business evolved, and a citizen's idea of the role of our federal government in the technology and the business. We will look at high definition television, integrated circuits, supercomputing, and computer networks. There are other races and other technologies, but these offer a depth of experience as well as opportunities for the future.

Reporters are usually in a hurry to say something about a subject they have not mastered; scholars do not write their books until they have thought for a long time and believe they have something important to say. This is a book by a journalist and it falls, I hope, somewhere in the middle: I have not mastered the subjects of the computer industry and international economic competitiveness, but I have been watching the American industry and writing about the issues in this book for more than a decade. I am in a hurry to say something about these subjects, because our country is at a turning point in business policy.

The perpetual crises of the American economy during the 70s

and 80s—recession, inflation, wage and price controls, more inflation, oil price shock, deep recession, more inflation, another oil shock, another recession, "malaise," credit crunch, tight money, tax cuts, deep recession, bull market, budget deficits, trade deficits, foreign investment, tax reform, Market Meltdown—these economic events left deep scars on the political culture of the country.

With so many people to blame for such deep troubles, blaming somebody for everything became a national necessity. We blamed the Arabs, we blamed the Iranians, we blamed the Russians, we elected Jimmy Carter and then we blamed him, we blamed high-taxing, big-spending Democrats in Congress and then we reelected them, we elected Ronald Reagan and blamed supply-side economics, we blamed the Japanese.

This book attempts a different task. By looking at several key technological industries, ones that are likely to continue to grow in importance, we may come to understand our mistakes and our successes. We may see that technology and business drive each other, that the fuel is investment, and that the reward is profit. We may see that government has the power to oil the machinery, or to put sand in the gears. If we see these things, perhaps we will see that return on investment is the best indication of economic success and the best leading indicator for government policy.

We begin with an introduction to high definition television, an industry being born in the 90s. It is a symbolic industry in several ways, particularly because it resonates so well in the economic war with Japan that some people in both countries believe is being waged. Japanese companies defeated American companies in television manufacturing; Japanese companies took another American invention, the video tape recorder, and turned it into a successful consumer product often sold under American brand names.

HDTV has become immersed in politics, so we are led to a section on the role of the federal government in developing and nurturing new technology. Lawmakers and bureaucrats spend our money directly on research and development; they also have created incentives to reward private individuals and companies for their research. This leads to a discussion of our tax system, chief vehicle for economic incentives in our government.

The third section is for those who came in late to the world of electronic technology. Where did computers come from? The answer to that leads to the story of what's inside the computer—the story of the integrated circuit, or microchip. How they are made and marketed is a fascinating story of the way technology and business drive each other.

Microchips have become the subject of an international trade war between the United States and Japan, and the roots of this competition are the subject of the fourth section. Trade negotiations, trade politics, and how they are fed by the practical business of manufacturing integrated circuits are this part of the story.

The supercomputer, one of the important tools of the current industrial revolution, is the subject of the fifth and sixth sections. Supercomputers today are where the rest of the computer industry will be in a few years—not just in computer power, but in economic position, political importance, and technological character.

These main subjects—HDTV, government policy toward technology, integrated circuits, and supercomputing—come together in the seventh section, which deals with the creation of computer networks. Networks are the means by which computers communicate; they are the highways of the information industry. The national telephone network is evolving into something more like a string of computers, while computers are being strung together in a skein of growing complexity.

In the eighth section, we confront the potential of a network, worthy of the name "supertech," of enormous speed, carrying capacity, and reach, and we confront the problems of reaching that potential. Storing information is getting easy, processing information is getting quicker, but managing information remains an enormous challenge. One way or another though, people are going to learn to live "life as a node," plugged into the global network. The eighth section also brings us back to the present, with some proposals for ways to win the technology race. By the end of the journey, the reader should be well prepared to judge these proposals and the other opinions scattered throughout the book.

A Word about Sources

There's no way to identify all the newspaper, magazine and newsletter articles, press releases, studies, reports, and speeches

I have read about the electronics industry in a decade of reporting on business and economics. Some of the most important are cited in the footnotes. Among the periodicals that I use to keep up are: *Aviation Week, Barron's, Business Week, Byte and its BIX bulletin board system, Congressional Quarterly, Defense News, Electronics, Electronics News, Forbes, Fortune, High Technology Business, National Journal, The New York Times, Spectrum* (the magazine of the IEEE), *The Wall Street Journal,* and *The Washington Post.*

For intensive research, I use the Dow Jones News Retrieval and Nexis databases, and on technical points, the inexhaustible resources of the databases on Dialog. There is no better evidence for the increased productivity that the electronics industry brings than the experience of working in these databases.

Washington think tanks and interest groups fill my mailbox each day with analyses of every major issue from every side. They put their experts on parade, often over lunch. A journalist cannot fail to thank them for their efforts. Those whose labor I collected for *Supertech* include: Aerospace Industries Association; American Council for Capital Formation; American Electronics Association; American Enterprise Institute; Brookings Institution; Cato Institute; Center for Budget and Policy Priorities; Center for International Business and Trade; Computer and Business Equipment Manufacturers Association; Council on Competitiveness; Council on Research and Technology; Economic Policy Council; Heritage Foundation; Institute for International Economics; Institute of Electrical and Electronics Engineers; National Association of Broadcasters; National Cable TV Association; National Venture Capital Association; and Semiconductor Industry Association.

One reason for writing this book was the nervous excitement in government about issues of technology policy. Those executive branch organizations whose studies fill several file cabinets include:

Department of Commerce:
  Technology Administration
  International Trade Administration
  National Telecommunications and Information
    Administration
  National Institute of Standards and Technology
National Advisory Commission on Semiconductors

National Research Council
National Science Foundation
The President's Commission on Industrial Competitiveness

Congress is an endless resource. The various congressional committees and caucuses and their staffs do studies and, even better, hold hearings at which some of the biggest names and best brains in whatever field come to give the government a piece of their minds. This is often not quite as rewarding for either side as one might hope, but it's the best thing in the world for a researching journalist. The witnesses are usually asked to boil down their thoughts to three minutes, leaving 20-page or 50-page statements on file with the committee. The full statements are often very valuable. And during the many breaks in hearings, reporters can ask the witnesses the questions they wish the congressmen might have asked. I must thank many such witnesses for the almost unfailing patience they give to an inquisitive reporter.

In addition, Congress employs several brigades of researchers. I thank particularly: the Congressional Clearinghouse for the Future, the Congressional Research Service, the General Accounting Office, and the Office of Technology Assessment.

Thanks to all these sources and the researchers behind them.

There are many others whom I would thank for their more fundamental contribution to the making of this book:

Christopher Adams, who taught that writing has a dangerous and compelling permanence.

George Nesbitt, the college writing teacher who taught that clarity is superior to elegance.

Ann Crawford, who taught the craft of reporting by her example.

Ed Orloff, who taught that there is room for art in writing for a newspaper.

Shlomo Maital and Charles Berry, who taught the language and analytical structure of microeconomics.

Uve Reinhart, who brought life to the mysteries of accounting.

Stu Hunter, who created a voracious consumer of statistics.

Alan Abelson, whose suspicious nature and enthusiasm for bad news is a worthy professional beacon.

Kate Welling, Jim Meagher, and Rich Rescigno, who have edited 10 years of my copy.

Hundreds of colleagues and competitors, who have encouraged, challenged, and tolerated me.

Carol Knopes Donlan, my wife, my best editor, my best friend.

Contents

Section I
BETTER PICTURES

High definition television is coming. It's the technology of the 90s, an entertainment medium and more. It's being bottled up in Washington while the government and special interests try to decide if it will come from America or Japan. But HDTV is a product of the global economy.

1

HDTV and Regulation

Pictures and Politics

In January 1987, television broadcasters tried to rent a monster called HDTV to do a little dirty work. Then they were surprised when the monster would not go back into its cage.

The broadcasters were trying to head off a power play against them at the Federal Communications Commission. The people who make and sell beepers, pagers, and portable telephones were trying to get the FCC to give them more room on the airwaves for their services. Their target was several channels of the UHF band allocated to television broadcasting. The UHF channels are the ultra high frequency ones above channel 13. If you are over 40 years old, you probably remember that your family's first television set only had channels 2 through 13. If you are over 30, you probably remember when your television set had a UHF tuning dial that was nearly impossible to use, and the stations up there on the high dial were snowed under with interference. Your kids, though, especially those 10 and under, have probably been watching cable since birth. They would never notice that Sesame Street was on a high-number channel—on cable, all channels look alike.

When anybody suggests to the FCC that some part of the radio spectrum is not being put to its highest and best use, those who have been assigned those channels react immediately to protect themselves. If they are unable or unwilling to use what they are trying to protect, they are all the more vicious and vehement in defense—like the dog in the manger in Aesop's fable.

Broadcasters could not deny that cellular mobile telephones were becoming extremely popular and would soon need more channels to meet consumer demand. They could not deny that pocket pagers were extremely popular and would also need more channels. They could not deny that a single UHF television channel could provide bandwidth for hundreds of telephone or pager channels. And they could not deny that UHF television was a marginal business at best, long overshadowed by network television and recently by cable networks.

Since these things were undeniable, the National Association of Broadcasters (NAB) had to find a creative way to deny them. Most of the NAB's members are not networks. They are mere affiliates of networks or outright independents, many broadcasting on UHF channels. The NAB's answer was to show that the broadcast industry needed to save those unused channels for a wonderful new service that was just coming along—high definition television, or HDTV. The association got a special FCC license to demonstrate HDTV in Washington, D.C. Broadcasts on two unused UHF channels went to receivers installed—with a fine sensitivity for power—in the offices of the FCC and in the U.S. Capitol.

Edward Fritts, president of the NAB, proudly demonstrated the wonderful pictures and high-fidelity sound to regulators and lawmakers. He said if UHF channels were taken from the broadcasters, that would "preclude America's broadcasters from developing HDTV as a free over-the-air service to the nation. It is a fact that consumers will be able to enjoy this improved broadcast technology in the near future. The question is whether the FCC will let them."[1]

This monster called HDTV was effective. The NAB easily achieved its short-term objective. The raid on UHF channels died quickly. But the broadcasters had created a monster they could not control, that would come back to haunt them—worse, to compete with them. The HDTV picture is remarkably sharp. Its superiority to conventional television pictures is obvious and makes anyone say, "Where can I get one of those and how much is it?" That is what congressmen were saying as they walked away from the NAB demonstration.

But the congressmen learned that this new technology, with all its appeal, with all its promise to revolutionize television the way color TV did in the 50s and 60s and the way video tape machines did in the 70s and 80s, was MADE IN JAPAN. It was a 100 percent Japanese product, developed by NHK (Nippon Hoso Kaisha), the Japanese national television network. Fritts's promise to the contrary, U.S. researchers were still in the labs and showed no signs of emerging with a product to sell.

This was 1987, when the trade deficit with Japan was reaching new heights, and the power of the trade deficit as a political issue was growing proportionately. Two years of driving down the dollar under the administration of Treasury Secretary James Baker had done little to increase American exports or decrease American imports. Many Democrats were trying on campaign positions with a protectionist style. The time demanded the question: Why is the U.S. electronics industry ignoring this great new industry?

Over the next few years high definition television would become a practical economic issue and to some, a symbol of the decline of the United States. The debate over HDTV incorporated technical, industrial, economic, and political issues. Understanding the competition in electronics in the 90s requires that those issues be understood.

Inside the Television

The National Television System Committee was organized in 1940 to establish technical standards for black and white television in America.[2] For reasons that seemed good to engineers at the time, they established that U.S. television stations would broadcast an amplitude modulation (AM) signal, like the radio signals of the day, on a channel that would be 6 megahertz wide. (Translation: The signal would send a radio signal vibrating at the rate of 6 million waves per second, and information would be conveyed by the size of the waves.) As with the motion pictures of the day, the picture would be 4 units wide by 3 units high. The picture would be composed of 525 scanning lines per frame, with 42 lines blanked out for separation, leaving 483 lines of picture information. Each line would contain 440 dots. The frames would be sent at 30 frames per second, but to achieve a better picture, the signal would actually be composed of half-frames sent at 60 half-frames per second. Each half-frame would incorporate every other line of the picture. This "interlacing" speeded up the flow of picture information to the eye, making the picture seem sharper than it could otherwise be, given the amount of information a 6 megahertz channel can carry.

In the early 1950s, another National Television Systems Committee agreed to add color to the broadcast signal without increasing the 6 megahertz bandwidth or changing existing black and white sets in any way. They did this by coding additional information on the existing signal in a technique developed by RCA called subcarrier modulation. Drawbacks, which you may have noticed on your own set, included a loss of brightness on black and white sets, and an annoying tendency for bright colors to produce interference in the sound or to produce ghost images.

Television grew to a worldwide medium. The Japanese adopted the NTSC standard whole; the Europeans changed one feature, choosing a 625-line frame and getting a slightly sharper picture.

Since color was added, improvements to television have been limited to improvements in television receivers. Transistorized circuitry has replaced vacuum tubes; three electron guns write different color elements of the scanning lines making up the picture; a black mask surrounds each picture element and makes it seem sharper; filters and coding circuits clean up and enhance the signal to reduce noise, static, and false images. This last category, cleaning up and enhancing the signal, has been propelled by the power of the computer to the point where the interior of a top-of-the-line TV is essentially a picture tube and a specialized computer.

What We Don't See

As we sit and watch our favorite shows, we don't notice the flaws in NTSC television. We have been conditioned since childhood to accept them. Some of us, in fact, feel that programs made on videotape are more "real" than the objectively higher quality pictures made originally on film. We learned that live TV "looks like that," and live TV is what's happening. But anyone who has tried to follow a hockey game on TV knows that television pictures have a problem with fast-moving images. The picture is also sensitive to interference, which produces ghosts, flicker, distortions, and false colors. We live with it all, because we don't know any better.

Another flaw is historic. The 4 by 3 screen is no longer the movie industry standard. Wide screen movies came in about 1955. So when a movie is adapted for TV the wide image is either chopped off at the edges or scrunched together like an accordion, or a little of both. To see the wide image, try renting a recent Woody Allen movie on videotape. Allen refuses to allow chopping or scrunching, so his movies come with big black stripes at top and bottom. The remaining picture has the proportions of the wide screen.

Other flaws are easiest to see on a big screen set. When the TV picture is enlarged up to a 50-inch screen, the kind you find in sports bars, each picture element—the dots that make up the picture, called *pixels* for short—grows bigger in proportion. To appreciate the big screen, paradoxically, you must sit proportionately farther from it, until its apparent size is back down to the apparent size of a home TV screen when viewed from 6 to 10 feet away. (Six times the height of the picture is considered ideal for NTSC.) Sitting close to a big screen set makes most viewers feel that the image is dissolving into a moving swirl of dots. (Conversely, the NTSC picture provides excellent definition on a Sony "Watchman" or other very small screen.)

There's no such problem with movies, even if you have to sit up front. That's because film has a much greater density of picture elements. Each one is much smaller, so the film can be projected onto a much bigger screen. Even on a small screen, the quality of the picture is far better. It could be that good on television, too.

A Technological End Run

There have been a number of proposals to improve the existing NTSC signal, but broadcasters were unwilling to disrupt their operations for limited benefits. And large benefits, that is, vastly improved pictures, would require expansion of the information carried on each television channel. Doubling the number of possible pixels in each direction quadruples the number of pixels and quadruples the quality of the picture. But quadrupling the amount of information would require either expanding the bandwidth of the channel to more than 6 megahertz or totally reconstructing the way television information is encoded on the radio signal. Either is technically feasible, but since broadcasting everywhere is owned or at least heavily regulated by the government, powerful political considerations have overridden mere technical feasibility. Making 160 million television sets in the United States obsolete seemed the very essence of political poison.

In the 80s, however, two unregulated technologies reached maturity in the United States and a third was born. Cable television is available to more than 80 percent of U.S. households and more than half of them are actually connected to a cable.[3] And videotape machines, propelled by the brand new videotape rental industry, became a commonplace item in the average home, with 66 percent of households owning at least one unit.[4] Just coming into existence is a third vehicle for television transmission, the direct broadcast satellite, sending signals from space to a rooftop antenna. The first commercial direct broadcast satellite system in the United States ran for about a year in the mid-80s, but was a commercial flop. The market, potentially spread out over the whole United States, was too thin and hard to serve for a fledgling company with limited resources. But about 2 million U.S. homes are part of an unofficial satellite broadcasting system, using large dish antennas to pick up satellite signals being transmitted to cable systems. New satellite systems in Japan and Europe were just getting off the ground at the end of the 80s and new U.S. ventures were announced, with service to begin, perhaps, in the mid-90s.

Videotape is a wholly unregulated industry. Except for ubiquitous rules about shielding stray radio energy, nobody tells the manufacturers how to build their machines, how to hook them up, or what to charge. Nobody requires the tape rental shops to offer tapes in a particular format or at a particular price. Despite governmental neglect, standard formats have evolved and the medium prospers. Cable was never subject to technical regulation and in a 1984 law, Congress freed the cable systems from local price regulation. Direct broadcast satellite TV is subject to national licensing and allocation of radio frequencies, but not to any particular set of broadcasting standards.

As these new systems for distribution of television programming grew in importance, not just in the United States but in Europe and Japan, experimentation with whole new systems of television broadcasting went on in labs around the world. Laboratory engineers are sometimes free to ignore the world of politics and regulation and hundreds of millions of conventional television sets.

In the Labs of NHK

Japan Broadcasting Corp. scientists tried to find out first what people needed in a television set. They tried different frame rates, screen sizes, angles of vision and aspect ratios, different interlacing patterns, numbers of lines per frame, and so on. Then they designed a system that seemed to meet their "psychophysical" requirements.

This was not entirely an ivory tower operation. The Japanese designers believed they needed more than 1,000 lines per frame to come acceptably close to the resolution of contemporary 35 mm movie film. They selected 1,125 lines. Double the U.S. standard would have been 1,050 lines; double the European standard would have been 1,250 lines; NHK settled for something in between, apparently because they wanted to avoid charges of favoritism. NHK kept the 30 frames per second rate with interlaced half-frames—to reduce the amount of information that would have to be stuffed into the channel, and the engineers picked an aspect ratio of 5.3 units wide by 3 units high—close to but not exactly the contemporary wide screen movie proportion.

The Japanese studio system requires about 30 megahertz per HDTV channel, the equivalent of five NTSC channels. For broadcasting, NHK adopted a signal compression system called MUSE (Multiple Sub-Nyquist Sampling Encoding), which crammed the signal into 8.4 megahertz at some cost in sharpness and realistic portrayal of images in motion. The MUSE system also can be decoded to produce an NTSC signal, but that would require the consumer with an NTSC set to buy a decoding box. Japanese TV makers are putting two receivers in the same TV set, so that purchasers of new HDTV sets can also watch conventional programming on the same screen.

NHK's choices left plenty for engineers to argue about. Sending the whole frame, instead of interlacing, would have been a big improvement, but would have required twice the bandwidth in the channel, more than it seemed videocassette recorders could handle. But in the mid-80s, NHK had the only system far enough

along in development to argue about. NHK proposed its system
to the International Radio Consultative Committee (CCIR for its
French initials) for adoption as an international studio standard,
and Japanese diplomats won the support of the U.S. State Department, much to the subsequent dismay of American nationalists.
European interests, however, derailed the proposal in 1986, aim-
ing to protect the European TV system and the European TV industry. Almost immediately, European electronics companies announced their own HDTV program with a format incompatible
with the Japanese system. A nine-nation European consortium
called "Eureka Project 95," led by NV Philips of the Netherlands
and Thomson SA of France, is developing improvements to conventional TV and a satellite broadcasting HDTV system. Eureka is
backed by government and industry funding in the billions of dollars, though they have little to show for it.

The international competition may be enough to ensure that no
studio standard for HDTV will be adopted worldwide by the
CCIR. However, the 1,125-line, interlaced, 30-frame per second
NHK studio system has been used to make movies, television
programs, and commercials in the U.S., Canada, Japan, and Western Europe. Sony sells cameras, monitors, and tape machines
using the NHK system. What an international bureaucracy cannot agree to do, the market has a chance to do.

The FCC Bars the Door

A U.S. bureaucracy is intent on doing what the market might
have been able to do alone. In the United States, at least nine
competing versions of broadcast HDTV emerged and the Federal
Communications Commission appointed a panel of experts,
drawn from the production, cable, broadcasting, and engineering
industries, to study and evaluate them.

The Advisory Committee on Advanced Television Service
seems mostly designed to prove that the United States of America
is still Number One in what Shakespeare called "the insolence of
office and the law's delay." It's chaired by Richard Wiley, a former chairman of the FCC and a Washington lawyer with many
clients in telecommunications. (He likes to make the self-depreca-
tory—and accurate—remark that "Washington's growth industry
is the high-tech, regulatory lawyer—a guy who's pretty good with

numbers but doesn't have the personality to be an accountant.")
The Advisory Committee brings together 34 representatives of
production companies, broadcasters, cable system operators, system designers, trade associations, and bureaucrats, plus dozens
more people who only serve on ancillary subcommittees and
working parties. Except for the bureaucrats, it duplicates a private
sector group that had been treading water since 1983. To some, it
is important that this disparate group manages to agree; others
say they have agreed on nothing important.

The advisory committee, and the FCC that created it, did agree
on something extremely important. They agreed that they were
not choosing the best HDTV standard but the best HDTV standard that could be *broadcast* compatible with the NTSC system.
Compatible here means what was done when color TV was introduced: the HDTV television system that the advisory committee
chooses *must* include an NTSC signal that conventional televisions can receive.

Why? The FCC is like most regulatory bodies; it has become a
defender of the interests it regulates. In this case, the FCC is defending local broadcasters and trying to make sure they can compete on an equal technological footing with cable, tape, and satellite television.

Making HDTV Fit

There are three basic ways to produce HDTV compatible with
conventional television: widening existing channels from 6 megahertz to 9 megahertz or 12 megahertz; simultaneously broadcasting NTSC and HDTV on two separate 6 megahertz channels; or
somehow condensing and coding to combine the HDTV information onto an existing NTSC signal in 6 megahertz. FCC Chairman
Alfred Sikes decreed in March 1990 that the commission wants a
simulcast system.

An advantage of simulcast is that a system designed from
scratch with powerful signal processing and memory chips could
produce a far better signal because it could pack much more information inside a separate 6 megahertz channel than could be done
by adding high definition information to a standard signal. In addition, a completely different HDTV signal could be broadcast on
channels that are not used now because an NTSC signal would
interfere with programming in neighboring cities. Zenith was the

first to propose such a system to the FCC, and Sikes's endorsement of simulcast was taken to mean Zenith has the inside track. Early in 1990, Zenith put all its remaining resources behind HDTV and consumer electronics. It sold its profitable personal computer business and kept the TV business, which has been losing money since at least the mid-80s. Also, it entered a joint venture on HDTV with AT&T.

The FCC's decision on simulcast narrowed down the field and required others to go back to the lab for some more engineering. NHK had a simulcast system ready; the U.S. division of Thomson got together with North American Philips, the NBC network, and Sarnoff Laboratories to field another entry called Advanced Television Research Consortium. Strictly American applicants were Faroudja Laboratories of California and the Massachusetts Institute of Technology.

Digital Surprise

On the last day for filing at the FCC, General Instrument unveiled a surprise entry, an all-digital system. GI based its technology on the video scrambling devices it invented for HBO and other cable TV channels to protect their satellite broadcasts from unauthorized listeners. All the other HDTV systems are based on the analog systems of conventional television; only GI is completely digital.

What's the difference? An analog signal is a continuous, constantly varying voltage or current in which the size and frequency of the peaks and valleys carry information about the brightness of each point on the picture. A digital signal is carried by binary digits, or bits, which can have only two values, on and off, 0 and 1. It takes 24 bits to express each possible value in the analog signal, and to make the digital equivalent of an analog signal requires many thousands of digital evaluations of the signal per second. As complicated as this sounds, it is duck soup for a computer equipped with special digital signal processing circuits.

Once a TV signal is digitized, it can be manipulated by more specialized computer circuits. The information in it can be refined and compressed without losing accuracy. Compressing analog signals always results in a loss of quality. General Instrument compresses the information in its HDTV signal by a 50 to 1 ratio, but it promises that its system will not lose quality in broadcast or satellite transmission, stages in which the other systems rely on an analog signal. "If you had digital NTSC, you'd think it was HDTV because the clean digital signal makes so much difference," says Larry Dunham of General Instrument. "For HDTV, you should digitize at the camera and never go back to analog until you reach the picture tube."[5]

The other applicants used digital circuitry in part, and many observers of the HDTV scene had been saying that digital TV would eventually usurp whatever hybrid system the FCC might choose. But it came as a surprise to find a small cable TV equipment company offering digital technology in 1990.[6]

Within a few months of the General Instrument announcement, digital television went from pie-in-the-sky to state-of-the-art. Compression Labs produced its own version of digital video compression and found a partner in a satellite broadcasting venture called SkyPix. Comsat Labs, MIT, Sarnoff Research Center, and North American Philips all said they were working on the technology.

When They All Get Together

All these interests and the interests of broadcasters, producers, and various government agencies, including the Defense Department, are represented on the FCC's advisory committee. With so much in conflict, they fight about many things and resolve very little. Especially, they fight about money. In March 1990, the advisory committee wrangled over whether the companies proposing HDTV systems should pay for the testing process. The guy from Zenith, Robert Hansen, started it. He said Zenith hasn't been very profitable recently and can scarcely afford something like a million dollars as its share of the testing procedure. "We got into this to save terrestrial broadcasting," Hansen nobly declared, adding that broadcasters ought to pay for being saved.

Ward Quaal, a consultant, favored the broadcasters: "The true gainers in the long run are the proponents." He suggested that when one proponent wins, he pay back the fees of the losers.

Joe Donahue of Thompson Consumer Electronics, and John Henderson, of Sarnoff Laboratories, said the idea of charging the proponents is self-defeating. "To go back to the proponents [for money] will subtract too much from R&D," said Donahue. "Such fees will come straight out of our development budget," Henderson echoed. Jay Ling of MIT, also offering a system, said the university has no budget for such fees. "The major beneficiaries are the TV broadcasters and the consumer electronics industry," he said, so they should pay.

These representatives of major U.S. companies strained at a million-dollar ticket to a competition for control of a business they claim to believe will be worth $20 billion a year within a decade. But ultimately they prevailed. The FCC made the entry fee $175,000. Taxpayers are putting up more than $2 million a year for the testing.

Still, the exercise is going nowhere, slowly. In March 1990, two years after the advisory committee was formed, FCC Chairman Alfred Sikes announced that the FCC will boldly push for fast adoption of a technical standard for HDTV broadcasting—in the second quarter of 1993. The advisory committee members agreed that was pretty tough, but they accepted Sikes's admonishment to finish their testing and advising by September 1992. They all congratulated one another on their bravery, determination, and efficiency.

"We don't want to hold up HDTV," Sikes said. "We want to avoid endless legal proceedings in the midst of a dynamic market development." Amazingly, nobody laughed. Holding up HDTV is the purpose of the entire exercise. Sikes and the members of the advisory commission are involved in a government-sponsored conspiracy in restraint of trade. They have combined to assure the exclusion of the NHK system from the American broadcast market.

Adopting the NHK system right away is a practical solution to every interest except that of the local broadcasters. Nationwide network programming, such as CBS or HBO, is now carried on communications satellites. The satellites could just as easily deliver HDTV programs to the 85 percent of homes that can receive cable; anybody else could stick a dish on his roof. But local broadcasters would be stuck with second-class pictures, and probably second-class programming. They might even lose their access to cable, if cable operators had to kick something off the system to make room for HDTV.

Joseph Flaherty of CBS put the issue this way:

A terrestrial HDTV broadcast system must be devised to maintain the American system of broadcasting. . . . Terrestrial broadcasters need to deliver a quality of picture and sound that is competitive with other media delivery systems. Anything less than this basic principle will be detrimental to terrestrial broadcasters and the public we serve. . . .

The capability of competing home delivery systems to deliver a full quality HDTV signal emphasizes the need to develop a terrestrial HDTV broadcasting system which will maintain competitive parity with all other services of HDTV program distribution. A failure to provide sufficient radio frequency spectrum for the terrestrial broadcaster could put terrestrial broadcasting in a position of irreversible inferiority.[7]

Analysis of Flaherty's sentiments shows that he carefully equates the public and the American way of life with broadcasting interests. That's understandable for a representative of broadcast interests, but members of the public ought to ask whether their happiness depends on the continued profitability of local television stations.

Many local broadcasters paid big bucks for their licenses during the 80s, a period of frenzied trading of broadcast properties. Some of them are big media conglomerates who own newspapers. All of them are politically powerful. The FCC is afraid to tell them to take a hike. Zenith Chairman Jerry Pearlman was honest about it: "In my view there's no way we are not going to protect the terrestrial broadcaster, because he's the guy who gives free news coverage to the politician."[8] Commissioners and staff echo the pap from the National Association of Broadcasters about Americans' "right" to receive free broadcasts, and about the local stations' devotion to local news and public service. Consumers should be glad the FCC at least rejected the broadcasters' most outrageous suggestion: Robert Wright of NBC urged that FCC rules be extended to ban incompatible HDTV cable and tape systems as well.

What the Networks Say

In June of 1988 Rep. Edward J. Markey, D-Mass., chairman of the House telecommunications and finance subcommittee, took testimony from the chief executives of the three major networks. Thomas S. Murphy, chairman of Capital Cities/ABC, Laurence A. Tisch, president of CBS, and Robert C. Wright, president of NBC, came out foursquare for preserving the current system. Although they sit at the top of the current system providing national programming, they described the system as a hometown, mom-and-apple-pie service.

Murphy declared: "Local broadcasting is unique, both in its ability to respond to local issues and local community needs and in its ability to provide the public with diverse national and local entertainment, news, and sports."

Said Tisch: "The public should not have to bear the risk that HDTV would not become fully available to the local broadcasters and networks who have made the investment and built our system of free over-the-air broadcasting."

Wright of NBC made the best plea: "Broadcasters and the FCC have a responsibility to protect the 140 million sets currently in use, representing a consumer investment of approximately $70 billion [that's $500 per set]. Second, if we are concerned about free over-the-air television and its role in serving the needs of the American public, then broadcasters must be able to respond swiftly to the arrival of advanced television as rapidly as their competitors in rival media." Never was a question more strongly begged:

What if we are not concerned about free over-the-air local television? What if we cannot think of any local program we like? What if we think our local cable companies, with several channels of local news, local government coverage, local entertainment, are already doing a far better and far more localized job than the local broadcasters?

Rep. James Cooper of Tennessee put some of those questions on the table: "I am worried that what we are seeing on this panel are three very large, very powerful dinosaurs who are protecting their feeding grounds. It worries me very much that due to your vested interests and a very narrow channel bandwidth, you are willing and interested to do virtually everything within your considerable power to slow the access of the American consumer to this magnificent new technology."

Wright replied on practical and idealistic grounds. Practically, he denied the charge, asserting that networks could easily survive. Each network sends its signal to satellites and need not care how it's received or relayed. The response, while true, overlooked a fundamental secret of network economics. In most years, ABC, CBS, and NBC make more profit from their owned and operated affiliate stations than they do from their networks. Their interests are in large part the same as the independent broadcasters.

Idealistically, if that's the right word, Wright said he and his fellow network executives were defending "the portions of the public who do not have access to that hard [cable] wire who have chosen not to spend the money," which sounds as if he wanted the congressman to believe he cares about people who can't afford to buy the products advertised on his network. "If the statement is that we are desperately trying to preserve the ability of that non-cable customer to receive an adequate and technologically acceptable picture, then we will plead guilty to that."

Cooper, who said many of his constituents in the hills of Tennessee have satellite dishes, translated. The view of the networks, as he put it, is "Don't let the consumer vote with his pocketbook because he might put us out of business."

Tisch weighed in with the warning that Cooper was heading down the road to universal pay TV, but Cooper's cross-questioning produced this frank concession: "We're here to preserve free television because we do preserve shareholder value through the medium of free television."

Markey, however, didn't buy Cooper's argument. "This is clearly an issue that cannot just be left to chance, that cannot be left to some invisible hand to resolve. This is clearly a case where the government has to work closely with the leaders of our private industry to achieve the goals which we establish, which I believe at heart include the maintenance of the over-the-air free broadcasting system in this country."

The FCC's Experience

There is a close historical comparison, in radio, to the HDTV issue of today. The FCC acted more wisely in guiding the transition from AM radio to FM radio. It accepted industry standards for FM broadcast, and later for FM stereo, without much worry over the damage that would be done to owners of AM stations. The commissioners probably didn't expect FM broadcasters to offer such attractive programming in the higher fidelity format: the whole baby boom generation abandoned Cousin Brucie and Murray the K for the better sound of album rock stations. Would the FCC of the 60s have openly allowed the financial damage that was done to AM station owners?

Certainly, today's FCC would not do so. With its interminable technical evaluation, the FCC has decided to reinvent the wheel, and it's trying to evaluate competing technical proposals—for

wheels with wire spokes, wheels with steel spokes, wheels with
no spokes, wheels with disc brakes, wheels with drum brakes,
wheels with large tires, wheels with soft tires, you name it. The
slower this process goes, the better the chance that an American
wheel will outperform the Japanese wheel. The emergence of the
General Instrument digital system suggests the strategy is working, but it is just the same, and just as misguided, as the European strategy for slowing down adoption of the NHK studio standard.

During the process, no business, Japanese or American, is
likely to take a chance on an HDTV system for cable or tape or
satellite that would be made obsolete by an order of the FCC.
Thus, while the process goes on, local broadcasters are safe from
competition. Any bets on how long the process will go on?

Here's a clue: the advisory committee is constructing a lab in
Alexandria, Va., to do exhaustive engineering tests of HDTV systems. It plans to drag a whole lot of people into an auditorium
and play all the types of HDTV at them, asking which one they
like the best. This, of course, has to be set up so as not to favor
one system over the others by some technical accident.

As part of its elaborate protection against favoritism, the technical subcommittee unanimously agreed not to use a direct view
set (one like conventional sets, in which the works are behind the
screen and the viewer sits in front). They chose to use only a
projection set, similar to those seen in bars, and in the homes of
real TV sports fans. Why? Especially why when all agreed that
most early purchasers of HDTV systems will buy direct view
monitors? They couldn't find a direct view set that would accommodate all nine systems that was also big enough to put a reasonable number of people in front of for the subjective screenings. A
38-inch Sony monitor would not accommodate the fast scanning
rate needed by the systems submitted by Zenith and MIT. But the
technical staff would rather have a consistent test than a useful
test.

A Lesson from the Past

More than 20 years ago, AT&T Bell Labs brought a new technology called cellular mobile telephony to the FCC for approval. It
took the FCC more than 10 years to decide to test the new tech-

nology, four more years to run the test and evaluate it, two more years to decide how to allocate the precious radio spectrum, two more years to award the first licenses for big cities, and three more years to award licenses in smaller cities and rural areas. The popularity and the potential market for cellular telephones was never in dispute. The only issue was whether the FCC would let the telephone company dominate the market.

HDTV presents much the same issue, and it's being decided much the same way. Today, instead of being frightened of Ma Bell's monopoly, the FCC is frightened of Japan Inc. and of communications media the commission does not control. Once again, the commission is determined to protect a narrow slice of American business interests at the expense of a great many American consumers.

There is no question that the American public will buy better home entertainment systems as soon as they are available. There is no question that the people who sell them, and the people who produce the programs, and the people who advertise on the new medium will be serving a huge market worth billions of dollars a year. The only issue is who those people will be.

The FCC has decided those people will be today's American local broadcasters. Them, or nobody. The FCC is working against the interests of American consumers in favor of those few individuals and corporations owning television stations. Is this regulation in the public interest?

The FCC should boot the whole HDTV issue out onto M Street. Let the proponents settle their differences themselves, if they can. Let them hire a hall and lock themselves in until they agree on one standard. Once a similar process got started in cellular telephone licensing, it didn't take more than a couple of months. But if they cannot agree, let them invite the top executives of trade associations of broadcasters, cable system operators, videotape renters, TV producers, and so forth to view the systems, as best each proponent can muster. If the trade associations cannot agree, let them write the names of the competitors on slips of paper and draw one from a hat. And if that won't do, the U.S. electronics industry will have to let the Japanese have the business.

Or, if the FCC must be involved, it should be on entirely different terms. The commission should disband the advisory council of special interest representatives, close the HDTV evaluation lab, and hire an auctioneer, who will take bids from all proponents of standards, including the Japanese. The winning bidder would receive the FCC's blessing for 10 years. After that, another auction. In a system of open bids, the business will go to the HDTV system whose owners and financial backers have the most confidence and expectation of profit.

2
HDTV and Competitiveness

Technological Potential

HDTV has become a national economic and political issue. It is one focus of a great national debate about industrial policy—the idea that the government should intervene in business to keep the economy strong. HDTV is also a focus of a national debate about competitiveness, the idea that the United States economy is declining, especially in comparison to the Rising Sun of Japan.

What's the point? Why all the fuss about a new way of looking at soap operas? The dominance of the FCC in HDTV up to now obscures the fact that HDTV is more than just a TV set. HDTV technologies are the most important computer, communications, and electronic component technologies of the 90s. Some advocates have dropped the acronym HDTV in favor of HRS, for high resolution systems. The new term is meant to avoid the idea that this new technology is merely an entertainment medium, and to promote the idea that it is a core technology of the future. We will stick with HDTV because it is familiar.

HDTV systems will include major subsystems of great use in other electronics products. High resolution displays (the picture tube or liquid crystal display unit) and digital signal processing chips (the microcircuits that clean up and enhance the picture) are or will be just as important in computers. In fact, high resolution displays are here now in graphics workstations; thus computer markets are pulling HDTV components along. But if HDTV becomes a mass market, the entertainment medium may lead computer technology. Similarly, digital signal processing chips now are required for military radars and guidance systems but may find a market in HDTV.

HDTV technologies will be used in integrated systems merging several different existing products. At home, the TV set will contain enough processing power and memory to serve as a standalone computer or as a node on a national information network. It will be the gateway for services ranging from videotext to movie rentals to TV telephone systems. The merging of product technologies will lead to a merging of the products themselves. The HDTV set can be the terminal for multimedia database systems in which moving pictures, still pictures, voice and sound data, and text data from a variety of sources can all be accessed and processed on one machine. Telecommuting—connecting a worker at home to the computer at work—is already a reality; there's room for much more of it.

HDTV systems will be the platforms for a wide range of peripheral devices, such as printers, copying machines, cameras, and video recorders. In the new system, images from all sources can be assembled, edited, and processed in the computing part of the machine.

HDTV also will be part of scientific computing through the common application and development of underlying technologies. Examples are electronic packaging (methods of assembling components to work together reliably and effectively), parallel processing (a computer technology that handles many streams of data at once, especially well suited to imaging), and image-generating algorithms (mathematical formulations that underlie computer programs). "These three example technologies are among the most important underlying technologies in supercomputers, computer graphics, and computer-aided design," concluded a group of analysts working for a consortium of high-tech companies.[1]

HDTV technologies also will be part of visual computing, in which a powerful computer applied to a difficult problem gives its solution in a picture instead of hundreds of sheets filled with numbers. Simulation systems such as pilot trainers are already a remarkably useful substitute for "real" experience; HDTV technology linked to supercomputers makes some people start talking about "artificial reality."

Political Potential

High definition television has been nurtured as a political issue by several congressmen, including Rep. Edward Markey, the Massachusetts Democrat; California Democratic Rep. Mel Levine; Pennsylvania Republican Rep. Don Ritter; and Sen. Al Gore, Democrat of Tennessee. Markey held the first HDTV hearing in October 1987.

"If we do not get a handle on where we as a Nation are going with this technology, by 1990 or 1991 the marketplace will take care of it for us," Markey declared in opening the hearing. "But we must recognize that the marketplace decision may not be the best decision for the American broadcast and cable industries, domestic manufacturers, or consumers." Markey's lack of trust in markets was expressed a few minutes later in more forceful terms: "We intend on making policies; we intend on making the decisions, and we don't want either the technology or the regulatory process or the courts to make those decisions." He concluded: "Either we put the Government and labor and the electronics industry and the universities together today, and we put together a policy and we understand what our strategy is, or we are going to go down the same road that we have gone with automobiles and VCRs and every other consumer product."

Rep. Ritter, a member of the subcommittee, addressed the competitiveness issue: "Why are we so far behind? Why have we come out so far behind on what is the next revolution in consumer electronics, the next revolution in television, which has put American broadcasting at a crossroads?"

Economic Potential

HDTV became a hot issue. During 1988 and 1989, the electronics industry and a related industry of Washington lobbyists, lawyers, and consultants produced stacks of reports about the importance of HDTV to the U.S. economy.

A study done by consultant Larry F. Darby for the Commerce Department's National Telecommunications and Information Administration[2] dwelled heavily on the time it takes for new consumer electronics products to penetrate the U.S. market, cautioning that acceptance of HDTV might be more like the tepid acceptance rate for audio component stereo, satellite dish antennas, or projection TVs, rather than the comparatively rapid acceptance of color TV, personal computers, and videocassette recorders. The former group took more than 12 years to reach 1 percent of U.S. households; the latter took less than eight. (Darby did not study two products closely related to HDTV: cable television with pay TV and compact disc audio, both of which grew faster than any of those studied.)

From the historical examples, Darby extrapolated a path for HDTV, in which the first million sets would be sold by 1997, reaching 10.5 million sets a year in 2002 and 18.6 million sets a year in 2008, by which time 93 percent of U.S. households would own HDTV sets and the market would largely be a replacement market. HDTV videotape players would track this growth at first, because the tape would be the only reliable source of HDTV programs in the first five years of the Darby model. Later, as broadcast HDTV became widely available, tape machine sales would trail set sales.

Darby conceded that estimates of prices for HDTV was "pretty much guesswork," and that without price information, the rate of acceptance and sales figures were not reliable. It would make a big difference, he said, whether HDTV sets will cost $1,500 or $600.

"This scenario is as realistic as the key assumptions which underlie it," he said. Those assumptions included healthy economies, high levels of consumer spending on electronics, favorable product development and pricing trends, timely and decisive standard-setting, vigorous competition among manufacturers, and widespread availability of programming.

"The details of the scenarios do not really matter. Under a broad range of alternative assumptions, the scenarios imply that future development of this technology may offer both enormous opportunity and significant risk to U.S. interests," Darby said.

Pushing the Panic Button

One contribution that computer programmers have made to the English language is the saying, "garbage in, garbage out." The

Darby report was at least guesswork in, guesswork out. So was a later study published by the American Electronics Association. It looked econometric, but it was a compilation of many guesses. It was a survey of members, esteemed in the industry, who almost unanimously pushed the panic button:

> There are chilling implications for nonparticipation. The United States needs to gain a proprietary position in key Advanced Television markets to ensure that technological know-how remains in this country. The end reward for those who design, manufacture, and sell to Advanced Television markets is dominance of computers and telecommunications.

AEA published its report with columns of numbers projecting sales out to 2010 (an 11 million-unit year), accurate to the last dollar. A footnote revealed they were simply the averages of market share projections by industry analysts and company executives—more guesswork.

Despite its shaky statistical status, the AEA study made two major contributions that would dominate the HDTV debate.

The AEA stressed that HDTV will not merely be a consumer entertainment medium. It said the technologies for making large high definition displays, for rapid processing of complex signals, and for manufacturing the product in high quality at an acceptable price are likely to be critical in computers and telecommunications and all up and down the electronics industry. HDTV technology would be likely to take root in medical imaging, scientific instruments, and computing as well as entertainment.

The AEA compared the U.S. electronics industry to a biological food chain, in which many interdependent segments may suffer if one link is lost:

> If HDTV technology makes U.S. semiconductor designs obsolete, the U.S. will lose its innovative edge in many markets—not just the direct $3 billion one in HDTV semiconductors.
>
> If the U.S. does not choose to reenter consumer electronics via HDTV, the country as a whole is likely to experience a continued declining world market share in automated manufacturing equipment, personal computers, and semiconductors. In addition, telecommunications and other strategically critical industries could follow.

Loss of these markets will contribute to the loss of both high and low end American jobs in nonconsumer electronics fields, significantly increase the U.S. trade deficit, increase the national debt, and lead to the erosion and eventual loss of a U.S. manufacturing base. As is already happening to the semiconductor industry, the U.S. will cease to be the primary innovator in significant end use electronics markets. Implicit in this decline over time is the United State's loss of position as a major world power.[3]

The AEA's vision of an industrial apocalypse included publication of detailed projections about the nascent HDTV business. Reporting what it said was the consensus of industry leaders and analysts surveyed, the AEA predicted that ignoring or losing high definition television would:

- Leave to "others" a world market for HDTV sets and videotape recorders with cumulative sales of $260 billion by 2010. Just a 10 percent share of the U.S. market would be a $1 billion a year business.
- Deny U.S. semiconductor makers the chance to sell $22 billion worth of chips to U.S. HDTV makers. AEA gave U.S. makers no chance to sell to foreign TV producers.

In addition to these direct effects, the AEA also predicted large indirect effects, worth hundreds of billions of dollars a year by 2010, on the whole electronics industry, including loss of U.S. markets in personal computers, semiconductors, and automated manufacturing equipment.

The Department of Commerce Joins In

These studies and others fed off each other by mutual citation until Washington reached a state of high concern about the electronics industry and HDTV. Congressmen Levine and Ritter even formed a House HDTV caucus, a high-tech counterpart of the coal caucus, steel caucus, footwear caucus, mushroom caucus, and other organizations by which members organize to lobby each other. Secretary of Commerce Robert Mosbacher encountered the new *zeitgeist* at his Senate confirmation hearing in 1989.

Senator Lloyd Bentsen, the Texan who was the 1988 Democratic vice presidential candidate, told Mosbacher he was "particularly concerned about high-temperature superconductivity and high definition television in trying to identify coming industries where we have to be internationally competitive."

A nominee always agrees with a senator if he can, and Mosbacher went all the way:

> I share with you the concern about our capabilities in the advanced high-tech areas and frankly we are losing the advantages we have started out with. . . . What we need is to allow a greater degree of consortium and unified work where, as a start, the commercial and private sector can work together without any government interference. . . . Although it's very, very late in the game, it's not too late.

"The private sector and the public sector working together" was a phrase several of the senators liked. Senator Ernest Hollings, chairman of the Commerce Committee, was concerned with getting leadership and funding out of the Defense Department and into the Commerce Department. And Sen. Daniel Inouye of Hawaii played into that, too. "Overall, we spend about 90 percent of our federal research for military purposes, and about 10 percent for the support of American industry," he complained. (The true split is about 75 percent to 25 percent.) "The opposite is true for our NATO allies and Japan. Japan spends less than 10 percent for military research and the rest for their industry. I would hope that you will be aggressive and insist upon spending more federal funds for business research and get your share of that pie."

Too Much for the Secretary to Swallow?

A few months after Mosbacher's confirmation, the secretary was really getting rolling in HDTV. The Commerce Department was setting up an "industry-led business-government partnership." He cautioned that the industry would have to carry the ball: "If the private sector doesn't want to pursue this without massive infusions from government, there is nothing we can do."[4] But one person's massive infusion is another's partnership.

The American Electronics Association and 36 of its members stepped up with the idea of creating a new consortium to be called the ATV Corp. Its board, selected from industry, government, and academia, would manage a $1 billion fund to back HDTV development projects. In addition, the Defense Advanced

Research Projects Agency would be given $100 million a year to buy research in key technologies, such as large flat-panel displays, signal processing computing, and the development of manufacturing systems.

Naturally the ATV Corp. would enjoy antitrust and tax exemptions, and the AEA added one more wrinkle: the ATV Corp. would hold title to the technology of whatever broadcast standard the FCC adopts. Thus it would be the gatekeeper of HDTV in the United States, possibly the most powerful cartel (it wasn't so named) since the National Recovery Administration was declared unconstitutional in 1936.

Captains of Industry

A Commerce Department aide, Jack R. Clifford of the Office of Microelectronics and Instrumentation, had a revealing exchange with Eric E. Sumner, a vice president of AT&T Bell Labs. Sumner's advice—personal advice, not official AT&T policy, he emphasized—was for flat-out protection. He swept away the protection that might be afforded by the FCC's standards-setting rigmarole:

> The popular assumption that a different U.S. standard will discourage or immensely handicap a foreign competitor is almost certainly false. Given the importance of the U.S. market, design changes would meet just about any standard in a matter of a few months. I am sure that present Japanese designs make conversion to new standards easy. I, therefore, believe much stronger protection is needed for an infant HDTV industry.
>
> I think our HDTV industry will need to be almost totally protected for about five years. Perhaps we should set up a government-owned operating company (GOCO) in the beginning. During the five-year infancy period no set other than those produced by the GOCO would be sold in the U.S.

Spoken like a true son of Ma Bell's monopoly. Sumner went on to predict a "very large negative cash flow initially" for this GOCO, estimating about $10 billion for R&D and manufacturing facilities. Private industry will not be able to come up with it, nor, he said, should "Uncle Sugar." His prescription: "I think it is reasonable and proper that this money be raised by a relatively small percentage duty on imported consumer electronics."

Did Clifford, representative of a nominally free-trading Republican administration, recoil in shock? Hardly. His response:

> As you are aware, we are deeply concerned about the absence of any major U.S. industry effort to develop HDTV and the lack of a major U.S.-owned manufacturing base position to compete in the emerging HDTV markets. Our concern is not only for the consumer market for HDTV but also for the industrial, commercial, and defense applications of this advanced video technology. We must maintain a leading position, in video imaging, storage, and display technology. The future of our semiconductor industry and the industries dependent on it, such as the computer and telecommunications industries, will hinge on the potential large-scale requirements for memory and other semiconductor devices that will stem from a flourishing U.S. HDTV industry.

The letters, from May of 1989, were released by the Department of Commerce under the Freedom of Information Act. Other letters and documents also show that the Commerce Department was trying to gather support from a broad spectrum of American business. Barry K. Rogstad, of the American Business Conference, was a sort of deputy cowpoke in the roundup. He collected comments from Orville Wright, chief executive officer of MCI; Edward C. Raymund, chairman of TechData; John Rollwagen, chairman of Cray Research (who emphasized that he had "discussed this issue at length with Secretary Mosbacher"); and Chet Brown, president of American Digital Imaging.

The opinions in this sample, however, fell short of wholehearted support. The CEOs were interested most in what was in it for their companies.

Wright was thinking about MCI's fiber-optic network. "There is not enough radio spectrum available to meet the need of HDTV, therefore HDTV will need cable bandwidth into the U.S. home. This may necessitate rewiring the cities and towns with fiber. It should be government policy to encourage this rewiring throughout the U.S." On the point, he added discouragingly: "While the market will be larger than the current TV market, the policy implications are no different than the move of TV manufacturing offshore, which has already occurred. This will simply be another product market where the United States does not compete."

Raymund said: "If we are going to have world-class companies and manufacturing, we have to start thinking on a world-class basis, not in a provincial way of just protecting our own market. We should encourage patent protection, and give some help to the initial start-off. But from then on, it seems to me that the manufacturers have to pull their own weight and American business has to make investments in the future. We have it in many other industries and we can do it in this industry as well. Just because the electronics industry has been subsidized for the last 40 years because of the defense situation doesn't mean that it has to be subsidized forever." He added that his views were colored by 35 years in electronics, mostly in the defense sector.

Rollwagen was thinking of Cray's pet project, a network to connect supercomputers with more users. He cited HDTV's potential for computer workstations and he emphasized the importance of a digital network to "promote the more efficient use of the nation's supercomputing power."

Brown spoke of the promise of a wide area computer network that happened to provide high definition television as one of many services. He stressed the importance of HDTV as a market for displays and semiconductors and he warned of the capability of the potential foreign competition. "I feel strongly," he said, "that the United States companies need to play in the HDTV arena, or in the future we may find ourselves being held hostage to the availability of critical technology."

Clearing Out the Underbrush

Mosbacher, on the McNeil/Lehrer NewsHour of June 26, 1989, sounded as though he was convinced:

> We are beginning to wake up to the fact that America is in one big world competition. Private industry in this country is beginning to think in terms of competing, not only in HDTV, which is just a part of the total picture, but an all new and major electronics revolution that's going to follow on from HDTV.
>
> We in the government need to clear the underbrush out of the way so that the private sector can get into this. It must be a private sector-led operation, but the government can do several things. It can make it easier for private companies to get together in groups, in consortia, or other methods. We can make it more exciting for them—and help-ful—through tax dispensations.

But as the Commerce Department grew more and more enthusiastic about HDTV, and as the ATV Corp. gained more and more support at Commerce and on Capitol Hill, they became targets. The Congressional Budget Office threw cold water on the excitement. The market studies were "at the high range of the industry's likely sales." CBO analysts questioned whether anybody would sell millions of HDTV sets per year at prices above $1,000 and they went so far as to construct a low-growth scenario from the Darby report, finding HDTV sales might be as low as 100,000 units per year, less than current sales of projection televisions. And "even the most optimistic market growth would be unlikely to affect other electronic industries in the way suggested by proponents of HDTV."

The CBO also observed that most TV sets sold in the United States are made in the United States, although by foreign-owned manufacturers, and that most U.S.-made personal computers contain foreign-made components. The internationalization of electronics would continue, CBO analysts said. They declared:

> It is not clear why a product made in Mexico by a firm owned by U.S. citizens is a U.S. product [the reference is to Zenith] while a product made in the United States by a firm owned by foreigners is a foreign product. R&D presents an equally vexing problem: while U.S. policymakers might want all firms to perform their R&D in the United States, many U.S.-based firms find it advantageous to perform their R&D in Japan or Europe.[5]

European and Japanese firms are performing R&D in the U.S. as well.

The CBO was skeptical of the idea that foreign firms could use HDTV technology to become dominant in other electronics markets, even though this is widely believed in the U.S. industry. Analysts questioned whether HDTVs would consume a dominating quantity of semiconductors, or even 1 percent of the world's output. They questioned whether HDTV would require such sophisticated semiconductors that the market would drive the pace of innovation in semiconductors. And they noted that the AEA's idealized image of the growth of a successful HDTV industry in America was not too different from the actual success of the U.S. personal computer industry in the 80s. Yet during the 80s, the U.S. memory chip industry declined.

The Congressional Budget Office is supposed to help Congress determine facts, not advise the lawmakers on policy. So the CBO

report on HDTV made no forecasts of its own, and drew no conclusions. Robert Reischauer, director of the CBO, even told Congress, "These conclusions do not necessarily mean that federal
support for HDTV is without merit. Support for HDTV might be
justified for reasons other than competitiveness in the electronics
sector—for instance employment, national prestige, or scientific
advancement. In addition, development of the HDTV market, although small on its own, might also have a role to play in a
broader strategy for government involvement in the U.S. electronics sector, including attempts to create a U.S. industry manufacturing a whole range of consumer electronics."[6] Translation:
the idea is technically silly but politics—that's your department.

Bureaucratic Football

The HDTV industrial policy also became a target of opportunity
on bureaucratic and philosophic grounds. Chief hunters were
Michael Boskin, chairman of the Council of Economic Advisers,
and Richard G. Darman, director of the Office of Management
and Budget. They shared a philosophical opposition to anything
smacking of industrial policy or corporate welfare, but philosophy rarely carries the day in Washington. They also shared a common interest in keeping Mosbacher under control and the Commerce Department a policy backwater.

In a flock of chickens, the only means of staying high in the
pecking order is to peck. In a bureaucracy, pecking is also a matter of the survival instinct. *The Wall Street Journal* and the *Washington Post* were soon reporting that Mosbacher's HDTV initiative
was as good as dead. It is a curious Washington custom that the
White House rarely delivers bad news to cabinet officers in person. Instead, the White House staff leaks the bad news to the
papers, so the unlucky official can choke on his morning coffee.
Mosbacher must have been astounded at the lead on David
Wessel and Eduardo Lachica's *Wall Street Journal* story: "The Bush
administration has all but scuttled Commerce Secretary Robert
Mosbacher's initiative for federal aid for the infant high definition
television industry, according to federal officials. 'I don't know if
it's dead, but it's not moving,' one administration official said."
The question seemed to be not whether it would be a tough day at
the office, but whether he would have an office at the end of the
day.

Mosbacher did stay in office, and the Commerce Department
line is that there never was any conflict with Darman and Boskin,

that the secretary was disillusioned by the refusal of U.S. industry to make a substantial investment in HDTV. His aides said the department was working on a broad initiative in high technology. No public Commerce Department program emerged, but discretion is still the better part of valor. In the field of U.S. industrial policy, working quietly is less dangerous. Also, working with the broadest possible coalition of interests gives a better chance of success.

In a letter to Markey dated Dec. 6, 1989, Mosbacher provided an outline of his new policy:

> HDTV represents the convergence of a number of technologies, each of which is likely to have a major economic impact on the nation. The exploitation of these technologies by the private sector could enhance our balance of trade position, could result in boosting our sagging consumer electronics markets, and could help to revitalize the U.S. semiconductor industry. How we deal with these issues will set the long-term course for high technology sectors characterized by high risk and long lead times. The problem before us, then, is not merely how we deal with U.S. competitiveness in all high technology sectors. Therefore, we do not intend to propose policies that only target high definition television. Rather we shall proceed with the development of a wide range of options to foster U.S. industries' ability to regain the global initiative by capitalizing on our innovative strengths.

The reader who suspects Mosbacher is trying to give Markey a snow job need only flip the page. Mosbacher shifts to the role of campaign spokesman, plugging President Bush's program:

> We have already begun pursuing some of the policies needed to increase the competitiveness of U.S. industry. For example, in the 1989 budget proposal, the president requested that a more favorable capital gains tax rate be reinstated and that the tax credit for research and development be made permanent. The administration has also been working to reduce the federal deficit. These measures could help to reduce the cost of capital in the United States. The Congress has had these proposals before it, and has debated them.

Markey could fill in the obvious, that Congress had also defeated them as part of the budget and politics game.

Mosbacher also summarized the other actions of the Commerce Department on HDTV: an effort to involve U.S. companies in a discussion with Japanese manufacturers about the design and specifications for Japanese HDTV components; research by the department's National Telecommunications and Information Administration and the National Institute of Standards and Technology concerning broadcast options for HDTV; and an NTIA study of the economic and policy implications of the standards before the FCC.

Behind the snow, Mosbacher's Commerce Department was arming those who would fight a battle for U.S. industrial policy. Department analysts put out a study on Emerging Technologies that claimed the United States was falling behind in 10 of the 12 technologies highlighted. And in the summer of 1990, the department published *The Competitive Status of the U.S. Electronics Sector*, a warehouse of arguments in favor of activist trade and business policies. Mosbacher and his Commerce Department declared that solutions would have to come from the private sector, but the reports went to Congress.

3

HDTV and Politics

Science Meets Politics

Some of the biggest names in the science establishment gathered with Sen. Al Gore in September 1989. Gore, a once and future presidential candidate, has positioned himself as a new John Kennedy, ready to lead America into a bright future. Gore often leans toward the view that a high-tech tomorrow requires government intervention today. But he has an open mind and he collects ideas like stamps. His hearing was like a seminar with several good teachers and one attentive, argumentative student.[1]

Dr. Erich Bloch, a 30-year veteran of IBM who headed the National Science Foundation, testified on universities and the need for federal support at all levels of education. But in the question period, he got into the desirability of federal support for corporate research. At IBM in the 1980s he had helped in the creation of the Semiconductor Research Corp. and at NSF he had helped in the creation of Sematech, two research consortia intended to improve the performance of the semiconductor industry. Bloch observed:

"Normally, it's not good for the government to take a hands-on role in research. But Sematech was good because it had the goal of preservation of the semiconductor industry." He also said Sematech was good because the companies involved had put up a substantial amount of resources. "If the companies wouldn't put up 50 percent, the government shouldn't have either."

That was a distinction he drew between Sematech and the AEA's HDTV program. "HDTV is on the table now; the government should not participate until industry produces a reasonable and feasible plan." Sen. Richard Bryan, D-Nevada, asked Bloch what went wrong with VCRs—if the federal government failed in some way. Bloch answered, "You can't blame that on the federal government. The companies didn't have the persistence of the Japanese to keep on working at the technology for 20 years until the technology led to a product."

Gore seized on this notion of persistence and compared the U.S. performance in high tech to the U.S. performance in the Olympic games. "It's like why the U.S., a country of 240 million people, wins fewer gold medals than East Germany, a country of 17 million people. East Germany's methods are inconsistent with our values, like picking pole vaulters in kindergarten and training them to the exclusion of all else." (This was just a few months before East Germany's values self-destructed in the peaceful December revolution.)

If we had to, Gore said, we could decide that winning gold medals was so important that we would learn some things from the East Germans. "And it is important to do well in international economic competition. So the time has come to look at what's successful in other countries. We still won't do exactly what the Japanese do but we will come up with a new approach consistent with our values that will work better than what we do now."

Bloch acknowledged that HDTV would be important, both as a building block and as a market for semiconductors and other components. He said, however, that supporting an HDTV industry would be futile unless there really was an industry to support. "We have to make sure there's an industry capable of building HDTV. That requires instrument companies, materials companies, semiconductor companies, and so forth. And you have to have a blueprint [for how these companies will work together]."

On AEA's specific plan, Bloch said, "I wouldn't put any money into the HDTV proposal; there's much too little money from industry. What came out of AEA was a bill for $1.5 billion."

HDTV and Strategic Defense

Gore complained that the Bush administration had "washed its hands" of HDTV and "abdicated any federal role" in this area. He added this zinger: "We are not willing to do for HDTV what we do for SDI." Bloch told him not to be hasty; he recalled that he had worked two and a half years on the Sematech plan and it often looked like it was going to collapse. "On HDTV, if the industry would get together with a new proposal, there would be another round of discussion." He said it's up to industry to come forward with a plan that is "believable."

Gore: What probability do you assign to that event?
Bloch: A low probability.

Gore asked with evident frustration what to do, then, since we know it's unlikely that anything will be done even though we also know that it's very important. Bloch said maybe it would be useful for Congress to call the officials and the industry together. "You make progress through talking, you know it better than anybody," he said. After the laughter died down, he said he didn't mean it that way.

Gore complained that the last time Mosbacher was on Capitol Hill to talk about HDTV, he acted as if he had adhesive tape over his mouth (alluding to a grisly drug murder reported in the paper the previous day, in which a witness had been killed and dumped with adhesive tape over her mouth as a warning to other squealers). "Somebody in the White House [gagged] Secretary Mosbacher. He stopped talking because the White House made a policy decision."

Gore also observed that "our current science and technology policy emphasizes a decentralized non-policy. We need a reexamination of that fundamental choice. We are confronted with a new model [the Japanese partnership between government and business] that is obviously far more successful in achieving certain objectives than the U.S. model. HDTV focuses the debate: should U.S. non-policy be changed to allow us to be more successful?"

Note the jump in logic, in which Gore assumed that a change in policy will make us more successful. There is also the assumption that we know what "success" is.

What Should We Be Afraid Of?

Lewis Branscomb, director of the science, technology, and public policy program at Harvard University's Kennedy School of Government, recalled that one postwar outline for technology policy called for a kind of federal department of science. He said

the National Science Foundation was invented instead, because
"business and academics were afraid of government involvement
in research."

Ironically, business and academics now seek what they feared
a half century ago, while government shies away from the role it
created for itself in the nuclear age.

Many electronics industry partisans argue that failures of the
U.S. government are killing the high-tech industries. These failures are harmful economic and tax policies, and weak opposition
to dumping and other predatory trade tactics.

Jerry Pearlman, president of Zenith, put it this way:

> For the last 20 years, inaction on the part of our own government has
> let an industry born and bred here slip away. Severe price erosion,
> caused by unpenalized dumping, duty circumvention and other un-
> fair trade practices, has made the industry unprofitable here. Zenith,
> which has not made a full-year profit since 1984 [It did post a small
> profit in 1989, after these comments] is the last of a dying breed; every
> other major brand has been forced out of business or acquired by a
> foreign firm. People leave the industry because they cannot make
> money in it.
>
> HDTV will not be the profit panacea, just as stereo TV was not, so
> long as our market is the world's dumping ground. Unless there is a
> profitable environment, investments cannot and will not be made in
> the United States by U.S. companies.

Economics and Investment

The push toward a government HDTV effort was killed by economics, but not the way Pearlman describes it. One factor in particular has been missed: In an economy at full employment, one
sector gains employment at the expense of other sectors. Translated into political terms, this becomes a challenge. One must explain why other sectors of the economy should be taxed $1 billion
or $10 billion or 10 cents in order to aid a privileged industry. In
terms of investment, the market is supposed to direct capital to
the highest returns, and if HDTV promises high enough returns,
the capital will get there on its own.

There are as many opinions as there are players in the industrial policy and competitiveness debate. But one of the paradig-
matic stories that all raise is the story of the VCR. How is it, we

ask, that Americans invented the video cassette recorder and yet today we import all our VCRs from the Orient?

In 1969, Richard Elkus, manager of the industrial products division of Ampex Corp., gave the president of the company a plan for a new product—a home videotape recorder. The plan was accepted and Ampex introduced the product under the name Instavideo in 1970. Ampex then was the dominant factor in the small videotape recorder market; virtually all the basic patents in the field were its property.

Elkus, now with another company, bitterly recalls that the company's top management decided to cure cash flow problems by transferring Instavideo technology to Toshiba, rather than getting involved in a joint venture with a stronger U.S. partner.

"This event was the beginning of the downward slide of U.S. consumer electronics dominance," he told Markey's subcommittee in September 1988.[2] Today, U.S. producers of video recorders represent less than 2 percent of the total market—a market of approximately $15 billion a year worldwide.

Elkus's bitterness, however, finds no home at Ampex today. Ampex spent substantial sums in 1989 on newspaper ads warning against precipitous action to aid development of an HDTV industry in America. Though still a small company, Ampex is a world leader in studio and professional TV recording equipment. One ad declared, "The combined revenues of the more than 1,400 American-owned television stations and nearly 10,000 cable systems are almost $40 billion—more than six times what Americans spent buying television sets last year."

Searching for Profits

In the same period, 1975–1990, that American companies walked away from TV manufacturing industry, two new industries emerged. Cable television required a large infusion of capital to string the wires, capital that otherwise might have gone to modernizing television factories. Similarly, the opening of thousands of videotape rental stores had large financing requirements, whether mom and pop opened a store or a wild-eyed entrepreneur opened hundreds. But financing cable TV and video stores was so simple that it is rarely remarked upon: the cash flows generated were enormous and even a small-town banker could see the opportunity.

It is a sign of the times that neither of these industries is dependent on the U.S. manufacturing economy. Coaxial cable is a commodity product made by the mile, and decoder boxes are a well-developed technology that has not advanced much in a decade. The videotape rental industry is more dependent on hardware, but videocassette recorders also represent the full flowering of 1980s technology and are available from several manufacturers in dozens of styles and brand names aimed at every conceivable price point.

As the 90s open, we should be able to see that the cable TV and video rental industries have made our economy stronger, in large part because they are not dependent on manufacturing. Even if we are only interested in jobs, these industries far overshadow the old television manufacturing industry. They directly employ hundreds of thousands of people: blue collar technicians and installers; part-time and odd-shift sales people; managers, accountants, lawyers, and support staff ad infinitum. And indirectly, their prosperity and the markets they have created have enriched the U.S. entertainment production industry, which spews out movies and television programs in great numbers. That industry is profligate with its employment of skilled and unskilled labor and is famous for putting wealth in the hands of conspicuous consumers.

But more: manufacturing is a dangerous, chancy business. In a service industry you need only satisfy the customer. In a manufacturing business you must satisfy the customer with the same product long enough to earn back the costs of developing the product, setting up a production line, training the workers, and so on. You are a slave to your invested capital.

Marxism is fortunately out of style at the moment, but we should not be afraid to risk sounding a bit Marxist if we recognize that the owner's enslavement to his source of capital requires that, in turn, he squeeze the maximum productivity from his other factors of production, chiefly labor. It is no accident, as Marxists are fond of saying, that manufacturing industries are more heavily unionized than service industries. Only by creating an artificial monopoly on the supply of labor can unskilled workers hope to wrest a middle-class wage from employment in manufacturing. (Extractive industries, such as mining and farming, are even more tyrannical.)

As American steel workers and auto workers and, yes, television workers learned to their sorrow in the 70s and early 80s, this is not a stable situation. Only just so much profit can be made in a competitive industry, and in the long run, all companies must compete. Those that extract more profit from consumers will find those consumers turning to other sources or to substitutes. Thus the U.S. steel industry paid a high wage and generous dividends, but failed to modernize and lost markets to aluminum and plastic.

The still-unfolding story of HDTV and American competitiveness demands that we ask in all seriousness if we should spend billions of dollars to re-create a U.S.-owned consumer electronics industry. We should instead be following the trail of profit blazed by the companies and investors who turned away from television manufacturing and consumer electronics in general. They sunk billions of dollars into stringing cable television wire, creating cable television channels, opening videotape rental stores, and producing the movies and programming that would be seen on these new media. It was a simple fact that profits were higher in these businesses than in manufacturing, and we can rely on them to find the profit-making opportunities of the future.

Section II
THE FEDERAL STEW

Some say "the president proposes and Congress disposes." It would be far more accurate to say that everybody proposes and nobody disposes. The federal government in Washington is not one institution. And its many institutions are not monolithic. Policies, laws, and regulations often turn on disputes within agencies of the Executive Branch, subcommittees of Congress, or bureaus of independent agencies. The federal government is like a giant stewpot, kept on the back of an old wood stove. Something from every meal is put in the stewpot. Every now and then, the pot is brought to the boil (to kill the most dangerous germs) and a nourishing meal is ladled out. The federal government ladles out about 40 percent of the nation's spending on research and development. In 1989, federal spending on R&D was $52.9 billion. Private industry spent $63.8 billion, while universities, colleges, and other nonprofit institutions spent $15.5 billion. The aggregate 1989 figure represented a 4.9 percent increase over 1988.[1]

4

Federal Research

The People Who Throw the Money

If, as Shelley claimed, poets are the unacknowledged legislators of the world, then a couple of hundred people in a shabby office building in Arlington, Va., are the high-tech equivalents of poets.

These men and women work for the Defense Advanced Research Projects Agency, known as DARPA. They do not invent anything, or build anything, but they legislate an industrial policy for American defense. Project managers at DARPA hire private companies and academics to do research. When you talk about the Defense Department throwing money at a problem, these are the people who are doing the throwing. DARPA has a budget in excess of $1.1 billion dollars, and is only vaguely accountable to the Secretary of Defense and the Congress for what it does. About half of DARPA spending is devoted to the development of weaponry, but the remainder, including about $100 million a year on basic research, makes DARPA by far the biggest venture capital fund in the world.

What DARPA officials decide is important becomes important. Or, as one researcher put it, "DARPA's goals, because they are so well funded, tend to be science's goals. People like to do things where the money is available for support, and so DARPA has really had a major influence on the way science is done."

In the 30 years it has existed, DARPA has been a guiding influence in the space and missile programs, in the development of computer hardware and software, in telecommunications, radar, lasers, and a host of other technologies with military applications. But DARPA has also turned its attention beyond the military, beyond science, beyond engineering. While continuing to encompass all these traditional areas, in the 80s DARPA officials also nurtured new computer technologies. They believed better computers would mean better scientists, better science, and better products, including military products. And that drew them into a business effort to assure the health of the U.S. electronics industry. DARPA attempted to legislate U.S. industrial development as it legislates U.S. military innovation.

DARPA decided in 1988 to fund a major effort to push the development of high definition television. In part, officials justified this venture into commerce and entertainment by pointing to the military need for sharply focused computer screen displays. But a more important reason was that DARPA officials believed HDTV to be the "technology driver" of the 90s—the key product that stimulates development of the whole high-tech world the way personal computers did in the 80s.

Dr. Craig Fields, DARPA director and a 15-year veteran of the agency, said DARPA must keep the U.S. electronics industry healthy in order to achieve its basic goal of keeping the United States ahead of its enemies in military technology.

Some DARPA initiatives support development and production of products and manufacturing technologies that only the Defense Department wants to buy, at least for the time being. Examples include some high-speed computer chips for microwave radio, infrared radiation detectors, and some ultralight, super-strong composite plastics for aerospace construction. All of these probably have commercial futures too, but would not be developed so quickly if the Pentagon did not want them now.

DARPA played this role in the past, supporting the development, for example, of numerically controlled machine tools and computer-aided design. Three decades ago only the military had need of such equipment; today the technology is widely dispersed throughout manufacturing.

"To industry in some fields, the Defense Department is a small and unpredictable customer," Fields said during an interview in March 1989. "As they do not wish to serve such a customer, they are not making investments we need. That means our unit costs are high because our yield is low. You need large scale production to have low costs, and to have large scale production, you need to be part of commerce."

Fields became too much a part of commerce to suit the Bush Administration. He was shunted aside to a make-work job in the Pentagon in the spring of 1990 and soon quit to join Microelectronics and Computer Technology Corp., an industry-sponsored research consortium. The HDTV project, however, continued and the controversy engendered by Fields's virtual dismissal actually strengthened DARPA's support in Congress.

Support of high definition television could combine several of these major areas—certainly computing, materials, and manufacturing. In the 1989 interview, Fields ticked off some of the reasons that he decided to push HDTV within DARPA:

HDTV is related to DARPA's direct military work in optical sensors and in graphics displays; existing displays might get a lot cheaper if they were produced in a large commercial industry; commercial sets will consume an immense quantity of semiconductor chips; the complexity of HDTV sets will rival personal computers, posing a threat to the computer industry.

Fields said he prodded DARPA into an HDTV project after seeing unsolicited proposals from U.S. companies that were very attractive. He wouldn't name the companies, but Zenith, which happens to be the last major American-owned television manufacturer, sent DARPA two proposals in 1988. The next step was for DARPA to put out an open request for proposals, and the agency received 87 submissions. They were divided between new technology proposals for important components like large flat-panel screens and proposals for low-cost manufacturing techniques.

"The contents are absolutely outstanding," said Fields. "The best ideas here in these proposals are better than any ideas I've seen anywhere else and without that we don't have anything. So I'm extremely pleased with it." He bristled at any suggestion the HDTV battle was lost. "I reject categorically the idea that it's too late," says Fields. "If you saw the energy of the proposals of American industry you wouldn't think it's too late."

DARPA followed through on $20 million worth of the HDTV project even after Fields's departure. It funded 16 companies researching different ways of building large high-resolution displays.

Strength behind Walls

For some, the DARPA effort on HDTV represents a straightforward attempt to encourage "competitiveness"; for others, it's a form of trade war, a retaliation against unfair Japanese trade practices that caused U.S. losses in television manufacture and U.S. failure to make successful videocassette recorders.

Fields himself sounded as if he has bought into the second idea as strongly as the first. He stressed that a successful HDTV project will require antidumping tariffs that raise the price of imported goods or rules that bar discounts. And he said flatly in testifying to Markey's subcommittee, "We intend this to be an American program."

Fields did not see himself as a protectionist. In fact, he said he had mellowed:

> When I started this, I was about as xenophobic as possible. I wanted to have an all-American solution. And it quickly became clear that that was a more complicated issue. It's an issue of finding an American company that doesn't buy any foreign components—some are no longer produced in the United States—that doesn't have any foreign subsidiaries for production, any foreign research labs, or employ any foreign citizens, and that's simply impossible.
>
> The way we've decided to deal with the issue is to try to see to it that research and development occurs in the United States, research and development results are licensable in the United States, U.S. components are used, production occurs in the United States, and, to the extent possible, profits that are derived are plowed back into U.S. enterprise.

Direct Government Research

Outspending DARPA by more than 20 to 1 are more than 700 federal laboratories doing research. Those operated through the Department of Defense consume about $10.5 billion a year; those of the Department of Energy, about $4 billion (of which $2 billion goes for nuclear weapons development); the National Aeronautics and Space Administration's labs consume about $2.5 billion; the National Institutes of Health have labs consuming about $1 billion. Smaller labs scattered through many agencies consume about $3 billion a year, bringing the total spending on federal labs to about $21 billion.[2]

Military labs are concerned with development of weapons. Naturally they operate behind a veil of secrecy. By the time technology emerges from military labs, it is usually incorporated in new weapons. For example, radar-absorbing materials and designs are embedded in the B-2 and F-117A stealth aircraft. Some technology developed for military purposes may have such wide applications that civilian enterprises also discover it and implement it. One recent example is lightweight carbon fiber/plastic composite materials, developed in the military world to build aircraft parts and in the civilian world for tennis rackets and golf club shafts and fishing poles.

Technology flows in both directions between the military world and the commercial world. It is reasonable to speculate that some of the 68 military labs are now engaged in research that has civilian applications. For example, most observers agree that a Star Wars defense against missiles would require immensely complicated software to program the computers that would guide antimissile missiles or beams. So major quests in the Strategic Defense Initiative almost certainly include new computer architectures that are easy to program and new ways of automating the tedious task of writing reliable software. Yet if such research projects are successful, and the technology developed applications, there will be no "Made for SDI" sticker on them and most users will never know to credit the Department of Defense.

Grant Loebs, a Heritage Foundation researcher, made a tally of spinoffs for civilian technology that have already come out of SDI. Heritage practically invented SDI—it backed the original High Frontier study that convinced President Reagan of SDI's promise—so anything Heritage produces on SDI carries a potential conflict of interest. But we can accept this as an advocate's view. Loebs credits SDI labs with: a new way to deposit thin layers of diamond on cutting surfaces that could increase the precision of industrial saws; new high-carbon ceramic materials for rockets, jets, and other high-temperature applications; a new "bioglass" material for bone-grafts that might reduce tissue rejection; and a method of producing radioactive compounds used in medical diagnostics. In addition, Loebs says one SDI laser, the Free Electron Laser, can vaporize diseased tissue with great accuracy and avoid harming healthy tissue nearby.

Making things that go bang is not the only military technology; sending the things to the target is also important. In the 60s, missile guidance systems were the entire market for the nascent semiconductor industry. Today the whole defense sector uses immense quantities of integrated circuits, yet the military market is less than 10 percent of the whole integrated circuit market.

Military Purchasing

While defense managers frequently tell Congress and the public that the nation's high-tech defense requires reliable domestic sources of the most advanced components, it is more often the case that the military is still using components that civilian industry junked long ago.

Military products last a long time, often without significant improvement. Current Air Force and Navy jet fighters, their frontline weapons for air superiority, first flew in the mid-70s. That means major electronic components, such as radios and radars, were selected in the early 70s. Parts for these subsystems were selected even earlier. Electronic systems are upgraded and replaced occasionally, but often the attitude is that if it ain't broke, don't fix it. Under such a system, the U.S. military was the last user of vacuum tubes in the country. (The Soviet Air Force has not yet gotten rid of all its vacuum tube radars.)

In addition to its many enterprises at the leading edge of technology, Texas Instruments does a thriving, and highly profitable, business making and selling military electronic components that are a couple of decades out of date. Fairchild Semiconductor was deemed so important to the national defense that the Pentagon refused to allow it to be bought by a Japanese company. Fairchild produced virtually nothing state-of-the-art; it was just another important source of outmoded components.

Even when things they buy are up-to-date, the military services often buy in the worst possible way. The armed services require custom gear and special testing to be sure that equipment will operate in polar and equatorial climates, even equipment that will never see service outside an air-conditioned building.

Several integrated circuit companies carved out a niche selling computer chips to the military back in the 70s by investing in all the special testing equipment the military required. People found two ways to beat the system. In one, hurried workers simply lied about doing the testing in order to get the products out the door. In the other, the manufacturer tested all chips according to the military specification. Then it sold chips to the military at the inflated prices the military had come to expect, while it sold the rest of the same batch at far lower prices prevailing in the civilian market.

National Labs

Though weapons research, like other specialized research, often produces results that have wide, and even commercial applications, military spending is less effective at creating new technology for civilian applications than spending in the private sector. In the 80s, the military share of federally funded R&D rose from 50 percent to 70 percent. (Another 6 percent went to space science, and 11 percent went to health, which has a disproportionately weak effect on economic growth because so much of its benefits are conferred on the elderly.) In Japan, the military share of government R&D is 3 percent, and in West Germany it's 12 percent.

The Department of Energy has the famous National Laboratories, Oak Ridge and Los Alamos, that were created for the World War II research that built the atomic bomb. Those labs became the first of a network of Atomic Energy Commission laboratories and the Department of Energy inherited them. Now there are four big weapons labs—Los Alamos, Lawrence Livermore, Sandia, and Idaho Engineering; five more large ones that perform basic research in energy—Oak Ridge, Argonne, Brookhaven, Lawrence Berkeley, and Pacific Northwest; and 28 smaller labs. The Department of Energy also inherited from the AEC a World War II-style management system. All but a couple of the 37 DOE labs are operated by independent contractors—some universities and some industrial companies.

The DOE's National Laboratories have been the subject of much study and criticism and much attempted reform. As many as 50 studies have been done on the problem of extracting technology from the national labs and getting it adopted by American companies. Bureaucrats like to refer to this as the problem of "technology transfer." It is a problem widely recognized, studied, and yet still not solved. Congress passed a Technology Innovation Act of 1980, a Patent & Trademark Amendments Act the same year, a Federal Technology Transfer Act of 1986, another one in 1989, and more bills than ever are pending in the 90s.

These laws were supposed to pull down legal barriers to technology transfer and make it easier for companies to use the discoveries of federal scientists. In addition, the contractors managing the national labs were urged to think more about commercialization.

Results, in the words of the Congressional Office of Technology Assessment, "have been modest." According to OTA, "One main reason is that the labs' efforts at encouraging commercialization have not been adequately funded. Without line-item funding, such efforts are often considered by personnel at the labs and their parent agencies to be mere distractions from their primary missions.[3] In other words, the managers have to take money away from research in order to place the results of research in the hands of those who will use it.

The OTA did not mention it, but the problem runs deeper. When a government agency like a national lab manages to make some money, say by licensing an invention, the income does not benefit that agency. It goes into the U.S. Treasury, where it is of no use to the agency. If anything, Congress is likely to reduce their budget by the amount of income earned, even though the income doesn't benefit the agency. There was a classic example of this not long ago at the Federal Energy Regulatory Commission, which was seeking an outside contractor to make stenographic records of commission proceedings. Several contractors bid zero, since they can supply FERC with the records it needs and cover that cost plus a healthy profit by selling copies to interested parties. So healthy is the profit, in fact, that one bidder offered to pay FERC for the privilege of handling transcripts. Sorry, said FERC, we don't want your money—handling your payments would be cumbersome and costly, and besides, the agency would get none of it. The Federal Technology Transfer Act of 1986 paid some attention to this financial problem at national labs, allowing federal lab researchers to receive 15 percent of the royalties from their patents. But it did nothing to pay lab managers or benefit lab programs.

A glacial pace of negotiation, involving the company that wants the technology, any potential competitors, the lab that developed it, and the parent agency of the lab, is another barrier to commercialization. This was supposed to be made simpler by the 1986 law, authorizing the delegation of negotiating to the lab director, but it seems to have also required a 1987 executive order and a 1989 amendment to the law. That suggests the problem remains. And once negotiations are complete, what does the company have? Many government negotiators are reluctant to grant exclusive rights to government inventions, whether patents, copyrights, or just agreeing to keep certain data secret. Some bureaucrats believe that inventions made with public funds are public property; others distrust the monopoly powers that a patent confers on a company. Unfortunately, they overlook the further development costs a company may have to undertake to bring a discovery to the point where there is a commercial product. And, of course, not all commercial products are successful. "Excess profits" on one product cover the costs of others that never reach market.

During the 1989 Washington convention of the Computer Software and Services Industry Association, a few dozen optimistic people attended a conference on technology transfer and the national labs. What they heard was no assurance that the labs have acquired any business spirit. One after another, six scientific bureaucrats from six national laboratories dimmed the lights, put organization charts up on a screen, and set their listeners to dozing as they explained who reported to whom, and why. The closest any of them came to discussing access to technology was to point out the relevant bureau on the organization chart. There was no sales pitch, no zeal for the deal, no marketing, no products, no results.

Those Untapped Resources

Martin Marietta, which took over management of Oak Ridge National Laboratory in a flash of enthusiasm about mining the lab for hidden discoveries of commercial potential, came a long way and

has a long way to go. Active license agreements with private industry at Oak Ridge rose from 2 in 1985 to 33 in 1989. It was a
good percentage increase, but still dreadful performance.

One of Martin Marietta's best ideas was the establishment of a
local Tennessee Innovation Center. With $3.5 million from Martin
Marietta, the center provides budding entrepreneurs with lab or
office space, management help, and a little startup capital, typically $30,000 to $100,000, in return for a minority interest. One of
those investments was worth $7 million after a few years.

Argonne National Laboratory, run by the University of Chicago, copied a method that succeeded at MIT and Stanford. A
nonprofit ARCH Development Corp. receives patent rights to virtually all inventions at Argonne and at the university. ARCH
completes the patent process, tries to license the patent, or even
forms a startup company to commercialize the invention. Results
are not in at Argonne, but at MIT, this strategy produces about
the same number of licensing agreements and new firm startups
each year as do all the DOE labs combined, and this from an MIT
research budget of about $700 million, compared to $5 billion for
the DOE labs.

Admiral James D. Watkins, the secretary of energy in the Bush
administration, acknowledged that licensing of technologies developed by the national laboratories brings in revenue much below 1 percent of the money spent on the labs. In a speech on the
subject, Watkins urged that federal officials and people in industry "bridge the gap" by bringing industrial researchers and industrial money into the labs.[4] He also recognized the importance of
being able to protect commercial secrets and of doing business
quickly before the hope of commercial advantage is lost.

But when the crunch came, he pontificated: "If our nation can
unite around the goal of renewing our competitive edge, we can
enjoy unparalleled strength through a decade of advances in the
1990s. At a minimum, we can turn these advances [in the national
labs] into a source of competitive advantage for the United States
in the fields of energy, environment and trade." Watkins never
said how to bring industry and national laboratory researchers
together, even though the answer is plain: The easiest way to put
an industrial focus on the national laboratories is to sell them—
lock, stock, and Ph.D.s—to industry or universities. The stagnant
condition of the labs calls for a major shake-up in the way of life of

the people at the labs. If they can't sell themselves and their work, they shouldn't stay on the payroll. They should get out on the street and find productive jobs in teaching or industry. If the national labs consume one sixth of the entire research budget of the United States, they should be giving the taxpayers their money's worth.

Privatizing the national labs is no cure-all, of course. The difficulty of transferring technology is not confined to national laboratories. Private industry's laboratories also encounter difficulties. AT&T's Bell Labs were long the most productive industrial labs in the world, but many of their inventions made it to the outside world as a matter of chance. Even six years after the breakup of AT&T, Bell Labs researchers still make wry remarks about how hard it is to get anyone in the business end of the company to pay any attention to their neat inventions. In the 70s, the Xerox Corporation's Palo Alto Research Center was the birthplace of many of the best ideas and inventions about personal computers, yet Xerox made no successful use of them. We know they were good because they were lifted wholesale by Apple for the Macintosh. But the most aggressive attempt to turn those ideas into profit for Xerox came when Xerox sued Apple for copying them.

A Success Story

In a former life, NASA was the National Advisory Committee on Aeronautics, a federal agency that was created in 1915 to help the United States catch up in aviation design after falling behind the war-driven European powers. NACA was able to select projects for the advancement of flight, such as the construction of large wind tunnels. Experimenters tested an enormous variety of airfoil shapes, creating a library that aircraft designers could trust and adopt to suit their purposes. In the 20s and 30s, when aircraft companies were operating hand-to-mouth, NACA did the experimental work they could not afford. A NACA classic was the design of an engine cowl that reduced a radial engine's aerodynamic drag by 75 percent at almost no loss in air cooling. Such discoveries were made available to the whole industry. NACA also set up a system in which aircraft companies licensed their patents to each other.

After World War II, the aircraft industry was big enough to

stand on its own, although the military effort to develop jet engines and jet-powered airplanes diffused a great deal of new technology into the commercial sector. The outstanding example was the metamorphosis of Boeing's KC-135 tanker aircraft into the Boeing 707. But by the early 60s, military requirements had flown beyond civilian needs, Boeing and Douglas were funding their own commercial designs, and the federal research effort looked higher, into space.

Commercial applications of the U.S. space program are many and growing. By the National Aeronautics and Space Administration's tally, the Apollo space program produced 60,000 spinoffs for the civilian economy that are worth more than $600 million a year. The biggest is nearly ubiquitous, though rarely noticed by its users. A large share of telephone calls and nearly all television programs make part of their journey from sender to receiver by communications satellites, both domestic and international. On the other hand, there is no direct commercial use for man in space, though space enthusiasts see chances for new manufacturing techniques involving zero gravity, the vacuum of space, solar power unobstructed by earth's atmosphere, or the dramatic extremes of heat and cold available in orbit. Three books, *The Second Industrial Revolution*, by G. Harry Stine, *The High Frontier*, by Gerard K. O'Neill, and *The High Road*, by Ben Bova, explored these industrial ideas in the 80s. They are as timely now as they were then, because little progress has been made.

Advocates believe the U.S. space station will be the right environment for the experiments that will lead to establishment of space industries. But the space station will be built in the late 90s, at best. Constructing a space station, servicing it, and putting it to use will require $30 billion or more, possibly much more, and that does not count building more space shuttles or a new heavy lift cargo rocket.

How Big Is Too Big?

The space station is symbolic of the seductiveness of big projects. Everybody is at least a little bit vulnerable to the edifice complex, that desire to build the biggest and best thing in the world. Congressmen are a little bit more vulnerable than most people, because the construction of giant edifices produces giant payrolls.

As those giant payrolls spend their way through the economy of a congressional district or a state or even many states, the multiplier effect (in which money spent is respent and respent and respent, stimulating the whole economy) goes to work in a most tangible and prosperous way. Such projects, whether dams or highways or superconducting supercolliders, are known to their opponents as pork barrel, and to their supporters as vital contributions to national economic health.

Justifying these big projects is the assumption that only the federal government can amass the vast quantities of capital and have the patience necessary to wait for the big dividends that will follow. We ought to ask, however, if some other way of accomplishing the aims of these projects might not be found if the federal government declined to support them. Consider some examples:

Federal taxes paid for 90 percent of the interstate highway system, including some interstates on which few cars or trucks ride, and including some others that did more to destroy the cities where they were built than to strengthen them. State highway taxes and tolls were already building superhighways where the demand for swift, efficient roads was clear. Without President Eisenhower's vision, we would surely have a smaller superhighway network and there would be a greater disparity of quality and number of roads between rich states and poor ones. We would probably also have more missing links in the network. But it would be going too far to say that only the federal government could have built or would have built something like the highway network of today. The parts truly needed would surely have been built, with tolls if necessary.

Communications satellites are the accepted standard method of carrying electronic messages over long distances. But in the early days of communications satellites, the U.S. government created, subsidized, promoted, and protected the world satellite network. Satellites became cost-effective only in the 70s, as the electronic senders and receivers installed on them became capable of carrying thousands of messages simultaneously. But even as that day arrived, the day of fiber-optic cable, capable of carrying even heavier traffic, was dawning also. In the 90s, fiber-optic cable is the better, more efficient medium for many messages, and the governments of the world are back to subsidizing and protecting their investment in communications satellites. Satellites do seem to retain an advantage for broadcasting, but that use is just getting under way. The invention of fiber-optic cable could not be foreseen specifically in the 60s, but now it seems that developing satellites for telephonic communication was an evolutionary dead end, and an expensive one, at that. Would patience, in the sense of waiting for something better, have been a virtue in this case? Or were all the benefits of instantaneous global communication, among which we could number the collapse of the Soviet system as well as the popularity of NFL football in Britain, too great not to subsidize?

We also ought to ask whether some big projects are being undertaken more for the bigness than for their importance. The space station is an obvious example—most space scientists and even would-be space industrialists say that the things they might want to do in space would be done better in smaller spacecraft designed to their unique purposes. Are we going to build a space station just because all of the 1950s science fiction we grew up on included a space station?

The superconducting supercollider doesn't even have the support of all physics researchers. Arno Penzias, whose Nobel Prize came for research into the origin of the universe, the very purpose for which we would spend $8 billion to smash protons together, is skeptical. "If we end up beggaring our universities to build this thing, I think we're on the wrong track." He noted that supporters say the collider will attract researchers and students. "But if we can't educate them properly because we've spent our money on big machines instead of universities, where's the point? As a nation we must take a new look at our scientific priorities and ask ourselves what we really want."[5]

Another physicist opposing the collider, Paul A. Fleury, adds: "A frog suddenly dropped in a beaker of boiling water jumps out and saves itself, but if the water is heated slowly, the frog fails to notice the heat until it's too late. That's what's happening to most basic research in America and one of the reasons we don't notice it is that we're spending so many research dollars on big-science projects like the SSC."[6]

If, in fiscal 1991, Congress had taken the president's requests for big science projects—$2 billion for the space station, the $859 million for planning a trip to Mars, the $218 million for the superconducting supercollider, the $254 million for the X-30 hypersonic spaceplane and the $87 million for the Human Genome Project (spending on all these are in early stages and will rise in future years if they are continued)—what could it have done instead with the $3.4 billion thus collected?

Another Way to Spend

Congress would most likely spend that money on something else big, and not necessarily something scientific. Paying for prescription drugs for the elderly, or rebuilding after some natural catastrophe consume such sums and ask for more. But Congress could divert the money from these big projects into 3,418 annual grants of $1 million to university science and engineering departments, or into 34,180 grants of $100,000 to Ph.D. researchers, or into 341,800 grants of $10,000 to postgraduate students in the physical sciences and engineering. Any of these conversions would have long-lasting effects. Doing all three would carry an annual cost of just over $10 billion. But in 1990, Congress and the administration only began to deliver on a 1987 pledge to double, over five years, the budget of the National Science Foundation. NSF, the agency of the government that awards grants of this type, received $1.6 billion, a 12 percent increase. It is a measure of the diminished expectations of the scientific community that NSF officials expressed great pleasure.

Budget trends at the NSF show that fewer new applications for grants are being funded, that the average size of grants is not keeping up with inflation, rising from about $59,000 in 1985 to $61,700. After inflation, that's a 10 percent decline.[7]

One reason grants to individual scientists are diminishing is that the NSF established during the 80s a network of regional engineering research centers at 18 universities. Each receives about $2 million a year from NSF to cover about half their costs. The idea was to bring industry into engineering education and to bring universities into the real world in which their graduates must work. NSF sponsors of the program said they hoped a long-range benefit of the program would be that more engineers would be prepared to move into management.[8]

The NSF also is part of a structural problem that is a classic of American politics. Congress reviews programs in committees, which are divided by cabinet department. Independent agencies,

such as NSF, NASA, and the EPA, are lumped in with the smallest cabinet department, the Department of Housing and Urban
Development. The spending plans of each government office are
reviewed by subcommittees of the Appropriations Committee divided on the same lines. Since the congressional budget process
operates by assigning each subcommittee a target, the science
agencies vie with housing, a traditional pork barrel agency, for
funding.

Partnerships with Industry

The National Institutes of Health are a model of cooperation
among government, industrial, and academic researchers. In the
burgeoning field of biotechnology, where a few basic discoveries
about gene-splicing and cloning have led to a decade of progress
and products (and profits), NIH coordinates and funds research
and helps put new products through scientific testing. But NIH is
taking grief for cooperating with industry all too well. Rep. Ted
Weiss, a New York Democrat, held hearings in 1989 on conflict of
interest in arrangements between federally funded researchers
and industry. In general, the researchers were testing procedures
and treatments proffered by firms, and the problem was that the
researchers had financial interests with the firms.

NIH published guidelines in the fall of 1989 that satisfied Weiss
and drove the biotech and medical research communities bonk-
ers. NIH researchers would have to follow prohibitions against
holding a financial interest in any company that would be affected
by the outcome of their research and against taking any money
from companies whose products or services they were evaluating
in a federally funded project.

Researchers, especially AIDS researchers, and firms, especially
biotechnology outfits, said that rapid progress and rapid transfer
of technology require close ties between researchers and the companies that would turn research into products. And there is no
closer tie in our society than the tie of a monetary relationship.
Money gives credibility: when the firm pays, it believes in what it
has bought; a researcher's powers of concentration are enhanced
by a source of college tuition for his kids. The protests, directed
over NIH to the top officials in the Department of Health and
Human Services, Department of Commerce, and the White

House Office of Science and Technology Policy, were successful in getting the guidelines withdrawn.

The NIH problem is a common one in government, where many people believe that a pound of prevention is worth an ounce of cure. A library full of procurement regulations are supposed to make it impossible to cheat the government, or steal government property, or bribe government officials, or create situations that involve a conflict of interest. In fact, the regulations only make it impossible to do business with the government on a rational basis, and tens of thousands of prosecutors, investigators, and auditors still find enough work to fill their days.

5

Research and Tax Policy

Gimme Gravy

In the federal stew there is more than what's grown in government research labs and nurtured with federal grants and contracts. There's gravy, too. If you think of tax and economic policy as gravy, you won't be far off. Gravy covers everything with a rich, warm, uniform taste, having a similar effect on everything it touches. Fiscal and regulatory policies, and particularly those that are intended to improve and expand the U.S. business climate, have an effect on American businessmen that is at once uniform and uncontrolled.

Consider the tax credit for research and development. Business lobbyists and congressmen adore tax credits—not because they work so well but because tax credits are an instrument of policy that they uniquely control. They are so much easier to work into a voluminous tax bill than the equivalent subsidy would be to work into an appropriations measure. In addition, tax credits work impersonally, by holding out an incentive for future behavior instead of paying a direct reward that could be seen as a form of corruption.

Such was the tax credit for research and experimentation, usually known as the R&D tax credit.[1] It was slipped into President Reagan's big tax cut bill of 1981—a small item at a time when Democrats and Republicans were competing to offer as many incentives for business as possible. Although it sounds simple to give corporations a bit off their taxes if they spend money to innovate, the R&D tax credit couldn't be much more complicated, or unsuccessful.

Complicated? It reduced a company's tax by 25 percent of the company's increased R&D spending, but only "qualified" spending for innovation, not for mere product development, not for research done outside the United States, not for research in the humanities or social sciences, not for research funded by somebody else.

Though it may have been a boon to some companies, it was a big headache to the nation's tax collector. The Internal Revenue Service questioned the credits claimed by 79 percent of the corporations that were audited. About 20 percent of the amounts were questioned. It took the IRS a year and a half to propose regulations that sharpened the definition of what "qualified," and the issue wasn't really settled until Congress tinkered with the tax credit law in 1986. The revised version was more definite about qualified expenses, but it lowered the credit to 20 percent. Even after the clarification in 1987, the IRS argued with about 70 percent of the corporations claiming the credit.

For example: Aerospace companies claimed that they funded their own research in preparation for Defense Department contracts, while the IRS claimed that they would eventually be paid back from profits on the contract. Utility companies claimed credits for payments to industry research institutes, but the IRS objected that the institutes' spending was not all qualified research.

Another complicating issue was the way Congress set the base from which the increase should be computed. The base was to be the greater of a three-year average of qualified spending or half the current year's expenditure. What that meant was that young, rapidly growing companies without a three-year track record fell under the second standard, and received half the tax credit that older companies did. The point of the R&D tax credit was to encourage creativity, and yet the youngest, most creative companies received a lesser incentive. Worse still, unprofitable companies received no benefit until they became profitable. The companies that need help the most are the ones still struggling to make a profit.

Computing the base on a three-year average also reduces the

incentive. An increase this year raises the average and thus reduces the benefit next year. Consider a hypothetical ABC Corp., with spending on qualified research of $20 million last year, $15 million the year before, and $10 million the year before that, for an average of $15 million. If ABC spends $25 million on research this year, it will receive a tax credit of $2.5 million (25 percent of the $10 million increase), in addition to a deduction for the actual expense. With a 34 percent corporate rate, the after-tax cost of qualified research this year is $25 million, less $8.5 million for the tax benefit of the deduction, less $2.5 million for the tax credit, or $14 million. Without the tax credit, it would have been $16.5 million. Thus the tax credit lowered ABC's costs of qualified research by 15 percent.

At this point we should ask if ABC's behavior was really modified by the tax cut, since in our example it was raising research spending by $5 million a year anyway. If ABC was going to spend $25 million on research regardless of tax policy, then Uncle Sam just tore up $2.5 million. If the tax credit were really working, ABC would be spending $27.5 million on research. In the extreme case, ABC can receive a tax credit of $1.25 million (25 percent of the difference between the $15 million base and $20 million) if it does not increase research spending at all this year and reduced amounts even for reduced research spending.

Nothing on the Bottom Line

The General Accounting Office took a close look at the R&D tax credit in September 1989 and estimated that each dollar of lost tax revenue had stimulated between 15 and 36 cents of research spending. The gross numbers, in the period 1981 to 1985, were lost tax revenues of about $7 billion, stimulating between $1 and $2.5 billion of additional qualified research spending, out of a total of $154.7 billion spent on research in the private sector.

Among the other GAO findings from a sample of 800 corporations:

- 75 percent of the tax credits benefited companies that were raising R&D spending anyway.
- Another 11 percent of the credits went to companies that *stopped* increasing R&D spending during the period.

- The average actual tax benefit from the tax credit to a company for spending an extra dollar on research was about 4 cents.

(Critics of some of the GAO's accounting argued that the tax credit benefit should be compared to posttax, not pretax, profits, producing an estimate of the incentive of about 7.4 percent, and that the incentive would have greater effects in the long run than the short run.)

The GAO has the politically protective habit of writing inoffensively. Thus it concluded:

"It is commonly held that the average social rate of return on research and development is greater than the average social return on non-research spending."

(Translation: A lot of people say research is good for the economy, but they are just guessing.)

"If the activities that are encouraged by the credit are, in fact, more beneficial to society than the activities that are discouraged by the additional taxes needed to fund the credit, then the credit is acceptable tax policy."

(Translation: If the guess is correct, then we get more than we give up, and that would be okay.)

"However, the fact that the credit may be acceptable tax policy does not necessarily imply that it is better than alternative forms of government incentives to research. We have not evaluated tax incentives other than the credit, nor have we examined nontax incentives to R&D spending, such as research grants."

(Translation: Even if there is some incentive, a 4 percent incentive is obviously pretty shabby. You could get a 100 percent incentive by taking in the taxes and throwing back the money to researchers. Or you could let everybody decide their best investment opportunities for themselves by reducing corporate taxes. But we weren't told to talk about that, so we won't.)

Getting Worse

Since the 1981–85 period studied by the GAO, the effectiveness of the R&D tax credit has diminished. First, the rate of the credit was cut to 20 percent. Second, the corporate tax rate was cut, reducing the value of all credits and deductions. Third, the R&D tax credit has been set to expire three times in five years, and each time it was revived only at the last minute and only for brief extensions.

Under such uncertainty, most executives admit they cannot factor the R&D tax credit into their investment plans. Its incentive to increase their investment was zero. It was a simple gift, after the fact, to fortunate companies.

That hasn't stopped Congress from continuing to play with the R&D tax credit. The latest version, adopted in 1989, creates an even more complex formula that factors in R&D as a percentage of sales and caps the tax credit allowed to the fastest growing companies. Even consultants hired by supporters of the tax credit could not find much stimulus to this, and to find any they had to assume, falsely, that the law would be definitely enacted and stay in force for five years.

In truth, R&D spending already enjoys a favored position in the tax code without any credit at all, because it can be deducted as a business expense, even though it is supposed to be an expenditure to create a business asset. Most such expenditures are depreciated; that is, expenses are taken only gradually during the life of the asset created.

The deduction of R&D spending as a business expense, normally not controversial even though it reduces corporate income tax revenues by $1.75 billion a year,[2] has been attacked, but only in the eternal Washington war among interest groups. In the summer of 1989, Rep. Andrew Jacobs, an Indiana Democrat, got the Ways & Means Committee to tack on an amendment that would have required corporations to spread R&D write-offs over five years for work done *abroad*. It was a raid on multinationals, to punish them for exporting jobs. Multinationals led by IBM—which has major research facilities in Japan and Switzerland—were powerful enough to get the amendment dropped later, but at some cost to the reputation of the United States as a good place to do business.

Tax Incentives

The United States has other tax options open if the country wishes to send more investment capital in the direction of high-tech industries. It could give more incentives to the accumulation of long-term hoards of investment capital:

- The Individual Retirement Account, a very popular provision that allowed working individuals a $2,000 tax deduction for savings, may not have spurred much new savings, but by shielding from tax the dividends and capital gains earned in the IRA, while placing a tax penalty on withdrawals before age 59, it acts to keep some savings locked up and available for long-term investing. Many IRA investors are aware that the long-term returns to investing in the stock market exceed the returns to bonds and bank accounts, so they have put a generous share of their money in growth-stock mutual funds.
- Proposed variations on the IRA include Individual This-and-That Accounts, aimed at encouraging people to save for, variously, college tuition, a first home, old-age medical benefits, and what-have-you. The best variation is the most sweeping: an Individual Investment Account that would allow tax deductible deposits and tax deferral of dividends and interest earned in the account's investments. Withdrawals of principal and earnings would be fully taxed as income, plus a 10 percent penalty on the withdrawal of principal, which would be assumed to be withdrawn first. This provides a sweeping incentive to save and invest for the long term.
- Business and financial leaders prefer incentives that operate to help firms, rather than individuals. Thus Treasury Secretary Nicholas Brady—and many before him—want to eliminate the "double taxation of dividends." Corporations pay taxes on their income, and then pay dividends, which the individual pays taxes on as income. Naturally, rather than make dividends tax-free to the individual, advocates of this change want to give corporations a tax deduction for paying dividends. Under our current system, this is a perverse incentive as far as the individual is concerned. He pays no tax on the increased value of the corporation's stock if the corporation does not pay a dividend and reinvests the money in its business. Or, if his investment is held for him in a pension fund or IRA, he already pays no tax on the dividend. Eliminating the double taxation of dividends is just an award to corporations that pay dividends. That would not be an incentive to economic growth because the corpora-

tions that pay dividends usually are those that are not expanding rapidly. They pay dividends as a substitute for increasing the value of the firm and its stock.

A Modest Proposal

It might make more sense to reduce the corporate income tax or eliminate it altogether. That would leave corporations substantially wealthier but not affect their outlook on whether to pay dividends, taxable to the individual, or reinvest earnings in the business, with resulting gains taxable to the individual when he sells his appreciated stock.

A proposition like killing the corporate income tax seems so sweeping and unaffordable, especially in the perpetual budget crunch, but consider the true cost. In fiscal 1991, the corporate income tax, at a maximum rate of 34 percent of taxable income, was expected to bring in revenues of $129.7 billion—about 10 percent of the total federal tax take. The federal government forgoes $75 billion a year of taxes to support residential real estate,[3] and that should be the first place to look for revenue.

Every year, in a little-noticed addendum to the U.S. Budget, the Office of Management and Budget publishes figures on tax expenditures. That's the amount of revenue the Treasury loses when Congress legislates a tax credit or a deduction from the income tax.

In planning for fiscal 1991, the deduction for interest paid on mortgages on owner-occupied housing was estimated to cost the Treasury $46.5 billion and the deduction for property tax on such homes was worth another $12.4 billion. The deferral of capital gains on the sale of such houses was worth $13.2 billion and the partial exclusion of capital gains on home sales by persons over 55 was worth $3.2 billion. Total: $75.32 billion.

There are other legislated benefits for home ownership. There's FHA insurance on many home mortgages, implicit guarantees for mortgage-backed securities, created by Fannie Mae, Freddie Mac, and Ginnie Mae, and VA guarantees on mortgages for veterans. OMB only recently began computing the subsidy equivalent of these and other guarantee and insurance programs; their cost on that basis runs more than $2 billion a year. But, as the system of deposit insurance has illustrated, the ultimate cost of such programs is unforeseeable. Making good on deposit insurance for savings and loan associations is costing the taxpayers about $200 billion, plus hundreds of billions more for interest. All these subsidies are ultimately self-defeating—for when the government attempts to make housing more affordable, those advantages are quickly used to bid up the price of houses.

The subsidies for home ownership come at the expense of the whole economy. Investments in homes tie up hundreds of billions of dollars of American capital that could be freed for more productive investments if home ownership were not such an overwhelmingly favorable tax shelter.

There are, of course, tax shelters for commercial real estate, too: $8.5 billion on accelerated depreciation of rental housing and other buildings; $6.5 billion on investment credits on real estate; $4.2 billion in favored treatment for rental losses. Total: $19.2 billion.

The largest tax shelter in the whole tax code is the one that allows employees not to count as income their employers' contributions to their pension funds or the earnings of those funds. It costs the tax system $46.9 billion a year. On the other hand, it is a major stimulus for the accumulation of wealth in long-term investments.

The exclusion from personal income of employer contributions for medical insurance costs the Treasury $33.4 billion. This tax break is so common that most people don't even know it's a tax break. Nevertheless it just pushes up the general price of health care and causes people to be less interested in the cost of their coverage.

Politics aside, the United States could offset 80 percent of the corporate income tax by eliminating two pernicious tax breaks for individuals—on homes and health insurance. In the financial readjustment that would follow, interest rates, and prices for homes and health care, would probably fall even faster than other prices, while business profits would rise. The other 20 percent of the corporate tax take would come back to the Treasury eventually, because business profits ultimately would be captured in the form of personal income taxes on capital gains and dividends. In addition, there should be a large stimulus to the economy as businesses fund more investment and more hiring with their greater profits.

Two little words stand in the way: "politics aside." Making people pay more so business can pay less might be good policy, but it's suicidal politics.

More Likely Proposals

When Congress and the president negotiate at budget summits, such major reforms are never on the table. Nobody can imagine selling them to the electorate. More moderate income sources also exist, but the 1990 budget follies showed how hard they are to legislate.

Raising the motor fuels tax is worth $1 billion for every penny—50 cents a gallon would raise real money and provide an incentive for less thirsty cars and trucks and the efficient use of the transportation system.

Quadrupling the 16-cent tobacco tax is worth $8 billion—maybe less if the high tax causes people to quit smoking, but that will save money on reduced health care cost in the future.

Quadrupling the tax on alcoholic beverages is worth $6 billion—maybe less now and more later on the same rationale as the cigarette tax.

How about a new tax? Those who wish to use the tax system to increase savings, investment, and economic growth often turn to consumption taxes, a sales tax, or a value-added tax, because savings and investments escape taxation. State sales taxes are almost everywhere less unpopular than state income taxes or local property taxes. But at the federal level, the value-added tax is considered anathema. Rep. Al Ullman, an Oregon Democrat who was chairman of the House Ways and Means Committee in the late 70s, was defeated for reelection after supporting a VAT. This combination of two rare events—a senior congressman supporting a new tax and a senior congressman being defeated, are assumed by his more cautious successors to have a cause and effect relationship. They won't touch the VAT. It was hard enough to win even modest increases in the excise taxes during the budget crisis of 1990.

But a value-added tax—a percentage levy on the difference between business sales and purchases—has real power. The General Accounting Office estimated in 1989 that a 5 percent VAT would raise $125 billion. That's just about enough to replace the corporate income tax. Even a 5 percent VAT exempting food, housing, and medical care, in order to hold down prices of those basic necessities, would raise $72 billion.[4]

European countries generally have value added taxes in excess of 10 percent. An attractive side issue is that the General Agreement on Tariffs and Trade allows a VAT rebate on goods for export, which is not allowed for corporate income taxes. That pushes a substantial tax wedge between the prices that U.S. exporters must charge and the prices charged by their European competitors. An American VAT in European proportions can balance the federal budget and dismiss the annual fraud of a budget crisis. Or it can replace whatever tax we believe harms the economy the most.

The Social Security Mess

There is another tax that is a clear candidate for cutting. It also presents the greatest challenge to American economic stability.

The Social Security tax (FICA on your payroll check) finances Social Security retirement and disability benefits and the basic hospitalization benefits of Medicare. In 1990, the rate stood at 15.3 percent of taxable payroll, paid in equal shares by employer and employee. Any payroll tax is a disincentive to work and to hiring workers, but this one works an especially pernicious effect on the U.S. economy.

The first bad feature is that it is flat rate, rather than progressive. It takes 15.3 percent from a worker making $20,000 and 15.3 percent from a worker making $50,000. The personal income tax is progressive, taking 15 percent from the $20,000 worker and 28 percent or 33 percent from those with higher income.

The second bad feature is that the tax is only levied on incomes up to $51,300 ($54,300 effective January 1, 1991, and on up in 1992 and 1993). There is no Social Security tax on further income beyond the ceiling and no Social Security tax on income from sources other than wages, such as dividends and interest.

The third bad feature is that there are no deductions, exemptions, or adjustments. Earn a dollar, pay 7.65 cents. Pay a worker a dollar, pay 7.65 cents. A worker who later loses his job gets no rebate; an employer whose business is unprofitable pays just as much as one whose business can afford it.

The fourth bad feature is that the Social Security tax is simply set too high for current needs. The Social Security system nearly went broke in the late 70s and again in the early 80s because benefits had been raised faster than the stagnating economy raised receipts. Two "reforms," one under President Carter and the other under President Reagan, restored the system to solvency by a series of tax increases. The Social Security tax rate was increased, the wage level was raised, some benefits were subjected to the income tax, and the retirement age was raised for 21st century retirees. The second reform, however, also tried to handle the future retirement of the baby boom generation.

In theory, the Social Security trust fund will amass extra balances for about the next three decades, accumulating a surplus that is being invested now to pay benefits to baby boomers during their retirement years.

In practice, however, the Social Security trust fund is invested in Treasury bonds. Surplus Social Security tax revenues are being used to buy bonds that would otherwise be sold to the public as part of the federal deficit. Nearly $75 billion of deficit bonds were handed off to Social Security in fiscal 1990. The Social Security trust fund will eventually accumulate about *$14 trillion* in tax receipts and compounded interest, all invested in Treasury bonds. When the baby boomers retire, Social Security will pay their benefits by cashing in bonds, so then the Treasury will have to find the money elsewhere—either by borrowing from other lenders or by raising taxes.

At current spending levels, our policy is to have the Social Security tax set too high so that income taxes can be set too low. Starting around 2025, policy will reverse: income taxes will have to be set too high, so that Social Security taxes can be set too low.

If current tax policy makes sense, then our plan for the future is stupid. Or possibly the reverse is true. Actually, both current tax policy and our plan for the future are flawed. We are currently deluding ourselves that the federal budget deficit is $75 billion a year lower than it actually is. We also are deluding ourselves into thinking that President Reagan actually delivered on his promise not to raise taxes, when in fact the reforms of 1978 and 1983 provided automatic Social Security tax increases every year into the 90s. And we are deluding ourselves into thinking that we have provided for the baby boomers' Social Security benefits.

Make Lemonade

An interesting experiment would be to take a piece of the Social Security surplus and treat it as pension fund money—place it with private venture capitalists and investment managers, with instructions that they must take a long-term, buy-and-hold strategy. No junk loans—they should take equity positions. And they should try to attract money from other sources and funds to go in with them. The International Finance Corp., an arm of the World Bank, does this with Third World countries, establishing single-country mutual funds to attract investment for countries with immature markets. From the investment point of view, there's not much chance that this would produce abnormally good returns. Investment advisers' results on the average private pension fund usually don't quite measure up to the returns on the S&P index of 500 stocks. Still, it might provide a source of patient equity capital for American business without too much distortion of the investment economy.

Economist Barry Bluestone and some colleagues offered a similar idea aimed at training the American work force. Writing for the Economic Policy Institute, they offered the idea of taking a chunk of the Social Security surplus to create a revolving loan fund that would finance the costs of higher education or vocational training. Repayment over 25 years would be handled on the income tax withholding system. There is no chance that this would be a good deal for the Social Security trust fund, and it's not really clear that existing programs are so inadequate that many Americans are held back from their highest potential by the cost of an education. Still, the idea of using the Social Security trust fund for long-term investment has merit.

Another Alternative

Anyone can make suggestions for turning the Social Security trust fund into a bank to finance one's favorite cause. In fact, the ease of putting forward a competing idea is probably one reason the trust fund may remain entirely in government bonds. The question is, should the trust fund exist at all?

Congress could cut the Social Security tax take by $75 billion a year, putting Social Security and Medicare on a pay-as-you-go basis. It could enact automatic tax rate adjustments up and down each year to keep pace with economic growth. The 1991 combined employer and employee Social Security tax would be cut from more than 15 percent to about 12 percent. Eliminating the ceiling and taxing all wages, and levying the income tax on all Social Security benefits, would allow the flat rate to be cut to less than 10 percent. The disincentive to employment and productivity would be reduced accordingly.

The whole Social Security problem is rooted in the baby boom. When the boomers retire, there will only be about two workers for every retiree. More than three workers' taxes support each retiree's benefits today. There is a solution that does not require tax hikes: raise the number of workers. No, not with fertility drugs—with immigration. Raising the number of workers allowed to immigrate to the United States could settle the Social Security funding debate.

U.S. policy admits most new residents on the basis of kinship with a U.S. citizen or resident alien. The government tries to exclude people who might become a charge on the public welfare system, but selecting immigrants for their potential contribution to the U.S. economy could have larger economic benefits. A few congressmen have suggested giving preference to persons with skills in short supply or who are willing to settle in regions with a labor shortage. This concentration on jobs is a vestige of the fear that immigrants will displace American workers.

A better concentration would be on the aptitudes and skills that applicants would bring to the country. Australia and Canada, for example, use a point system to rate applicants on their likelihood of economic success. Points are earned for language proficiency, years of education, professional standing, and wealth. If we think it's a privilege to live in the United States, why should we not award that privilege based on standards that will enhance the privilege? A new immigration law enacted in November 1990 took a small step in this direction.

A Presidential Favorite

What about reduction of the capital gains tax, which President Bush made a key objective of his first term? It sounds simple: reducing the tax rate on capital gains, thus increasing the after-tax earnings of capital, should stimulate more savings, thus creating investment. President Bush's economists even said the capital gains tax cut would pay for itself, because investors would be so much more willing to cash in successful investments if they had to pay a lower tax rate that the volume of gains taxes would overcome the loss from the lower tax rate. (Stock brokers agree, with enthusiasm for the commissions that would be generated.) Democrats in Congress had their own economists, who argued that this effect would diminish in a few years, creating a large, permanent loss to the Treasury.

Another way to reform the capital gains tax was offered in the blueprint for tax reform produced by the Treasury Department in 1984.[5] This called for reducing reported capital gains to exempt the illusory gains created by inflation. This would reduce the effective rate levied on assets held for long periods without going back to a differential rate.

Actually levying the tax at the time of the gain might also enhance revenue. In addition to the tax-free rollover on homes and the deferral for a home sale after age 55, current law allows heirs of property to value the property as of the date of death of the giver, but does not require the estate to pay a capital gains tax. In other words, capital gains on property that's held until the death of the owner are never taxed, costing the Treasury $14.5 billion a year. (The first $600,000 of an estate is exempt from tax and any lawyer worth his fee can devise shelters for much more, so the estate tax brings in less than $10 billion a year.)

A lower capital gains tax is no simple matter. It has different effects on different people, and some of those effects are contradictory. For most of the period after World War II, a portion of capital gains were excluded from income, thus lowering the effective tax rate. In the 1986 Tax Reform Act, the exclusion was repealed. Sen. Bill Bradley, the New Jersey Democrat who was the architect of tax reform, wanted the capital gains tax differential abolished as much as he wanted the other key point, lower individual tax rates. The reason was that U.S. taxpayers had become adept at converting ordinary income into the semblance of capital gains, through tax shelters.

In a simple tax shelter, an investor purchased an interest in property, such as real estate. The investment would have high expenses for such tax-deductible things as interest and depreciation and would "throw off" losses to the investor for tax purposes, thus reducing his taxable income. Later, the property would be sold for a profit, which would be taxable as a capital gain to the investor.

Real estate was always a good tax shelter investment, because

the tax code contained hundreds of extra quirks favoring real estate that had been enacted by lawmakers hoping to encourage
more private investment in housing without spending money on
outright subsidies. Energy properties, from oil wells to windmills,
were also particularly favored.

President Bush, a veteran of the Texas oil business, sees nothing wrong with using tax policy for social engineering. Bradley
finds it wasteful, inefficient, and possibly, if he were frank, just
not aesthetically appealing. He would prefer an orderly government policy, made by "policymakers," even though he has been
quite adept at the messy political business of building compro-
mises.

The High Cost of Capital

The president's capital gains tax issue appeals to many commen-
tators and businessmen who say the big advantage Japanese industrialists have over Americans is a lower cost of capital. The
Japanese government provides small businesses with low-cost
loans and leases for capital equipment; the Japanese banks and
trading companies, linked together in combines called *keiretsu*,
provide low-cost capital to larger industrial firms. You can hear
this story from captains of industry, from academics, from venture capitalists, from the heads of small startup firms, from Wall
Street financial wizards, from professional Washington advisers
and industry lobbyists, from influential congressmen.

George Hatsopoulos, chief executive officer of Thermo Electron, a Fortune 500 maker of electrical equipment, chaired a committee on the cost of capital formed by the American Business
Conference. He wrote a book on the issue, plus numerous articles
and papers. He has become Mr. Cost of Capital to U.S. businessmen and politicians. He summarizes the disparity between Japan
and the United States[6] this way:

- Japanese companies obtain more financing by debt, with
  typical financial structures of 75 percent instead of the U.S.
  average of 25 percent debt.
- The Japanese people save three times as much of their
  income as Americans, which creates a pool of investment
  capital.

- Government policy in Japan does not tax capital gains, and encourages savings and investment.

Other observers focus on the *keiretsu*, the web of financial arrangements managed by large Japanese banks. There are elaborate interlocking directorates, long-standing supplier-customer relationships and other forces creating stable, patient financing for these corporations. IBM President Jack Kuehler told a congressional committee, "The long-term perspective of the Japanese investment community appears to free Japanese companies from a quarter by quarter results orientation."[7]

And what does the United States do? Many U.S. managers say that Wall Street demands constantly improving earnings, quarter-by-quarter. They condemn this as short-sighted conservatism that makes it impossible for enlightened managers such as themselves to make strategic investments that may hurt earnings in the short run but will strengthen the firm's competitive position in the long run.

This argument is at least a case of American business hoisting itself on its own petard, since the Wall Street institutions that are so narrow and short-sighted about American business are the very institutions that American business hires to manage its pension funds—and fires without a second thought when the quarterly performance of a fund lags a market average.

Further, there is a very strong case to make that Wall Street investors are not particularly oriented to the short term—they just bid down the price of shares in companies when they perceive that corporate managers are making mistakes. It should be obvious, from the lofty price-earnings ratios that favored companies sport, that investors will pay handsomely for the prospect of long-term growth. There's an old Wall Street joke about the price of a stock being so high that it discounts not only the future, but the hereafter as well. Somewhere between 20 times earnings and 50 times earnings, a stock price for a mature company is so rich that it cannot be justified by any conceivable estimate of growth. Yet at most times, institutions cheerfully accumulate such stocks. Unsatisfied managers are those whose companies are not so favored.

Besides, there is evidence that the best source of corporate capital is the corporation, not the private savings of individuals. Hatsopoulos and others who have worried about the decline of the

U.S. savings rate received a sharp rebuke in a recent study by Robert A. Blecker for the Economic Policy Institute in Washington.[8] Marshaling the evidence against the proposition that Americans are living beyond their means, Blecker noticed a very interesting statistical discrepancy.

A small decline in private savings and the large increase in government deficits did not account for the reported large decline in the national savings rate. A large part was attributable to a decline in business saving. That, in turn, was not attributable to a decline in corporate earnings, but to a large increase in capital consumption allowances, basically depreciation of fixed investment. Accelerated depreciation allowances were a major feature of the business tax cuts of the early 80s.

Adding depreciation to retained earnings produces gross corporate saving, which, Blecker notes, was 8.6 percent of GNP in the 80s, higher than in the 60s or 70s. "Clearly," he says, "there was no shortage of cash flowing through the coffers of American business." Interestingly, more of the cash flowed out again, as dividends and interest—especially interest—than in previous decades.

The High Cost of Debt

The evidence seems to point to the increasing propensity of business to borrow. Ask an industry-sponsored think tank in Washington called the American Council for Capital Formation. In testimony to the House Ways & Means Committee,[9] Council President Mark Bloomfield rolled out all the arguments against the Tax Reform Act of 1986.

Equalizing tax treatment of different investments, Bloomfield said, discriminated against savings and investment, compared to previous tax treatment. In particular, the effective tax rate on business equipment nearly quadrupled, while other increases were much milder. The reason was the loss of the Investment Tax Credit, the stretching out of depreciation schedules, and the imposition of a new Alternative Minimum Tax.

Bloomfield said that high U.S. interest rates are a major source of the difference in the cost of capital. On one level that sounds like the old saw about the cause of poverty being that people don't have any money; but Bloomfield was arguing that long depreciation schedules mean that tax benefits from depreciation are spread out over a long period of time, while high interest rates mean they are less valuable when discounted for the time value of money.

The most important argument that Bloomfield made was that the Tax Reform Act of 1986, by raising the tax rate on capital gains and lowering the tax rate on ordinary income, changed the American financial outlook further away from equity and further toward debt. "The potential costs of a highly leveraged economy are real," said Bloomfield. "A deeply indebted economy is subject to collapse in any substantial downturn."

The Sound of His Wings

While true, this observation applies even more strongly to Japan, a much more leveraged economy than that of the United States. Financial analysts have commented for many years that the chief advantage of the Japanese *keiretsu* system of interlocking ownership is that it locks up the supply of corporate equities, leaving comparatively small blocs of shares to be fought over by outside investors. Then as their fighting bids up the price of shares, Japanese accounting allows the corporate holders to include the appreciation of investments as earnings.

The price of Japanese real estate and the price index on the Tokyo Stock Exchange spiraled upward together in the 70s and 80s. Happy homeowners mortgaged their profits to buy stock, while happy shareholders took margin loans on stock to buy homes. This was unsustainable, but going short on the Tokyo Stock Exchange was a humbling, painful experience.

The Tokyo Stock Exchange peaked at the beginning of 1990 and fell 39 percent in the first nine months of the year. It was not obvious how much further it could go, but it was clear that the same leverage that was such an advantage on the way up could produce great losses on the way down.

While Bloomfield argued against debt, other advocates are more inclined to envy the Japanese their easy credit. Several advocates have proposed recently that the U.S. government should create a national high-tech investment bank that would lend money to strategic industries at a "fair" interest rate.

Rep. Mel Levine, D-Calif., put forward a proposal to create the

Technology Corporation of America. He envisioned a permanent venture capital fund receiving $50 million a year in federal funds, to be managed by industry recipients who would also match the federal largesse.

It is turning out, moreover, that the Japanese financial system is no "fairer" than the American system. Hit with losses on the equity side, major Japanese banks had to make money somewhere, and they turned to their loan portfolios. Market interest rates rose from under 5 percent to nearly 9 percent. Squeezing the cost of capital, however, is a two-edged sword, for higher interests rates force down the value of the bonds in bank portfolios. Fortunately for the banks' financial statements, there was no requirement to record these portfolio declines as earnings losses.

The Japanese system offered other ways for banks to camouflage their risky position. *Keiretsu* members are obliged to buy each others' shares, so a member in need of capital has willing buyers for his new stock issues. This is helpful as long as the issuing company has good prospects; in troubled times it will prolong the crisis and spread contagion through the whole group.

Daniel Kreps of SRI International, a former managing director of Chemical Sanwa Merchant Bank, reported that the 40 percent drop in the Japanese stock market translated to a $60 billion loss for the five biggest Japanese banks. "The damage that a prolonged bear market in Tokyo would conflict on the Japanese banking system is potentially staggering," he said.[10]

Making matters worse, the Japanese real estate market seemed to have reached a peak in 1990 as well. Then came higher interest rates.

Simultaneous crises in the stock and real estate markets will test any economy. The resilience and cooperation of the Japanese financial system have been the envy of the United States, but those very qualities may have only delayed an inevitable reckoning, and concentrated its effects. The savings and loan crisis in the United States has placed a heavy burden on housing and housing finance, but not on the whole economy. Japanese banks have financed real estate and industry with the same enthusiastic leverage, so a crisis could have far wider effects.

There may be much to envy in the Japanese system, but there is much to fear as well.

6
Research and the Cost of Capital

A Careful Look at Capital

In a 1990 speech to a National Academy of Engineering symposium on technology and economics, George Hatsopoulos divided the cost of capital issue into the cost of debt and the cost of equity.[1] Open capital markets and, since the mid–80s, cooperation between the Federal Reserve and the Bank of Japan, are driving the cost of debt in the two countries together, he acknowledged. But, he said, the cost of equity remains quite stubbornly about three times higher in the United States than in Japan.

The cost of debt is simple—it's the interest rate a borrower must pay to induce a lender to lend. That is simply the rate of return on (essentially risk-free) U.S. Treasuries plus a premium for the risk that the borrower won't make timely payments. Unless a borrower is obviously on the brink of disaster, this premium is rarely more than five percentage points and is usually much less, even for "junk" issuers.

The cost of equity is harder. From the investor's point of view, it's the expected appreciation in the market price of the company stock, plus the expected stream of dividends, all discounted to present value to reflect both the time value of money and the investor's perception of the risk that the expectations won't materialize. This concept is not even easy to say. Take it one step at a time:

1. Buy low, sell high. Is this stock going up? How much? When?

2. Current and future yield. Does the stock pay a dividend? Will the company increase the dividend?
3. The risk-free alternative. What would be the return on same investment in U.S. Treasury debt?
4. The risk premium. How much more return does the investor require to ignore the greater risk that the investment will not pay off as expected in (1) and (2)?

Stock market investors in the United States usually don't focus on this four-step calculation explicitly, except for current yield of dividends. For the other steps, most investors substitute earnings, and the multiple of earnings that they are willing to pay for a stock. Stocks that have rapidly growing earnings, and stocks that many investors *believe* will have rapidly growing earnings, usually command prices that are higher multiples of today's earnings. Stocks with poor prospects command low multiples.

From this "simple" process U.S. stock market analysts generate millions of pages of securities analysis each year. Opinions, of course, are far from uniform, but the mass opinion about each company is incorporated in its market price. Investors assimilate this advice, plus information about the overall market and the economy. Their actions in the market, buying and selling, then set the minute-by-minute price of shares in thousands of American corporations. (An attempt to purchase the entire corporation, or a controlling interest, drives up share prices because the buyer has different motives. In effect, he pays a "control premium" for his bulk purchase.)

The Cost of Equity

One way corporate managers can estimate their cost of equity is to take their companies' price-earnings ratios and turn them upside down. The earnings-price ratio, also known as *earnings yield*, is expressed as a percentage, and it is a measure of the corporation's cost of equity. By this method, a company whose stock is selling at six times earnings (pretty low for the U.S. market) therefore has a cost of equity of $1/6$, or 16 percent. A company whose stock sells at 25 times earnings, (pretty high for the U.S. market), has a cost of equity of $1/25$ or 4 percent.

This method makes a lot of sense, because earnings are the chief source of a company's equity and this method tells the manager how investors value his efforts. At the very least, a high cost of equity tells a manager in search of new financing to borrow rather than issue new stock. The extreme case, issuing new debt and taking the company off the stock exchange, is called a *leveraged buyout*, or LBO.

A persistent high cost of capital also is the market's signal to the board of directors to fire the manager. An unfriendly takeover bid is often a real-world substitute for firing the manager. Managers in the real world often take defensive steps such as using corporate funds to repurchase stock or hike the dividend. They may even maneuver the company into erecting takeover defenses. The golden parachute awards some of the company's remaining wealth to managers who lose a takeover battle; the poison pill contracts the company to give away a valuable asset if it's taken over. All such steps are defended as giving managers more time for their long-term strategies to succeed, but they are usually not that at all. Takeover defenses most often amount to theft of shareholders' property, or, when done with a shareholders' vote, gifts of their property to management.

A Capital Hurdle

Thermo Electron enjoys a price earnings ratio in the mid-20s, but Chairman George Hatsopoulos is still hungry for equity capital. Debt requires a corporation to make steady payments of interest and timely repayment of principal, no matter what. Equity transfers some risk from the corporation to the investor. So Hatsopoulos prefers a different way—a manager's way oriented to the cost of corporate projects—of figuring the cost of equity. He says corporate managers must "invest only in those projects that promise to return a pretax profit sufficient to provide the taxes required by law, the interest required by lenders, and the dividends and capital gains required by equity holders." Thus "the real net cost of capital for an investment is the least return that satisfies all of the requirements cited above."[2]

What's the difference? Hatsopoulos makes explicit the fact that managers must choose between reinvesting earnings in the business (or another business) and paying dividends. Paying dividends helps satisfy the requirements of equity holders. So would reinvesting earnings in the business, but only if the new investment is perceived by shareholders to add more value to the company and to stock prices in the future and to their wealth than the dividend would add to their wealth here and now. Managers know this required after-tax, after-interest return on investment as the hurdle rate. A project's return must clear the hurdle rate to win approval, as a racer must clear hurdles to reach the finish line.

Hatsopoulos and many allies argue that the hurdle rate in Japan is lower than it is in the United States, therefore U.S. firms have a disadvantage in the cost of capital, which is expressed in the inability of U.S. managers to undertake investments that Japanese managers can undertake. The assertion, however, begs a question: In what sense is the ability to undertake projects with a low rate of return an advantage over the restriction that investments must have a high rate of return?

This is a question that must be asked whenever we hear an American manager complain about some unfair advantage enjoyed by his Japanese competitors. It often turns out that the advantage is no advantage at all, but a willingness of Japanese managers of capital to put their capital to work at lower rates of return.

Debt versus Equity

William Farley, chairman of Farley Industries, a conglomerate, offered a classic example of muddled reasoning about capital, using the example of a startup that requires $5 million in financing and is expected to be worth $100 million in 10 years:[3]

> If you borrow [$5 million] from a commercial bank at 10 percent interest, over 10 years you will pay $5 million in interest. If you can sell high-yield bonds [as Farley did in his own business], you will pay $7.5 million in interest over 10 years. But if you had to give up a modest 25 percent in equity to get that $5 million—and if you pay no dividends—you will end up giving up $20 million in value.

Farley figures therefore that your cost of equity is nearly three times your cost of debt.

If Farley actually operated on analysis like this, there would be no Farley Industries. (Indeed, at this writing, Farley Industries was poised on the brink of bankruptcy because of its overuse of junk debt.) There are two points he overlooks—one straightforward, one more complex. On the simplest basis, he ignores the fact that an equity financing does not drain cash from a young company. In his example, the startup firm financed by debt must cough up $500,000 a year, whether or not it is profitable, whether or not it needs that cash to invest in its business. The startup firm financed by equity investment puts all the money to work.

In return for not receiving those interest payments, the equity investor receives, in Farley's example, 20 percent of the successful company. He also receives 20 percent of unsuccessful companies. His total portfolio of investments averages out to a return that is by no means exorbitant. Note Farley's assertion that the new company is expected to be worth $100 million 10 years down the road. At the time the businessman gets the venture capitalist's money, all that value is strictly in the businessman's mind. The businessman actually gets $5 million in exchange for some stock certificates worth a few cents in paper and ink. Not a bad deal.

Junk Debt

The weakness of the Japanese system of debt financing, at least if applied to American businesses, was illustrated clearly in 1989 and 1990, when hundreds of billions of dollars of junk bond financing began to shake and tremble. Companies that were overloaded with debt, like Campeau and Farley and Integrated Resources, found they could not make their interest payments and that they could not sell assets quickly to raise needed cash.

Behind the scenes, there was another reason for problems in the junk bond market. Michael Milken, the junk bond investment banker who virtually created the market for risky debt, was accused of trading on inside information about his deals and was pushed out of his firm, Drexel Burnham Lambert. Milken had done a lot more than simply advise companies and sell their debt. He advised his clients on financial and business strategy. He arranged for his clients to sell their debt to each other. He bought their debt for himself and his partners in order to keep the junk bond market stable and seemingly safe. In short, he acted like the Japanese banks at the center of the Japanese financial system.

When Milken became the target of civil and criminal investigations, he lost his power to stabilize the junk bond market. Highly leveraged American companies found themselves in a great deal of trouble, and they haven't recovered yet. There is no telling what might cause the Japanese banks to lose their power to stabilize the highly leveraged Japanese corporate financial structure. Other such structures have been brought down by real estate crashes, stock market crashes, waves of debt repudiation, and the discovery of fraud.

Throwing Away Capital

Whatever happens to the Japanese financial system, Americans need a new approach to the whole cost of capital issue.

Once upon a time the United States was the chief source of capital in the world. The rest of the world had blown its physical capital stock to bits in World War II, while sending its financial capital to the United States to purchase the weapons of war. After the war, the disparity was so great that the United States could afford to give capital away. The world is still readjusting away from this great imbalance.

As the world economy grew, it drew down the store of capital hoarded in the United States. This process was essentially complete by about 1973, what with the United States making it run faster by blowing up thousands of helicopters, airplanes, and young men in the quagmire of Vietnam. After that, the balance of capital power began to shift toward those countries that were laying up new stores of capital. The first signs of strain occurred with the oil crises of the 70s. The United States could not simply dig deeper into its pocket to pay the higher prices OPEC nations demanded. Nor did Americans quickly reduce their consumption, either of energy or of other goods. Instead, the United States debased its currency with a round of inflation, paying OPEC in new dollars that would buy less than the old dollars.

Although this was comfortable for the United States and amounted to cheating the oil producers, it was also of enormous benefit to Europeans and Japanese businesses. In the short term, they were required to adjust, painfully, to the higher price of energy. Thus they conserved energy more diligently and increased their industrial efficiency. Later, U.S. inflation caused the value of their currency to rise against the dollar, so the cost of oil priced in dollars fell in terms of pounds, marks, yen, francs, and guilders.

Until 1981, the United States was keeping up with Europe and

Japan, creating capital adequate for its internal needs plus investment abroad. Then came Reaganomics: the United States cut taxes, raised military spending, went into recession, and added large incentives for "investment" capital that found its way into real estate loans.

Things began to go wrong. Hundreds of billions of dollars of U.S. bank loans to Mexico, Brazil, Argentina, and other Latin American nations turned out to have financed fur coats instead of power dams, wage hikes instead of telephone systems, trips to Europe instead of oil wells. What should have been loans to productive Mexican businesses turned out to be gifts to rich Mexicans, for the Mexicans had no intention or ability to pay back the loans. The result, still not entirely admitted or accounted for, was the destruction of that much U.S. capital.

More hundreds of billions of dollars of loans were ploughed into U.S. real estate. On the residential side, easy money pushed up the price of homes, enriching those who owned them. On the commercial side, easy money and tax breaks facilitated the construction of office buildings and hotels nobody actually needed. The result, still not entirely admitted or accounted for, was the destruction of that much U.S. capital.

Meanwhile, the U.S. government sector ran deficits between $100 billion and $300 billion a year, while private citizens practically quit saving. It's impossible to explain why we ran huge government deficits; the collapse in private savings has three basic causes.

Savings and the Lack of It

First, the baby boom generation arrived at the age of family formation. Creating households and having children is an expensive time of life; hardly anyone saves money and most people borrow heavily.

Second, the rise of Social Security and Medicare benefits and the increased scope of employer-financed pension plans has (justifiably or not) reduced most Americans' worries about old age. Americans are (safely or not) substituting the promises of others for their own provisions. Corporate contributions to employee pension plans, oddly enough, are not considered savings in the national income and product accounts.

Third, the rise in the price of houses has given American home-owners a source of wealth that also reduces their worries about old age. Americans are substituting their mortgage payment for their deposit in a savings plan.

As to the first point, there are good prospects: the baby boomers are aging and moving into the period when their needs are well satisfied and their incomes are still increasing, so the savings rate is likely to increase. Prospects under the second point are dependent on the security of the pension promises and the wisdom of those who manage the investment of accumulated funds. On the third point, prospects are the reverse of those of the first point, since the baby boomers have worked their way through their period of household formation and home purchase, so the demand for housing is slowing down, and the price of houses is less a thrill than a source of anxiety.

If the United States wants cheaper capital, for development of high-tech industries or any other purpose, it must create more capital and waste less. It can tinker with exchange rates and interest rates from now to the end of the world, and they will not confer wealth upon the nation. Productive endeavor, creating goods, and performing services—adding value—does that.

Dale W. Jorgensen, a Harvard economist who has specialized in investment issues, divides the uses of capital into three parts: hardware, such as plants, equipment, and housing; software, such as research, advertising, marketing, and production techniques; and people, in whom is embedded the education and training that make productive assets out of warm bodies.

To create wealth faster, some of which can be saved and employed as new capital, we can invest in hard assets or new techniques or improved skills. These investments must have a positive return, preferably a large one.

International Markets

The cost of capital issue should be self-correcting. If capital is abundant in the United States and scarce in Europe, Americans will invest in Europe, where capital is the factor that will have a greater impact on production. (That was the pattern of international capital flows in the 50s and 60s.) If capital is cheap in Japan and dear in the United States, the Japanese will bring their capital here, where it commands a better rate of return. (A major economic story of the 80s was the increased purchase of U.S. property and government bonds by Japanese institutions.)

In the world's least fettered capital market, that for short-term debt, there has already been an equalization of the cost of capital. After adjustment for different inflation rates and changing exchange rates, U.S. and Japanese short rates have been moving in concert since 1987. Longer term debt rates also seem to be moving toward convergence.

Markets for equity capital, though, are much messier and harder to compare. Inflation and exchange rates are only part of the problem. There has been much Japanese equity investment in the U.S.—an estimated $48.6 billion from 1981 through 1988[4]— but only a few billion of that has been placed in U.S. stocks. Most Japanese equity has gone to real estate, to construction of Japanese-owned factories, and to private purchase of U.S. firms' nonliquid investments that are not continually priced in a market. But just because Japanese equity is not in the public market and not easily measured doesn't mean it's not felt.

Moving Money Around

Noting that American companies are moving much of their production offshore at the same time that foreign companies are creating new factories in the United States, economist Robert Reich sought a single explanation for these contradictory movements. His answer is based on the differences in productivity of workers in different countries.

American companies, he said, find higher profits in manufacturing in Europe and Japan because they find higher skills in the work force, making their capital investments more effective. For example, IBM and Texas Instruments have made substantial investments in research and production facilities in Japan.

Foreign investors in manufacturing in the United States, particularly Japanese managers, are better able to train American workers to be more productive. For example, Japanese carmakers require fewer labor hours to build a car in Ohio than do nearby U.S. automakers. Reich concluded:

> Some foreign companies are doing a much better job than American companies at increasing the value that Americans add to the world economy.

If I were an American worker today, given the option of working in a company with American managers backed by Wall Street capital, or working in a company with Japanese managers backed by Japanese capital, I would ask where am I going to get more job security, higher wages, and where is better product development going to be done. I would choose the Japanese manager and the Japanese capital.[5]

Reich, the Harvard economist who popularized the notion of "industrial policy" (meaning a conscious government policy of subsidy and investment to keep the ground fertile for industrial development), was led to an interesting conclusion. He said Americans and their government should not be too concerned about who owns companies, only about where they add value. If, for example, Zenith is the last American-owned producer of television sets, yet it makes most of its sets in Mexico, Zenith may be less "American" than the eight Japanese, Korean, and European companies that build 9 million TVs a year in the United States from components mostly manufactured in the United States. (Another 10 firms have substantial assembly operations in the United States, producing more than 5 million more sets.)

Productivity

All discussions about American technology, investment, and the cost of capital come eventually to a discussion of productivity—the ability of people in the United States to create goods and services.

Economists usually say that in the long run, wage increases cannot exceed the long-run growth of labor productivity. Attempting to deny this truth can result in stagnation, inflation, or both. For example, productivity in the steel and auto industries did not grow between 1960 and 1980, but real after-inflation wages grew rapidly. Result: mass layoffs, shrinkage of U.S. capacity, the rise of foreign competitors. But on the average, real after-inflation wages have not grown in the United States since about 1970, while productivity has risen at 1 percent to 2 percent per year.

Productivity is a misleading term, for it measures everything except what it seems to measure. That is, productivity does not measure the effort, or laziness, of the average worker. Instead, productivity is a measure of capital, of management, of workplace engineering and of the quality of raw materials. It is a measure of everything that can be substituted for labor. The more that management substitutes these other things for labor, the higher is the productivity of the remaining labor. If two workers are making one chair per hour, and management buys two chairmaking machines, each requiring one operator, so that output is now two chairs per hour, productivity has doubled. If anything, the workers are probably not working as hard, and they certainly are not using their old chairmaking craft.

Rhetoric about the productivity of the American worker, whether used to praise him or condemn him, rightly is aimed at the American manager.

Productive Changes

We measure productivity in dollars: the price of the object or service produced divided by the hours of labor put into it. This works all right as long as the things we make and the services we do change very little. But in our time, both are changing rapidly. Consider products:

We aren't buying the same things we bought 10 years ago, and some of the things, like computers, could not be bought for any price 10 years ago. If you buy an Apple Macintosh computer for $1,200 this year, the final sale is worth $1,200, and so it's tallied on the national income and product accounts. But is that really an increase or a decrease over the Apple IIe you bought 10 years ago for $2,000? It's clearly a much more powerful machine—in fact you couldn't buy a Mac for any price 10 years ago.

Harold Furchgott-Roth, an analyst at Economists Inc. in Washington, contends that when real GNP rose 28 percent in the 80s, there was actually a much larger increase in goods and services because technology drove up the power/price ratio.

Now, consider services. Service productivity is measured by what we pay for services, and doesn't reveal that much more service is produced for the same price. Take secretarial labor: it took many hours to type 10 perfect originals as little as 20 years ago. Automatic typewriters using punch tape and later, magnetic memories, cut the time to a few minutes for form letters. Word processing and laser printers allow any document to be printed as a "letter quality" original in a few seconds. What's more, word processing enables less highly trained typists to produce perfect documents.

As U.S. business employed more new workers and lower skilled workers in service sectors, such as clerical work, health care, and retail trade, reported productivity lagged the inflation rate. When we measure their productivity by what these new workers are paid, we find discouraging results. Some economists think that they are less productive, others think they are exploited. Either way, they are messing up the statistics but not the real economy.

A higher tech example of service productivity is the laptop computer. Writers, accountants, salespeople, and financial analysts have all made themselves more productive with laptop computers. Instead of reading the latest spy novel on an airplane, some people write them. Other people, especially those who manipulate and analyze data, now find that their work site is wherever their computer is—on the train, in a plane, at home, on vacation, in bed at night, at the breakfast table. Though workaholics have limits, such as the 24-hour day and the 7-day week, the laptop has drastically expanded their horizons.

Michael Boskin, chairman of the Council of Economic Advisers under President Bush, presents a simple question with no simple answer: Is there a productivity gain from the 24-hour teller machine, and if there is, how do you measure it?

Still in the Lead

Even with these distortions minimizing the reported productivity of the service sector, U.S. productivity still leads the world. In 1988 the dollar value of the output from an hour of labor in Japan was only 72 percent of the dollar value of the output from an hour of labor in the United States. Japan has about the same average productivity as Great Britain. France, at 86 percent of the U.S. level, and West Germany at 81 percent are more productive than Japan. The Japanese productivity growth rate, to be sure, was substantially higher at 5.8 percent per year, but the U.S. rate was 3.3 percent—better than France, Germany, Sweden, or Canada.[6] And on the labor cost side, as Bill Cunningham, an AFL-CIO economist, points out,[7] American wages actually dropped 0.2 percent, after inflation, between 1985 and 1988—the only industrialized nation where there was a decline in the period.

Long term, there appears to be even less of a U.S. productivity problem. A wide assortment of international economists have run U.N. data through their computers and found that productivity performance among nations has been converging for most of the postwar period. Since the United States is the leader, convergence means that other nations are catching up. One good reason for convergence of productivity rates is that technology is diffusing more rapidly and more widely throughout the world. But convergence does not mean that the United States is falling behind, or failing. The law of diminishing returns is at work: since the United States has long been a high labor-cost economy, its managers have employed more labor-saving machines and techniques than other economies. Much as oil drillers in the United States search harder, with less success, because so much oil has already been found, U.S. managers find it harder and more expensive to come up with new ways to save labor.

If an American industry has exploited all the cost-efficient ways of saving labor, there will be little new investment in that industry, permitting foreign competitors to catch up, especially if they have an advantage in some other factor of production, such as the cost of labor or raw materials.

William Baumol, a Princeton University economist, puts it this way: "Other countries are learning American techniques and are consequently pulling closer to the United States. That, in fact, is why their productivity can grow faster than America's."[8] Baumol finds it unremarkable that the world leader in productivity is not the world leader in productivity growth. To the contrary, he finds it surprising that the United States continues to register large productivity and output increases. He notes that the United States commands an increasing share of manufacturing output and industrial employment among the 24 industrialized nations of the Organization for Economic Cooperation and Development. Japan is also taking in a growing share of manufacturing. It's the manufacturing economies of Western Europe, particularly Britain, Germany, and France, that are contracting.

7

Research and Competition

In the decade of the 80s, the Reagan administration and the Congress agreed on few things, but one was to downplay the antitrust movement. Free market economists led the way. Even in the 70s, even in the Carter administration, there was a growing concern that antitrust actions be focused on business concentrations that genuinely harmed consumers. During the Carter administration, the Antitrust Division of the Justice Department actually hired a group of economists to give the division economic advice. Lawyers are not usually so modest, and indeed, many lawyers said the Antitrust Division had done a good job for 80-odd years without economists.

But the Antitrust Division and the other antitrust agency, the Federal Trade Commission, had in fact not done a good job. They had often prosecuted companies for (economically, not legally) defensible conduct, such as price-cutting, and they had often attacked mergers without any idea of whether the new, bigger company would gain any significant market power.

The Reagan administration took two significant, symbolic actions in the early 80s. First, it dropped a 12-year-old case against IBM, admitting that years of prosecution of the computer giant for allegedly unfair competition had been a waste of everyone's time and money. This gave a significant signal to business that mere success would no longer be a cause for prosecution. Second, it reached a settlement that called for the breakup of American Telephone & Telegraph. This provided an even more significant signal that the government's new chief aim was to spur business efficiency through the power of competition.

The Breakup of AT&T

Even only 10 years later, it is hard to remember how we used to joke about Ma Bell. "We're the phone company, we don't have to care," ran the gag line on *Laugh-In*. AT&T owned most of the significant local telephone companies and virtually all of the nation's long-distance facilities. It was a classic monopoly, guaranteed and enforced by willing state and federal regulators since 1913, when AT&T had exchanged freedom for a guaranteed rate of return.

There were many curious contradictions in the old AT&T. For our purposes Bell Labs can stand for them. Bell Labs consumed about 10 percent of AT&T revenues. It was America's largest research establishment and much of today's computer and communications technology was first thought of at Bell Labs. Many say, indeed, that the existence of Bell Labs was a sufficient reason to create the AT&T monopoly. But the contradiction was this: Bell Labs invented things faster than AT&T could use them. As a regulated monopoly, AT&T and its member companies were dedicated first to universal telephone service—wide access at low cost. New inventions could be placed in service only when they lowered the overall cost of service, and regulators were not interested in taking any risk of higher rates.

This reluctance took the form of an accounting exercise called long depreciation schedules. When a business buys a piece of equipment, accounting rules theoretically require that it spread the cost of the equipment over its estimated life. If your business spends $10,000 on a car, it might assign that car a five-year useful life, recording expenses—and reducing reported profits—of $2,000 per year. Gasoline expense, on the other hand, would be recorded in the same period it was consumed. The expense of building a garage, however, might be spread over 20 or 30 years. All this is in theory, because tax laws and regulations minutely set many depreciation schedules, and the whole issue is subject to endless manipulation. A company in trouble stretches out depreciation schedules to show more profit by reducing reported expenses; a healthy company with an aversion to taxation shrinks depreciation schedules and reports less taxable profit.

AT&T and its regulators wanted to make the company and its operating subsidiaries as profitable as possible, so that the lowest possible rates would give the company its guaranteed rate of return. Therefore, depreciation schedules for telephone equipment were set at 40 years. This was all right in the days of mechanical relays, which really lasted 40 years. When computers began to come on the scene and especially when Bell Labs began to design electronic telephone switches, AT&T's long depreciation schedules got in the way. Operating companies could easily install new electronic switches to handle new growth, but they often found replacement of outmoded equipment was financially impossible, because the total investment included not only the cost of the new equipment but also the remaining undepreciated cost of the equipment that would be replaced.

From about 1960 on, the U.S. telephone network lagged further and further behind the state of the electronic art. Only the indisputable fact of its superiority to any other nation's telephone network kept criticism within bounds. And even that fact would not keep competition away.

The long distance network was reasonably modern, but like a chain that is only as strong as its weakest link, it was only as fast and efficient as its oldest part. There was room for new competing networks to be built, entirely of more modern technology. Microwave Communications Inc., now MCI, constructed a radio link from St. Louis to Chicago in the early 70s and offered cut rates on private lines for businesses. Although MCI's lawyers had to spend as much time in court and before the FCC asserting the company's right to exist as its engineers spent in the practical business of raising microwave antennas, the upstart company flourished, and it built more such links between major cities. Within a few years, MCI had created the competitive telephone industry.

AT&T complained that the competitors were predatory, that they were "cream-skimmers," a term that meant they offered service only to select customers who were easy to serve, while AT&T

was forced by government regulation to serve everybody. The company's favorite example was the telephone service provided to a band of Indians who lived at the bottom of the Grand Canyon. AT&T of course was absolutely correct; it was the victim of "unfair" competition. Its first solution was to run to Congress seeking restoration of the total monopoly it and its supporters believed had been created in 1913. Congress in the mid-70s, however, was not ready to legislate any sort of sweeping privilege on the World's Largest Company. Many congressmen feared the monopolists of AT&T, whose economic and political power extended into nearly every district; most did not understand the issues. In such a situation, Congress usually dithers, holding endless hearings, introducing uncountable bills, passing some in one house, some in the other house, letting a few through both houses before they die in conference.

Congress, which in the past 15 years has legislated the reorganization of trucking, airlines, cable television, railroads, and energy twice, has in that span passed no telephone industry legislation. None of the reorganization of telephones can be blamed on Congress or credited to it; not the breakup of AT&T, not the write-off of more than $10 billion worth of outmoded network equipment and its replacement by advanced computers, not the creation of several new and modern long distance networks, not the introduction of new services like cellular mobile telephones, not the increases in the price of local telephone service, not the decrease in the price of long distance service.

Congress was far from silent on antitrust, and while not legislating on telephones, its members apparently learned a great deal from the AT&T breakup. They learned, for example, that companies really are more efficient, more responsive, and more likely to change when they are subject to competition. They also learned that in a competitive industry, where price is king and cost is the prime mover, there is not as much room for research. It's widely agreed that Bell Labs doesn't lay quite so many golden eggs as it used to; or at least, that more of the ones it lays are held to the exclusive benefit of AT&T, the slimmed-down communications service company. One of the most widely admired features of the Bell Labs under the old monopoly structure was that all research (except secret government research) was available at a low license cost to anyone that wanted it. This policy covered the transistor, the laser, and any number of electronic devices and the industrial techniques of manufacturing them.

Decentralizing Business

The American way of high tech follows the model of the milk-weed seed—one central, successful organism gives off hundreds of new organisms, or companies, each one of which takes an idea or a concept unsuited for growth close to the original organism and moves off into fresh territory. The advantage is that new ideas get a fair chance, developed and promoted by people who created them and believe in them. The disadvantage is that even companies that are successful with their first product often lack the resources—financial, intellectual, or entrepreneurial—to come up with a second-generation product.

Many American companies, especially the small ones that are the backbone of high-tech industries, publicly despair of their ability to compete against the Japanese industrial giants they confront in semiconductors, computers, telephones, televisions, and so on.

Hitachi, Fujitsu, NEC, and others are organized on the model of General Electric, which in its heyday pioneered the idea of the all-encompassing American conglomerate and still manufactures everything electrical from light bulbs to locomotives. The Japanese high-tech companies, as GE once did, invest in innovation for its own sake. And also like GE, they have enough cash coming in to support any amount of research they choose. GE itself, however, has reduced its faith in progress, abandoning any line of business in which it was not a leader, or at least number two.

Despairing of the state of high tech and of research, Congress legislated several times on antitrust in the 80s. The measure that has had the broadest impact is the National Cooperative Research Act of 1984. This law allowed companies to form joint ventures in research and development that would be immune from the potentially company-killing penalties of the antitrust laws. A joint venture whose members notified the authorities could not be assessed triple damages if it lost an antitrust case brought either by the government or by competitors. It explicitly applied a more difficult standard of proof from complainants and it warned off potential private plaintiffs by allowing successful defendants to recover their legal fees.

It is a measure of the timidity of American managers or of the ferocity of American lawyers that this law had any effect at all. Many antitrust experts, including some who were in a position to bring cases, have said that the previous law could never have been construed to bar research and development consortia. The government has rarely blocked joint ventures of any kind, especially not joint ventures in new technologies for which no market and no injured consumers exist. More often, in fact, arms of the government sponsored and even funded joint research ventures.

It is probably a measure of the true intent of some managers that they are back to Congress again, testifying now in favor of joint ventures in production, again to ward off Japanese competition.

The Virtue of Competition

Michael Porter, a Harvard University economist who has spent more than a decade studying international competitiveness, concludes that joint ventures and cooperation, whether among firms alone or among firms and the government, is an unlikely way to improve the performance of individual companies. "Industries and firms prosper because they are forced to," Porter says in one of his most widely quoted aphorisms. He emphasizes the importance of vigorous effective competition and even more, the importance of demanding, aggressive consumers.

> American policy in recent decades has often seemingly been based on the implicit premises that the value of the dollar, the intrusion of government, and unfair practices by foreign nations are the cause of any difficulties facing U.S. industry. Such a view of national advantage is, to say the least, incomplete. It has led to policies such as relaxing regulatory standards and allowing horizontal mergers, which usually undermine instead of help U.S. industry.[1]

Michael Porter concludes that the intensity of competition at home determines the competitiveness of companies abroad. The production of integrated circuits is one of the world's most hotly competitive industries and creates the basic building block of high tech.

Section III
ELECTRONIC RICE

The Japanese government targeted the semiconductor industry as ideal for the industry of a country with few raw materials and many educated workers. A saying grew up that integrated circuits were "electronic rice." Visually, little bits of silicon may look like rice grains. The Japanese, whose health requires a steady diet of rice, were also saying that the electronics industry would depend on integrated circuits in the same way that Japanese people depend on rice. The Japanese government has protected the rice industry, refusing to allow imports, even though American rice would be far cheaper. The Japanese say they should be self-sufficient in rice in order to be safe from foreign manipulation of the Japanese food supply. The American attitude about electronic rice parallels the Japanese attitude about rice.

8

A Computing Vacuum

Math Machines

Some of the ideas for a computing machine go back to the ancient Greeks; more are credited to the Renaissance mathematicians, such as Pascal, Kepler, Newton, and Leibniz. Charles Babbage worked most of his life on a clanking mechanical system he called the Analytical Engine. Though he never got it right, he developed most of the concepts a computer would need. George Boole developed the necessary mathematical expression of logic. Twentieth century mechanics developed calculating machines of amazing complexity; electric power pushed them ahead further. By the 40s, as engineers improved the mechanical calculator, the punch card reader, the mechanical code machine, and other devices using mechanical switches, the time was right.[1]

American scientists, liberally funded by the World War II military establishment, built electronic machines to solve single problems and these contributed to the growing body of knowledge about computing. Among the most important single problems were the complex calculations required for designing the atomic bomb and the repetitive calculations required to break enemy codes. (Even in the 90s, bomb designers at Los Alamos and codebreakers at the National Security Agency are among the most voracious consumers of powerful computers.)

Reinventing Arithmetic

A key to practical computing was the use of binary arithmetic, in which numbers are represented only by ones and zeros. Veterans of the New Math may recognize this as counting in the base two, in contrast to the common decimal system, which is counting in the base 10.

Binary	Decimal
0	0
1	1
10	2
11	3
100	4
101	5
110	6
111	7
1000	8
1001	9
1010	10
1100	11 . . .
10000	16
100000	32
10000000000	1024

As the later numbers illustrate, the round numbers in the binary system, those with a one followed by zeros, represent the powers of two, just as the round numbers in the decimal system represent the powers of 10. The number of zeros equals the exponent. So just as 10 multiplied by itself six times is one million and is written 1 with six zeros after it, so 2 multiplied by itself six times is 64 and, in binary, is written as a 1 with six zeros after it. This place-counting zero makes it easy in the decimal system to perform multiplications and divisions by 10 and its powers—you take the shortcut of adding and dropping zeros. So our currency system and the metric system are well matched to the decimal system. The binary system looks difficult to a mind oriented to the decimal system, but it's well matched to the computer.

The binary system reflects the easiest way to build a computer. The switch is the simplest device in electronics and in logic: make or break, yes or no, on or off, 1 or 0. Binary arithmetic matched the switch, and the computer is a collection of switches performing binary arithmetic operations. Holding the switches in a particular pattern amounts to memory, for storing information or instructions, and memory is the key advance beyond the calculator that distinguishes the computer.

The logic circuits that perform computer calculations are reduced to their simplest form in binary notation. There are only three mathematical processes: $0 + 0 = 0$; $1 + 0 = 1$; and $1 + 1 = 10$. In the 19th century, Boole had reduced logic to three basic operations: "and," "or," and "not." They were a perfect fit.

Computers reduce all operations to these three basic operations, but most operations we actually want computers to perform are much more complex. Thus computers perform these three simple operations over and over, thousands, millions, billions of times to complete a task. A typical circuit to add two numbers actually requires 24 Boolean operations.

Electromechanical switches—hinged pieces of metal moved by electromagnets—were good enough for many applications. The telephone system employed them into the 80s. Routing a call set switches that held their position for the duration of the conversation. Neither speed nor flexibility was required.

Both speed and flexibility were required in mathematical computation. A system that must, for example, multiply 1,000 times 1,000 by adding the binary number 1111100001 to itself one thousand times, must be very fast to beat the wheels and gears of a mechanical desktop calculator from the 30s. The accomplishment of the 40s, carried out in different ways in military and industrial laboratories, was to put a fast switch to work.

Electronic Switching

The vacuum tube is nothing more than a light bulb with a metal plate inside. Thomas Edison had built the first one in 1883 in hopes that the metal plate might do something to prevent darkening of the glass of the light bulb. It didn't, and Edison went on to try something else, but not before noticing that current was flowing in the metal plate. Practical Mr. Edison was uninterested, but physicists were bowled over by the apparent impossibility of current flowing from the filament through a vacuum to the plate. In 1897 J.J. Thomson, Professor of Physics at Cambridge University, explained the "Edison Effect," and to do so he showed that the atom was not indivisible, that what flowed through the vacuum, and through the filament, was a stream of subatomic particles he called corpuscles. We know them as electrons. Thomson's explanation was the founding moment of modern physics.

The vacuum tube, however, continued to be a curiosity for a few more years, until J.A. Fleming, professor of physics at University College, London, and a consultant to the Marconi company, sought a way of building reliable radio receivers. This would require converting the alternating current generated by radio waves into direct current. Years earlier, Fleming had noticed that the vacuum tube worked equally well with alternating current flowing through the filament, producing direct current through the plate. At the time, his discovery had only deepened the mystery of the "Edison Effect," but Thomson had cleared all that up. In 1904, Fleming found that he could use the vacuum tube to convert alternating current into direct current. He also found that the flow of electrons from filament to plate could be interrupted and restarted thousands of times a second by controlling the current flowing through the filament.

Radio receivers also needed to amplify the weak signals from distant radio transmitters and the American inventor Lee De Forest added a wire screen to the vacuum tube, between the filament and the plate. A positive charge on the screen repelled electrons and reduced current flowing to the plate; a negative charge on the screen attracted electrons and increased the current flowing to the plate. It was an amplifier.

Because it could convert alternating current into direct current, and because it could amplify direct current, the vacuum tube's place in the radio industry was assured. Because the radio industry became the first great medium of mass communication, the vacuum tube would be produced in mass amounts, in billions. Vacuum tubes would be ready to hand when engineers were ready to go beyond mechanical switching in the construction of computers.

Among the first such engineers were those employed during World War II by U.S. Navy codebreaking teams and U.S. Army artillery experts. The navy, working with National Cash Register, produced more than a thousand codebreaking machines incorporating electronics, though much of what was done was so secret that it was not revealed until long after the technology ceased to be amazing. The army's ballistic calculators were more out in the open and technologies descended from army war research received the bulk of popular attention in the late 40s.

Cold War Computing

In the postwar period, both services and other government agencies spent enormous sums on computer research at universities, often supporting the same researchers the services had employed during the war. Grants from the Office of Naval Research, in particular, helped develop general purpose computers from the specialized designs of wartime. Kenneth Flamm, compiling memoirs and contemporaneous accounts, puts U.S. government funding of industrial computing research at $15 to $20 million a year by 1950.[2]

The two men generally credited with the first electronic computer were J. Presper Eckert and John W. Mauchly of the University of Pennsylvania, who spent most of the war years building an electronic calculator for the Ballistics Research Laboratory of the army. They did not finish ENIAC (Electronic Numerical Integrator and Calculator) until after the war was over, but their report on the design and construction of the 17,000-tube monster was an instant hit on the scientific circuit. Among ENIAC's popularizers was John von Neumann, the chief mathematician of the atomic bomb project at Los Alamos. His papers on electronic computing were so basic, so complete, and so acute that digital computers using a stored program, memory register, and a central processing unit are often referred to as having von Neumann architecture.

Eckert and Mauchly's response to their initial success with ENIAC was to leave the University of Pennsylvania, which didn't seem to value their talents adequately, and form their own company. This pattern was to be repeated so many times in the history of American computing that it ought to be called the Eckert-Mauchly Maneuver; however, it has no widely recognized sociological sobriquet. Their first customer was the Northrop Corporation, which then, as now, was on the leading edge of aerodynamic design. In fact, then, as now, Northrop's big project was a flying wing bomber. (The one then, the B-49, was canceled after a few prototypes were built; the one now, the B-2, is well on the way to the same fate.)

Commercial Computing

Unfortunately, the Eckert-Mauchly Computer Corp. spent more on development than its customer paid for the product, another pattern to be repeated so often that it could be named after the two pioneers. The company received orders from another customer, the Census Bureau, which, if it did not make the company solvent, at least gave Eckert-Mauchly enough of a patina of hope that the company could be acquired. In 1950, Remington Rand, a company that was in the punched card office machinery and mechanical calculator business—and was bringing out a new electronic calculator—bought Eckert-Mauchly and its next computer, the UNIVAC (for UNIVersal Automatic Computer). The first UNIVAC was delivered late, but the Census Bureau found it to be the answer to their prayers. It handled a huge volume of data from the 1950 census, displacing older mechanical devices.

Other office machine companies, such as International Business Machines, National Cash Register, and Burroughs, held back at first from a commercial interest in computers, as did electronics and electrical firms such as RCA, Motorola, Zenith, and General Electric. Most of these firms had computer research efforts going, some of them large. But all were in the nature of services purchased by the defense establishment; profit-oriented executives were waiting to see a market develop. Similarly, AT&T's Bell Labs was in the thick of military computer development, but the telephone company itself showed no interest.

Eckert and Mauchly had associates who continued the computer work at the University of Pennsylvania. Von Neumann began a computer project for the army, navy, and Atomic Energy Commission at Princeton University's Institute for Advanced Studies, with additional funding from RCA. The National Bureau of Standards built two computers for itself and hired Raytheon to build another. An MIT project to build a flight simulator turned into a project to build a computer to drive a flight simulator and later to assist an air defense system. Navy codebreakers supported a new company called Engineering Research Associates, founded by some of their wartime staff.

Most of the basic elements of modern computing—its architecture—were developed in these early postwar projects. Designers developed different ways of handling magnetic storage of data, on tape, on drums, and on cores. They developed stored program techniques so that each problem did not have to be set up like a rural telephone operator's switchboard, with a maze of patch cords and switches. The next few decades would be spent improving components, not making new designs.

Watson's Vision

IBM was the first company to see the connection between its government work on electronic computers and its basic line of business machines. IBM scientists, with the support of Chairman Thomas J. Watson Sr., were involved in the wartime development of several experimental computers, including the ENIAC that Eckert and Mauchly were building at the University of Pennsylvania. IBM also pursued developments of its punched-card data processing machines from before the war. These machines read data encoded on cards and produced payroll records and other office information.

After the war, Watson was a technology sponsor in the way that the military was. He hired many scientists away from the military and university computer labs and put many more who wished to remain where they were on retainers and consultancies. IBM researchers combined electronic calculators with the punched-card accounting machines and came up, almost offhandedly, with a computer programmable from cards. When that turned out to be a commercial product, IBM entered the computer era for real. In 1949 the company began development of a computer using magnetic tape for program and data storage. In the heat of the Korean War this was adapted into a general purpose computer, development of several other models began, and by the end of the war in 1953 IBM was ready to enter the business computer industry.

Though Remington Rand was a little behind IBM in vision, its purchase of Eckert-Mauchly had put it at least two years ahead of

IBM technologically. A historian of IBM, Robert Sobel, has observed that UNIVAC came close to being a generic name for computer, the way Xerox became a generic name for copying. "A year or so later, and IBM would have found the Remington Rand position close to impregnable."[3]

But IBM had its own advantage, which proved decisive in the next few years: not in technology but in salesmanship. Whatever the company decided to sell, its highly motivated sales force could and did sell. Thomas J. Watson, Jr., the executive vice president and heir, supplied the vision and the urgency; his father had built the sales force and the corporate organization. Together, in the early 50s, the two Watsons more than doubled IBM's long-term debt to build computers, develop new models, and finance the customers' leases.

By the mid-50s, IBM had sold computers to most of the 25 largest corporations, plus the Social Security Administration and some other government agencies, and had begun to teach those companies how to use them—something the company was making up as it went along. IBM caught and passed Remington Rand in 1956.

In *Creating the Computer*, Kenneth Flamm argues strenuously for crediting the government for much of IBM's success in the 50s. In particular, IBM won a contract in 1952 to build 56 computers for the Air Force's SAGE air defense system. Citing several IBM accounts and memoirs, Flamm says IBM generally gained access to the most advanced technology sponsored by the military, including that developed by other companies. Also, the company learned how to mass-produce magnetic core memories and printed circuit boards, both of which would be key components of computers for years to come. In addition, the SAGE system was the first computer network, using digital data communication, and it was the first real-time transactions processing system. These three elements of system design have only grown in importance from that day to this. By 1964, in fact, IBM had turned SAGE into SABRE (SemiAutomatic Business-Research Environment), an airline reservation system. Virtually all commercial and scientific systems today incorporate these three basic ideas.

For SAGE, IBM also pioneered fault-tolerance, the practice of doubling up computers so that anything that failed would have a backup, and graphics displays on video monitors, progenitor of everything from video games to the PC displays of today. Not least in importance were the human and financial sides: at the height of the project, more than 20 percent of IBM's 39,000 employees were working and learning on the government's dime; and by the time SAGE was finished in the early 60s, IBM had also gained about a half billion dollars (5 billion dimes, if you want to look at it that way) in revenue.

The air force might have done even more for IBM: one of Flamm's sources told him that IBM was offered and refused the chance to be paid to write computer code for the SAGE system. The source thought IBM missed a major opportunity and certainly the company that did write the software, Systems Development, pioneered a whole industry of software writing, especially software writing for IBM machines.

Creating the Computer Business

Watson senior died in 1956; Watson junior almost immediately reorganized the company. He made sales and service one of the five basic divisions of the company, staffing it with a brew of salesmen and engineers. Their assignment was to steer punchcard and office-machine customers into the computer age. They were rewarded with pay and positive reinforcement commensurate with the importance of their task, and they were successful. Federal Systems—selling to the government, and World Trade—selling to foreign customers, set up along the same lines. Manufacturing was the fourth division. None of these were really a departure from past IBM practice; Watson junior's contribution was to establish the Research Division as an equal.

Research had already been growing in importance and in share of IBM financial resources, of course. The office machine company spent an amount equal to 12 percent of net income on research. Developing computers between 1949 and 1955 pushed that as high as 35 percent of net income. Watson's reorganization pushed research to nearly half of net income.

It is important to note that IBM did not become dominant in the computer industry by sheer financial weight. When the computer era opened, IBM's potential competitors had plenty of muscle: General Electric was nearly 10 times as big as IBM; RCA was twice as big; Sperry Rand was nearly 50 percent bigger and Bendix Aviation was 30 percent bigger. Though smaller than IBM, Burroughs, Honeywell, NCR, and Raytheon all had sales in excess of $100 million and were strong enough to compete.

Murphy's Computers

All the wonderful machines of the early and mid-50s, whether UNIVACs or IBMs or the products of other companies, still ran on vacuum tubes. And vacuum tubes burned out like light bulbs— unpredictably and in compliance with Murphy's Law (which says, "Anything that can go wrong will go wrong and at the worst possible time"). That a corporation or an army would buy a vacuum tube computer is a sort of historical proof that computers were badly needed in the postwar period. The first UNIVAC, for example, was out of service about 40 percent of the time.

Among the legends from that period is the military image of the army stationing soldiers around ENIAC with baskets of extra tubes in hopes of getting the machine to compute a whole ballistic trajectory (the problem being that it wasn't obvious which tubes had burned out). Another is that the term *debugging*, now applied to the process of finding mistakes in a program or a machine design, had its origin in the search for moth carcasses that had caused short circuits. (The moths allegedly were attracted to the innards of computers by all that heat and light.) Legends aside, it was true that vacuum tubes were unreliable in the best of circumstances and were much more likely to burn out in a computer cabinet, where every vacuum tube heated up the whole box. A critical mass of tubes could outdo the cooling system and turn a computer into a pile of glass and metal junk. (In fact, powerful computers have always skirted the edge of meltdown because it is always economically and technically advantageous to pack components as tightly together as possible. Heat generated by powerful computing was, and remains, the enemy of powerful computing.)

Vacuum tube computers were also expensive: IBM built computers for the air force that cost $30 million each in 1952 dollars.[4] That's about five times the inflation-adjusted price of the most expensive supercomputers available in 1990, which run about $25 million and are many thousand times more powerful.

A Better Switch

As the vacuum tube computer industry was just getting started, a basic invention was made at Bell Labs that would eliminate the vacuum tube from nearly all electronic devices. William Shockley, Walter Brattain, and John Bardeen invented the transistor at the end of 1947. Like the vacuum tube, a transistor could be a switch or an amplifier. Unlike the vacuum tube, it was not much more than a crystal with some wires attached. No glass tube. No vacuum. No filament. No plate. Magic.

In the 90s, all electronic products from radios to CD players contain transistors. And virtually every electrical machine, from refrigerators to toasters, is controlled by electronic devices containing transistors. Even Edison's incandescent light bulb, though it stands alone effectively and can be switched mechanically, is often controlled with electronic dimmers and timers containing transistors.

Most people have a pretty good idea about what makes a light bulb go. Other 19th century inventions, such as the phonograph and the telephone, are within the grasp of attentive elementary school students, even if they have no better understanding of the forces and laws governing electricity than did Thomas Edison. When we get to early 20th century marvels, we get a bit hazier. Ask yourself what radio signals are made of, or why some materials are radioactive, or even how electricity flows through a wire. Even if you have a pretty fair idea—which sets you apart from most of your fellow citizens—would you be willing to explain these processes to an audience of 12th grade physics students without consulting a reference book? The transistor is another level beyond these. For all most of us know, it might just as well be magic.

To understand the transistor, we must understand three types of solids: conductors, insulators, and semiconductors. Start with conductors and insulators because they are easy. Some elements, such as silver, gold, copper, and aluminum, conduct electricity quite well. Other elements such as selenium and sulfur, as well as compounds such as the oxides, are excellent insulators, refusing to conduct electricity. The good conductors have only one electron in their outermost orbit zones, or shells. These electrons are not tightly bonded to their atoms, and can be knocked off and sent along to another atom. That flow of electrons and the energy that makes it happen is what we call electricity. Insulators, on the other hand, have the maximum number of atoms in their outermost orbit zones. These electrons are hard to dislodge from their atoms. They do not break loose and travel, so there is no flow of electricity.

What about the elements in the middle? They are semiconductors, such as silicon, germanium, and gallium. With four electrons in their outermost layer, they are neither hard nor easy conductors. In the state of nature, however, these atoms form crystals, linking four electrons of one atom with four electrons of four other atoms, producing a very good insulator. But in the state of nature it is also true that crystals are not pure. Atoms of other elements form bonds, and if those other elements have some other number of electrons, there will be extra electrons and absent electrons in the crystal structure.

Where there are extra electrons, the semiconductor crystal carries a negative charge. Where there are absent electrons (which physicists call "holes" and talk about as if they have a material existence), the crystal block carries a positive charge. So the impurities in a semiconductor crystal are what make it electrically interesting, because if the semiconductor can be made positive or negative, current can be made to flow from one pole to the other. And by a process called *doping*, which means adding bits of impurities to the semiconductor, engineers can control the electrical characteristics of a bit of semiconductor crystal, deciding where it will be positively charged, where it will be negatively charged, and where it will be an insulator.

Shockley, Brattain, and Bardeen worked with germanium that had been doped to be negative on one end and positive on the other. The interesting border between the two zones—the "P-N junction"—had been explored by others. Current would flow from N to P, but not the other way. This was a simple diode, just like the earliest vacuum tube, and it was one that, compared to the vacuum tube, gave off almost no heat, required practically no power, would last a long time, and was not fragile.

Basic diodes, however, were not particularly important in the radio business nor in the rest of electronics. Germanium diodes were used only rarely. What the three Bell Labs scientists tried to do was take the doped germanium semiconductor to the next step and replace the vacuum tube amplifier.

Bardeen and Brattain put two wires on the P-N junction and discovered a simple, though quirky, amplifier. A few weeks later, Shockley made a new design, calling for a sandwich—a positive region with a negative region on either side. Applying current to one negative region would produce virtually no current flow. But if current were also applied to the positive region in the middle of the crystal, there would be a big boost in the main current across the whole crystal. This transistor could be both an amplifier and a switch at the same time, and, compared to the vacuum tube, it consumed almost no current, was virtually indestructible, much more sensitive, and could switch from on to off in an almost immeasurably short time.

Transitorizing the World

AT&T, the giant telephone monopoly, waived all royalties from transistors used to make hearing aids and charged $25,000 for licenses to use the technology. Bell Labs even ran training programs to introduce the transistor to manufacturers and circuit designers. Bell Labs collaborated on military projects incorporating the transistor, and transistorized products designed by the labs and built by Western Electric were incorporated into the telephone network. But the telephone monopoly, which was defending a government antitrust suit, left commercialization of the transistor to others. Within a few years, a little American company called Regency and a little Japanese company called Sony were building pocket radios. The world was changed, and it is still changing, because of the transistor.

In computers, transistors were the building blocks of a second generation of computers. Production of transistors rose from 1.3 million in 1954 to 47.1 million in 1958, while costs declined by about a third. Vacuum tube production in the same span held about steady, with costs increasing about 20 percent. For the first time, but not the last, there was an opportunity in the computer industry to put advanced technology to use ahead of the dominant player in the market. In 1958, Philco unveiled the first computer using transistors; RCA and General Electric were not far behind. IBM and Remington Rand were stuck with first-generation vacuum tube equipment; the new arrivals had leapfrogged ahead to the second generation.

IBM had to manage on sheer salesmanship at first. The computer it was bringing out at the time, dubbed STRETCH, was still primarily based on vacuum tubes and was a commercial flop. Transistorized UNIVACs hit the market, RCA entered with a transistor computer, and a new company formed by UNIVAC refugees called Control Data came out with the most powerful transistor computer of all.

IBM would not be able to compete technologically for some time. So the company lived off its leases and it announced powerful second-generation transistorized machines well before they were ready. Its salesmen were able to convince most customers to wait for the superior IBM product, even to take inferior IBM machines now with a promise of early delivery of the better ones, so they would not lose the superior IBM service and technical support.

(This tactic worked so well that IBM institutionalized it and elaborated it into an offensive gambit as well. Even when IBM was not playing technological catch-up, it would announce new models, constructing, out of thin air and good intentions, high hurdles for the competition to scale. Reproached and sued in the 60s for alleged antitrust violations, IBM refined the tactic to a system of deniable leaks still used in the 90s. Officially, company spokesmen never comment about new products, but IBM salesmen and a legion of independent Armonk-watchers speculate and predict endlessly.)

Remington Rand was not so fortunate. A merger with the Sperry Corp. was supposed to invigorate its management and provide abundant financing, but it produced only management diversion and confusion. The UNIVAC division responded well technically, but its salesmen lost battles with IBM at every turn. The company's market share dropped from 39 percent in 1955 to 19 percent in 1957. The profit situation was even worse: the UNIVAC division did not earn a nickel until the mid-60s, holding Sperry Rand's profit margin below 7 percent while IBM was making 25 percent.

"Customer loyalty, salesmanship, and vision turned out to be of vital importance," says Sobel, reflecting the IBM view of the world.

But even while IBM was coining money and becoming the dominant computer company, other companies were entering the business. Some may have been attracted by IBM's profits and simply hoped to gain a share of what looked like a lucrative business, but others surely were driven by technology, more precisely by IBM's lack of a technological edge. To such companies, the computer industry looked attractive in the era of transistors because it was technologically wide open. Transistors and other components were widely available; circuit designs were often published in technical journals and circuit designers could be hired; manufacturing technology was reasonably well known. There were no obvious barriers to entry. Even if IBM had its customers locked up tight, the number of potential new customers, buying their first computer, grew every year.

IBM's competition around 1960 included Philco (now a unit of Ford Motor), General Electric, RCA, NCR, Honeywell, Burroughs, Control Data, Bendix, International Telephone & Telegraph, Addressograph-Multigraph, Bunker-Ramo, North American Aviation, Litton's Monroe Calculating Division, Raytheon, Sylvania, and probably more. In addition, AT&T was beginning to computerize its phone network, using almost nothing but home-grown components designed at Bell Labs and built by Western Electric.

The Inevitable Weak Link

Transistors did not solve all computer problems. The new technology even brought some new ones. Computer designers and builders made their computers more powerful by making them more complex. Cool-running transistors could be packed together in great numbers. Unfortunately that wasn't so much a solution as a problem. Each transistor would have to operate reliably for the system to operate at all. Worse, each connection, and each connecting wire, would have to be made properly and operate reliably.

Designers faced the "tyranny of numbers," as Jack Morton of

Bell Labs put it in 1957, before the problem had even grown huge. Think of a computer as a chain of transistors and connections and remember that a chain is only as strong as its weakest link. Before a chain stretched between two points is even one mile long its total weight is so great that a link is almost certain to snap. The computer, considered as a chain, was similarly endangered.

In bridge-building, wire cable is the solution to the problem of chain. In a suspension bridge, each piece of wire runs the entire span of the bridge. Many wires, bound together as a cable, work together to hold up the roadway. There is no weak link that imperils the bridge.

The tyranny of numbers could have been called the tyranny of probability. The probability of one link failing may be vanishingly small, but it is not zero. To determine the probability of a system failing, one must multiply the individual probabilities of failure of each component that can cause the system to fail. Let us say that a transistor's probability of failure in a week or less is one in a million. So 15,000 components (the number of vacuum tubes in the ENIAC of 1945) are more than 98 percent certain to run for a week. Using transistors means a huge improvement in reliability for a machine of ENIAC's complexity. The machine doesn't blow out every time you turn it on.

But designers took the reliability of transistors as an opportunity, not just a solution. They immediately began to design more complex computers. And taking the complexity of the computer up 10 times means a 15 percent probability of failure in a week. Up another ten times, and the computer fails more than once a week. Up another 10 times and you're back to ENIAC in terms of reliability—although of course you are also doing vastly more complex problems, probably much faster and certainly much cheaper. But as they say in nearly every line of work, "What have you done for me lately?"

9

Solid State

The Integrated Circuit

The solution turned out to be much like the substitution of wire cable for chain in bridge-building. It occurred more or less simultaneously to two men, Jack Kilby of Texas Instruments and Robert Noyce of Fairchild. It was the idea of the integrated circuit: the way to eliminate the tyranny of numbers is to reduce the numbers. Kilby first saw that transistors and all other key electronic components could all be built out of the same semiconductor material, doped silicon. They wouldn't necessarily be the best devices that could be made, but they would work. They could be made simultaneously on a monolithic piece of silicon, which later would be called a chip. Noyce first saw that it was possible to connect different devices on the same piece of silicon by printing lines of metal on the silicon. Each man, having thought of his own idea, then quite quickly thought of the other's idea and thus invented the complete idea of the integrated circuit.

Circuit, here, means a collection of devices and connections that perform a task. Electronics engineers had seen their job as designing and building circuits. They would select tubes, in the old days, or transistors in more recent times, and resistors, diodes, capacitors, and other devices from a catalogue. Securing these on a board and connecting them with wire and solder according to a schematic design, produced a circuit. The circuit might be a radio transmitter or receiver, an amplifier, a computer logic unit, a controller for some mechanical device, whatever.

The integrated circuit meant, among other things, that the entire collection of devices and connections would be made all at once. It could be tested, thrown away if it wouldn't work, installed if it would, and thereafter treated as one device.

Because their ideas overlapped and intersected, Kilby, Noyce, and their companies were in for a 10-year struggle over patents. Fortunately, the world did not have to wait until 1970, when the U.S. Supreme Court ruled in favor of Noyce, to use the integrated circuit. Both companies exploited the idea immediately and both companies licensed other companies. And in 1966 Texas Instruments and Fairchild Semiconductor settled the whole thing, agreeing to license each other and agreeing on a common royalty levy on all other users of the integrated circuit idea.

Such users, however, did not spring up immediately. It took Texas Instruments and Fairchild about two years to convert their inventions into computer logic circuits. And even then, the integrated circuit would not be a solution to the tyranny of numbers until many devices could be crammed onto a single piece of silicon. The first products had less than a dozen devices comprising one logic gate, and Fairchild wanted $120 for it. A hand-wired transistor circuit could be made for less. Nobody in business, who hoped to stay in business, had a problem with the tyranny of numbers that was worth solving at that price.

But there was the U.S. government. The integrated circuit promised to be a key component for computers that would be lighter, more reliable, and less fragile, just what the military needed in a missile guidance system. Every pound saved in the guidance system might mean a kiloton more nuclear explosive delivered. And every extra percentage point of accuracy in the guidance system might reduce the amount of nuclear explosive required to be certain of destroying the target. The same considerations applied to rocket fuel: lighter, better guidance systems would allow longer range from the same missile.

Texas Instruments sought and received several million dollars of Army and Air Force money to develop integrated circuits. Fairchild used its own money for development, though with the security of knowing that military customers would beat a path to their door as soon as their new mousetrap was ready.

The National Aeronautics and Space Administration, with its charter to get to the moon by the end of the decade, regardless of expense, quickly became another ideal customer for the infant integrated circuit industry. Space travel is so close to impossible that the economics are daunting, to say the least. In the early 60s, putting a pound of payload in low earth orbit cost $100,000 in rocket fuel alone—not counting the rocket itself, the research and development costs, or an appropriate share of the ground control and launch facilities. So NASA could afford to pay a lot to save a pound in a computer or a radio or anything else electronic that was bound for orbit.

Minuteman II, in 1962, was the first missile to incorporate integrated circuits in the guidance system. The next year, Texas Instruments and Fairchild sold about 500,000 integrated circuits. Other companies soon entered the market, and sales were 2 million units in 1964.

The Integrated Circuit Business

The makers were fabricating replacements for pretty standard electronic circuits, with commercial applications as obvious as military ones, once the price was right. The 1965 Zenith hearing aid that was the first commercial product to incorporate an integrated circuit used the same amplifier circuit built for a NASA satellite. So there were immediate applications benefits and profits to be made inserting these military products into commercial products. As the price came down, the use of integrated logic circuits grew. And as the use grew, the companies learned how to make them more cheaply, and cut the selling price. Engineers call this a positive feedback loop. Some 8 million integrated circuits were sold in 1965 and 32 million in 1966.

If they had all been sold at $120 per unit, it would be a different world, one in which integrated circuits are reserved for the most high-value applications. But manufacturing integrated circuits turned out to be one of those problems that yields to a combination of time and money. Specialized production equipment could be made to produce integrated circuits more precisely and more easily. The new production equipment could handle new designs that would more tightly pack devices on each chip of silicon. The basic cost of production, though, which was already declining, was not much affected by the increasing complexity of the circuits.

Prices collapsed. From $120 in 1961, the typical integrated circuit cost $32 in 1963, $8.30 in 1965, and in 1971, the average selling price of integrated circuits was $1.27, 1 percent of the cost a decade earlier of a far less capable integrated circuit. Producers made it up in volume and lower production costs. Their profits grew as the price shrank, because the falling price opened new markets.

Semiconductor manufacturers were as astonished as anyone. Intel Chairman Gordon Moore, then at Fairchild Semiconductor, made a tongue-in-cheek observation in 1964 that for the past three years the number of components on a chip of silicon had doubled each year, and he said that might continue for awhile. It continued for so long that the prediction became known as "Moore's Law." Around 1975, Moore's Law was recast to a doubling every two years, but with that revision it remains an iron rule of semiconductor economics.

Industry leaders liked to describe this phenomenal improvement in the capacity of integrated circuit manufacturing as a productivity improvement. They made the almost irresistible comparison to the auto industry, saying that if Detroit had such productivity gains cars would speed at millions of miles per hour, get thousands of miles per gallon, last for dozens of years without repair, and cost a few dollars.

Productivity?

Improvements in integrated circuits are not productivity improvements in the usual sense, and economic statistics did not pick up all of what was going on. Productivity is measured as output per hour of labor. Output is measured in dollars. So if a chip factory employing 100 people on a 40-hour work week (right there the statistic is weak, because young computer engineers, like young, enthusiastic workers of any profession, put in 140-hour work weeks that are never reported), turns out 100,000 1K (holding 1,024 bits of information) memory chips per week that sell for $10, the productivity of this factory is perceived to be $250 per manhour. If the same factory a couple of years later, with the same workers and the same equipment, turns out 100,000 4K memory chips per week that sell for $10, productivity hasn't changed at all. In this example, the only thing that changed was the only important thing: the number of bits of memory storage per dollar increased by a factor of four. But statistically, this factory would be a drag on the growth of U.S. productivity.

Productivity improvements of this kind are lost in a statistical swamp. They are incorporated in computers and business equipment, where performance rises and costs fall in the same way. Eventually, people actually use the products incorporating all of this unmeasured productivity, and their productivity soars. But if, as is most common, the users of productivity-enhancing business equipment are employed in the service sector, their output is measured by their pay and by their employers' profits. Legal secretaries aren't paid more because they use word processors to type legal briefs perfectly the first time. They just type longer legal briefs. And so on: the productivity enhancements from computing are often lost in the counting.

Commercial producers of computers and business equipment and electronic products, fortunately, don't make business decisions based on productivity statistics. They redesigned their old products using integrated circuits, because integrated circuits had become cheaper than wiring transistors together on circuit boards. The commercial market for integrated circuits overtook the military market in size by about 1970.

Another Change, Another Opportunity

In the computer industry, the conversion from the transistor to the integrated circuit was another technological divide, another market opportunity like the one that occurred when the transistor could replace the vacuum tube.

The integrated circuit did not take IBM by surprise. Company engineers began a design program for a computer that would use integrated circuits in 1961, and the next year the top executives embarked upon a business plan built on integrated circuits that would revolutionize IBM for the second time in a decade. They decided that IBM would not just commit itself to building computers made of integrated circuits, it would design and build the integrated circuits as well. They killed off a new-model transistor machine that had been intended to carry the company through the 60s. They committed large shares of earnings to new capital investment, and they borrowed hundreds of millions of dollars more, mostly short term. They even reversed a long-standing aversion to dilution of equity ownership and sold $371 million in new stock.

Some $500 million went into research and development during the mid-60s, but more went into new factories, including major facilities in Europe and Japan. In the six years from 1961 to 1967, IBM invested nearly $5 billion in plant and property. The company added more than 50,000 workers worldwide, an increase of one third. And IBM, the largest consumer of electronic parts, became the largest producer. It was—and remains in 1990—the world's largest producer of integrated circuits, though all its production was reserved for the company's own products. IBM's first integrated circuits were actually hybrids, in which connections were laid down on silicon wafers onto which individual transistors were wired. Still, IBM had established itself as a world leader in components and that turned out to be a crucial element of success.

"What the Ford River Rouge plant complex had been for automobiles in the 1920s, the IBM worldwide network would be for computers," says Robert Sobel.[1]

The integrated circuits were destined for the 360 series of computers, which became the first truly successful line of computers. There were several sizes of 360, offering about the same price-performance ratio and using the same software. Thus a customer could start small and, as he and his IBM sales representative found new uses for the computer, he could easily expand his computer operations, just by leasing a bigger machine. The entry-level machines, moreover, were so attractively priced that new customers opened their doors and welcomed the IBM salesmen.

Success Fosters Competition

At the same time that the success of the 360 series was blasting competitors out of the water, IBM ignored other competitive developments.

One was the classic thankless child. H. Ross Perot, a young IBM salesman in Texas, reached his sales quota—beyond which he could earn no further bonuses—on the second day of January. He spent the rest of that year creating his own computer services business. On the one hand, he talked some of his customers into letting him use the computers he had placed during the late-night periods when they were idle. On the other hand, he told small businesses that weren't ready to afford a computer that he would do their computing for them. At the end of a year of 24-hour days, Perot had Electronic Data Systems off the ground. At first, he was nothing but a broker, bringing together buyers of computer time and sellers of surplus computer time, but he quickly hired people to develop computer programs for his customers, and the business grew. Perot and his imitators eventually built computer centers bigger than those of most corporations and relieved medium and small companies, and government agencies, of the terrible burden of dealing with IBM salesmen. EDS provided answers, not machines; its customers left the computer jockeying to the experts.

At the other end of the spectrum was Digital Equipment, a Massachusetts company started in a garage, which used integrated circuits bought on the open market to construct "minicomputers." They provided cheap machines, lacking all but the most rudimentary software, to sophisticated purchasers who could tame the savage electron without assistance. DEC disdained "handholding" and left the customer pretty much on his own to deal with his bargain-basement computer.

The computer industry was now big enough to encompass IBM, a host of competitors, EDS and a host of other computer service providers, and DEC and another host of minicomputer makers. The integrated circuit revolution had made it possible, and another revolution was on the way.

10

Fabrication

Making Integrated Circuits

The manufacturing revolution in integrated circuits is, at the moment, the last great revolution in computer technology. It is now some 30 years old, and it continues. The trend toward increased complexity, increased power, and decreased prices began in the early 60s. These trends have never stopped. Computer architecture has been much the same for the past 30 years. (A new way of designing computers, called parallel architecture, emerged in the late 80s and will be discussed in Section VI.) Practically all the significant gains in computing power in the period came as a result of improvements in integrated circuits. Those improvements were the direct and indirect results of the steady improvement in manufacturing technology.

Direct results were obvious: packing more devices on every chip made each chip more powerful. New designs were the indirect results of better manufacturing: complex circuits for some tasks had to wait until manufacturing technology allowed them to be squeezed to fit on a chip. Only then would they become economical.

In the early 70s two complex circuits were reduced to chip size.

Robert Noyce—coinventor of the integrated circuit—left Fairchild Semiconductor in 1968, dissatisfied with management. Several colleagues left around the same time, including Gordon Moore—propounder of Moore's Law. Moore had left because he couldn't interest Fairchild in developing semiconductor memory.

Logic circuits were highly profitable, and the existing memory technology, magnetic-core memory, was cheap and reliable.

Noyce and Moore incorporated Intel in 1968. Their reputations brought them financing and engineers. Within a year, they were making memory chips based on established technology. These chips would store only 64 binary digits, or bits, but there were enough customers to pay the bills while the new company developed a new technology.

Intel adopted a metal-oxide-silicon (MOS) transistor that had been developed at Bell Labs. MOS technology was a departure from the bipolar transistor technology of the previous 10 years. It used a different, somewhat slower, transistor design, but it permitted designers to create less complex circuits with fewer devices per memory cell. (Later, another advantage of MOS—that its transistors gave off much less heat than bipolar transistors—would turn out to be very important, a crucial advantage in making densely packed integrated circuits with many thousands of transistors on a single chip.) At the time Noyce and his colleagues started Intel, MOS chips were generally thought to be too hard to manufacture. Intel engineers solved a chemistry problem that made it possible to deposit aluminum in tiny holes in silicon oxide. That made connections in the MOS transistor more reliable. It took two or three designs, and another year, however, before Intel had a product that customers would look at. It was the 1 kilobit dynamic random-access memory chip and it was a wild success.

To its customers, Intel announced without modesty: "Intel introduces Type 1103, a history making 1024-bit RAM made by our silicon gate MOS process at such high yields that the cost dips below cores. Just tell us what core memories cost you, and we'll tell you how to build operational Type 1103 memories for less cost in any size from 50,000 bits to 10,000,000 bits. The Intel 1103 makes a fully assembled memory system that has a maximum access of 300 nanoseconds and a total cycle time of 600 nanoseconds. The chip is fully decoded and dissipates only 100 microwatts per bit, permitting dense packaging in compact configurations."[1]

Some explanations, since we have encountered new terms that are going to be with us awhile:

A *RAM* is a random-access memory chip, meaning it holds bits in memory cells, which a computer can access at random. A book is a random-access memory device, since the reader can turn to any page and find the information stored there. Its opposite is a serial-access memory device such as a cassette tape, on which each bit of information must be examined in turn.

A *DRAM* (pronounced dee-ram) is a dynamic random-access memory chip, meaning that it is barely a memory at all. The information bit is stored in a device that holds a charge, called a *capacitor*, and this charge weakens quickly. Thus the chip requires refreshing, like being reminded of the information stored in it, several times per second. Computer designers tolerate this because it allows a smaller memory cell than that required for a *SRAM*, a static random-access memory chip that doesn't need to be refreshed.

A *ROM* is a read-only memory, meaning that the information stored in it is there for good, like ink on the printed page. ROMs also come in blank versions and in versions that allow all the data on them to be erased at once.

Intel's 1103 DRAM was a solid success. "Our 1103 RAM circuit is now found in the products of 14 out of 18 mainframe computer manufacturers in the U.S., Europe, and Japan, and it is now the highest dollar volume semiconductor component in the world." Intel bragged in its 1972 annual report.[2]

Computer on a Chip

While Intel was concentrating on development of the memory chip, the company was picking up business as it could be found, just to pay the bills. A Japanese calculator firm called Busicom wanted somebody to design a set of integrated circuits that would drive a calculator. (The company was looking for some way to leapfrog more established Japanese companies that were making desktop calculators.) The Japanese figured about 12 special chips would do the job. Intel handed the job to a young engineer named Ted Hoff, who took the Japanese assignment as a license to design a computer. In 1971, Hoff created a design which incorporated all the logic circuitry for a calculator on a single chip. The most important feature, though, was that the logic circuitry could be used in other machines besides a calculator. So when Busicom demanded a lower price (to meet competition from a four-chip hand-held calculator invented at Texas Instruments) Intel took back its rights to sell Hoff's design to all comers.

This sideshow chip, known as the *microprocessor*, would quickly become as important as Intel's main event, the memory chip. Eventually it would be the most important product of the generation. The original microprocessor was a four-bit device, meaning it directly handled binary numbers up to 1111—0 through 15 in the decimal system. It was barely adequate as a calculator, but it was good enough for many simple tasks. It was well worth even the original price of $200 per chip to put rudimentary "intelligence" into temperature- and pressure-sensing devices used in industry. And as prices fell, consumers entered a new world of smart thermostats, smart ovens, smart air conditioners, even smart toasters. Automobile engines acquired smart sensors and microprocessors to control operation and keep emissions within environmental specifications. Four-bit microprocessors, at a cost of $3 or less, are used today by the million to control appliances, toys, automobile emission control devices, and so on. Calculators, a precious marvel less than two decades ago, are given away with magazine subscriptions.

By 1972, Intel improved the idea of the microprocessor enough to produce an eight-bit unit, meaning one that could directly handle numbers up to 11111111 in binary, 0 through 255 in decimal. That was enough for all the letters of the alphabet, upper and lower case, all the numbers, and all the other symbols on the typewriter keyboard. Instant computer.

It actually took about three years for Intel—and the competitors that sprang up with similar chips—to bring the price of the eight-bit microprocessor down from the original $200 to a level where hobbyists could start thinking about building computers. The first computer design in *Popular Electronics* was published in 1975 and could be made from readily available parts, including the Intel 8008 microprocessor, for about $800. Not included were any sort of display, such as a video screen, any sort of input device, such as a keyboard, or any sort of mass storage for data, such as a tape or disc drive.

Computer on a Desk

These drawbacks only entranced hobbyists. The period from 1975 to 1979 was the crystal radio set period of personal computing. Kids with the minds of adults and adults with the hearts of children tinkered with kit-built and scratchbuilt computers. Among the kids, of course, were a couple of California guys named Steve (Jobs and Wozniak) who founded Apple Computer.

The Tandy Corp. was a company that catered to such people, selling electronic parts at its Radio Shack chain of stores. In 1978 it produced the first fully assembled personal computer, including video screen, keyboard, and cassette tape storage unit available nationwide in a chain of retail stores. For roughly $2,500 the computer hobbyist no longer had to know how to solder.

Within a few months, the hobbyist did not have to know how to program, either. The first few personal computers were sold with an operating system and a programming language, and little else. The first customers would be able to write their own programs. Once written, however, a program can be copied and shared, or sold. There is no more work involved in copying a program than there is in using a Xerox machine to copy a newspaper article. Thus many of the first Apple and Tandy customers wrote programs. And the programs they wrote made the machines more useful for others, including those who did not know how to write programs. Many of the programmers got rich having fun, which became a lifestyle.

At least a dozen other companies joined Tandy and Apple in the newborn personal computer industry, filling the shelves of equally new personal computer stores with products. When IBM entered with its own PC in 1981, Apple ran a tongue-in-cheek ad welcoming the big company to the field. Partly by IBM design, its PC was easy to "clone." Now new entrants to the personal computer industry did not even have to design their own computer. Purchase of an Intel microprocessor, some other readily available electronic gear, and some key software put virtually anybody into the PC business.

Some were amazingly successful. Compaq, based in Texas, set records for the shortest time a firm ever took to have a billion-dollar sales year, and for the shortest time to be listed on the New

York Stock Exchange. It's still a leader in the industry. Many others flashed in the pan. At one point in 1983 there were about 80 clone companies, all predicting that they would prosper on as little as 5 percent of the PC market.

Columbia Data Systems, based in Maryland, beat even Compaq to market with a clone. But the company grew faster than its managers could handle. In particular, they could not handle the integrated circuit market. As sales soared, managers bought chips in quantities to match their expectations, paying top dollar in a hotly competitive market. But when the PC market cooled off a little, Columbia and all its competitors found they had enough chips in inventory to last them a year at least—for Columbia it was more like five years—at the new slower sales pace. Instead of double-ordering to make sure they could get enough chips, computer companies canceled orders. The chip companies could not just turn off the production stream, so they slashed prices to move the goods. Memory chips that cost $5 in the spring of '84 were selling for 45 cents at the end of the year.

This was no one-time tragedy: Apple Computer was caught with similar inventories that had to be written down in 1989. It is one of the most characteristic pitfalls in the computer industry. Apple, of course, had the financial strength to withstand an inventory crisis. Columbia was trying to grow its way to solvency and when that didn't work, company executives cooked the books. In order to spread skyrocketing costs over the maximum revenue, Columbia resorted to an end-of-the-quarter sale to a distributor that was actually a consignment deal. The distributor didn't have to pay until after he sold the computers, and he could return anything he didn't sell. Columbia's auditors and board balked at that; the sale was reversed in the next quarter, which was a bad quarter anyway. Equity was wiped out, the company likewise.

Growing by Shrinking

In both memory chips and microprocessors, Moore's Law was at work. The 1K DRAM memory chip was succeeded by the 4K in 1974, by the 16K in 1977, by the 64K in 1980, by the 256K in 1984, by the 1-megabit DRAM in 1987, and the 4-megabit DRAM went into production in 1990. Prototypes of 16-megabit DRAMs were fabricated in 1990 and introduction is expected in 1992. Microprocessors became more and more powerful, and more complex, handling 16 bits at a time in the early 80s and 32 bits at a time by the late 80s. Within each generation, the speed with which the chip processed its data doubled about every other year. The day of the 64-bit microprocessor—crunching numbers as big as those crunched by supercomputers—was dawning with the 90s. Moore's company, Intel, has forecast that the microprocessor of 2000 will be 30 to 60 times faster than those of 1990, and handle four times as much information at a time.[3]

In addition, there was developed a third class of dense microcircuits of particular interest to computer designers. Gate arrays assembled ever-increasing numbers of basic devices on chips for logic circuits. These chips could be made in great quantity, hence very cheaply. The computer designer could then customize them by specifying a final stage of production, connecting some devices and insulating others, to produce the circuit desired. Moore's Law worked as well with these to increase the power of computing.

If you compare the page you are now reading with a microfilm copy of it, you will understand how Moore's Law works. The microfilm copy retains all the information stored on this page— the letters and the pattern in which they are arranged and the place of this page in the entire book —while shrinking the information to the size of a 35mm slide. (The 4M DRAM available in 1990, by the way, will store this entire book in a space the size of your fingernail.) Advances in integrated circuits are almost entirely advances in the ability to shrink devices and connections, thereby packing more devices and more computing power on a chip of the same size.

When you shrink the dimensions of a device by half, you cut its area by a factor of four—you can put four devices where one used to fit. Since DRAMs require one transistor per bit of memory, this explains why DRAM capacity rises fourfold with each generation. Other chips also progress as the number of devices make fourfold jumps, but their circuits are more complex. For example, a static RAM requires four transistors per bit, so it follows behind the DRAM by a factor of four. When the 1M DRAM is state-of-the-art, the 256K SRAM is its equivalent in complexity.

This simple fact—that metal-oxide-silicon transistors and other devices comprising integrated circuits can be made smaller and smaller—is the driving force of the entire computer industry since the 60s. The technology changes have either been made to accommodate shrinking devices or have been made possible by shrinking devices.

In 1970 designers of advanced integrated circuits could expect reliable production of lines on chips about five microns wide. (A micron is a micrometer, one millionth of a meter or 0.000039 inch) By 1975, this design rule had been shrunk to about 2.5 microns, and to 1.75 microns by 1980. As the 90s opened, designers were underneath the one micron barrier.

Smaller, Ever-Smaller

Are there limits to shrinking microcircuits? It is presumably impossible to make a transistor out of a single atom. Other than that fundamental limit, most every guess that has ever been made about the ability to shrink devices on silicon microcircuitry has proved too conservative. Current guesses are hovering around a design rule limit of 0.1 micron, on the grounds that electrical connections can't be made much smaller without electrons leaking out.

We are leaving the world of microelectronics and entering the world of nanoelectronics. One micron equals a thousand nanometers. A tenth-micron is 100 nanometers, and so on.

So the bad news is that it may take a fundamental change in technology for the computer industry to progress in the 21st century. The good news, however, is that no fundamental discoveries about the laws of physics have been applied to the computer industry since the discovery of the transistor in 1947. The only attempt, even, was an effort to apply Josephson Junctions, devices employing some startling properties of superconductivity at temperatures a few degrees above absolute zero. IBM researched Josephson Junction for about a decade but by the early 80s it had become clear that good old metal-oxide-silicon was approaching the performance sought in the exotic, quirky realm of superconductivity. A few researchers still work on Josephson technology and it may yet bear fruit.

Researchers at Bell Labs and many other places around the

world are exploring an entirely different technology for computing, employing fiber optics instead of electronics. Already in wide commercial use in communications, optical fibers conduct photons generated by lasers. Optical fibers present two possibilities. The simple, conservative one is that fibers might be shrunk below 0.1 micron, so that connections on integrated circuits can be made ever denser. The more complex and radical one is that "photonics" may eventually replace electronics. Fast switches—the photonic equivalent of transistors—have been developed already at Bell Labs and assembled into rudimentary computer circuits. These circuits take up a surface the size of a desk, but those who work with them say they will be simpler when they are made the size of a chip. The opportunity is for incredibly fast switching, a thousandth or even a millionth of the times of electronic devices. The obstacle is in power consumption and dissipation of heat: at the beginning of the 90s the fast speeds were offset by the longer connections and greater complexity of photonic circuitry.

The economic obstacle to photonics is how far it must go—and at what expense—to become financially attractive. If electronics and photonics were starting off evenly in 1959, there would be a simple competition of technologies. But 30 years of electronics have passed. There are no uses for simple photonic circuits in computing, no uses for 1K photonic DRAMs or four-bit photonic microprocessors. Developers of photonics must duplicate and surpass all those intermediate steps, and the other intermediate steps still being developed in electronics, before earning a single cent of revenue from a commercial product. Photonics may have to find niches, perhaps in fiber optic communications, that electronic devices can't fill.

One of the newest fields in materials research is exploring the previously unknown properties of "clusters," solids made from powders in which each grain is a cluster of no more than 100 atoms. Clusters apparently have interesting chemical and electronic properties different from those of the same solids in normal sized chunks. It might prove possible to join and divide clusters to cause them to change state in some detectable way.[4] That would be a sort of switch, and the microcircuit revolution might get another boost.

Projections for the end of improvements to silicon have been wrong before. The integrated circuit industry has examined many techniques and dismissed them as not (yet) cost-effective. One example is the apartment house chip, making better use of the third dimension, height. All chips in the first 30 years of silicon integrated circuitry have been laid out in an essentially flat field. The heat generated by the devices on the chip had to go somewhere, and up was the most convenient direction. It's not hard to imagine—although it may be extremely hard to build—chips in which devices are stacked on top of each other as part of the fabrication process. They would require some method of removing heat and they would require extra channels of communication. Another example is tearing down fences between the chips. Also known as *wafer-scale integration*, this approach calls for building much bigger chips. It was tried in the mid–80s by Gene Amdahl, whose Trilogy Corp. was the best-financed startup in the history of the industry. Trilogy also was the biggest failure in the history of the industry, so its name and failure are attached to the very idea of wafer-scale integration.

Some imaginative engineers, well versed in quantum mechanics, say that if devices below 0.1 micron, that is 100 nanometers, have the unreliable characteristic of leaking electrons, that may not be a problem but an opportunity.

Quantum mechanics, the science of subatomic particles, teaches that electrons and other particles of similar size have either location or motion, but not both. This boils down, for our purposes, to the unsettling fact that electrons can "tunnel" through barriers. Scientists working in this area are trying to develop reliable ways of controlling tunneling. They say that if their ideas are successful, they could lead to new forms of diodes and transistors that could take the design rule limit down to 10 nanometers. In DRAM terms, that's a mega-megabit chip, a trillion-bit memory chip. Robert T. Bate of Texas Instruments suggests, however, that such chip geometry would be more likely be applied in logic circuits, because information traveling along a circuit of nanoelectronic devices would tunnel from one device to the next. The circuit would require no physical connections.

The Print Shop in Microscale

Jack Kilby's first integrated circuit used real wire to connect devices. Noyce's first integrated circuit used connections about a quarter the thickness of a human hair, exciting for the time. Some features on 4M DRAMS require design tolerances of 0.7 microns, less than 1 millionth of a meter.

To get from Kilby to the present day, there have been major changes in design—in particular, three different types of transistors have been "state-of-the-art" in the past two decades. But the big advances have all required improvements in manufacturing.

Microchips are printed, hundreds at a time, on round wafers of pure silicon crystal. The wafer is coated with a material that reacts to light. Then a photoprinting machine shines light on the coated wafer through a slide called a mask. The mask has part of the pattern of the chip on it. After exposure, the wafer is chemically treated to remove the exposed photoresist material. Then it's put in a machine for doping (remember, the semiconducting silicon is made either conductive or insulating by the purposeful addition of impurities). Then the process begins all over again with a different pattern for a different dopant.

The factories where all this happens are the cleanest places on earth. By comparison, a hospital operating theater is like a greasy spoon cafe. A floating dust mote could ruin the picture that the photoprinter projects on the wafer and it could destroy the purity of the dopants laid down on the silicon. Photoprinters called *wafer steppers* must move precisely, detecting alignment points on each chip so that the series of prints and layers of material made by the prints interlace correctly. At the beginning of the 90s complicated chips required as many as two dozen separate printing processes. Each time the printer passed over the wafer, the piece of silicon would have to be in exactly the same position and the stepper would have to be in perfect alignment with each chip as it printed the next pattern. Otherwise, the chip would be ruined. Wafers are transported from machine to machine by automated devices built to keep the wafers clean and to orient them correctly for each exposure or doping. The completed wafers are cut apart and each chip must undergo automated testing to determine if it is a state-of-the-art integrated circuit, worth from a few dollars to a few hundred dollars, or a useless crumb of junk. The entire factory must be isolated from movement—no small feat in earthquake-prone regions such as California and Japan. Factories are built on shock absorbers, but more than one factory has been plagued with unexplained failures that occurred as if on a timetable, until workers noticed the passing trains on a rail line hundreds of feet away.

Many of the manufacturing improvements in the fabrication of integrated circuits have come through automating the production processes—humans are too unreliable and too dirty for such delicate tasks. Even the design of integrated circuits has become automated. Engineers lay out the map of new chips on computer workstations that are programmed to test the design as it's being put together. Can it work? Can it be manufactured? The workstation advises the designer as he goes. The most advanced design workstations, called "silicon compilers," actually create designs for custom chips from an outline of their functions. The workstations compile previously established designs for subsections of complete chips, working from a library of such designs and a library of interconnections.

The silicon compiler seems to limit creativity, by restricting the designer to the subsections in its library. But those who use such design tools say that replicating established ways of doing things leaves them time to do the hard part of a new custom chip—tailoring the chip to the job it will do.

Equally important for the chip designer is a process of making and testing prototype chips. The silicon compiler's output includes manufacturing specifications, so that a specialist in fabrication of chips can take several designs and process them, returning them to the designers in a matter of weeks.

These techniques for rapid design and prototyping were developed by Carver Mead of Cal Tech and a few disciples, mostly with funding by the Defense Advanced Research Projects Agency. "In the 70s, it used to be that only foundries could do design," says a DARPA official who was involved in the project. "We felt that was like saying that only printing press owners could write books. The barriers of entry were too high; so the DARPA community created notion of multiproject chips and multichip wafers. Designs were sent over the computer network, so it only cost a couple hundred dollars to do a chip design, instead of $20,000."[5]

This is making a fundamental change in the balance of power

in the integrated circuit industry by giving "authors" the power to "write" their own chips. Before the advent of these new design systems, chips could only pay their way if they were made in the thousands and could only be profitable if made in the millions. Now a few custom chips can hold down the cost of a new product at the start.

Most of the U.S. semiconductor companies founded in the 80s, in fact, don't actually make chips at all. They make designs, either for clients or to sell on the open market. Some "chip foundry," specializing in low-cost manufacturing, does the actual fabrication. The designers are thus freed from heavy capital costs and avoid the tedious drive toward manufacturing excellence, just as magazine publishers hire excellent printers to manufacture their products so they can concentrate on writing stories and selling advertisements.

Printers and Publishers

This change is dividing the semiconductor industry into companies that manufacture chips and those that create designs. Those that do manufacturing face growing capital costs.

"The original tool which drew the circuit pattern onto chips— known as a contact printer, cost less than $35,000 just 15 years ago," IBM President Jack Kuehler told a House subcommittee in 1989.[6] "Today, this process has been automated in a device known as a [wafer] stepper. Each stepper costs $1.7 million, and every production line requires 10 to 50 steppers. Most other production processes and testing, all formerly manual, are now automated. Each process requires many tools costing hundreds of thousands or millions of dollars. So it's easy to see why a state of the art, commercially viable chip factory can cost $500 million."

The National Advisory Committee on Semiconductors lists 20 key types of equipment and specialized materials, but the stepper, mentioned by Kuehler, is the most impressive and the most crucial to the production process.[7]

The first steppers were produced by a Massachusetts company called GCA in the late 70s. They replaced projection aligners, which used lenses to reduce the design pattern from the size of the mask to the size of the chip. The lenses brought distortion at the edge of the chip and were hard to keep focused.

Steppers required masks the same size as the chip, but that difficulty was not as great as the one posed by the distortion of lenses in projection aligners. Steppers were the key piece of equipment in producing 64K DRAMs for both U.S. and Japanese chip producers. The Japanese government and industry, however, sponsored a stepper development program while GCA essentially stood still. Nikon, and later Canon, proved formidable competitors even as Japanese chip companies took a greater part of the chip market from GCA's American customers. GCA, now owned by General Signal, has but 20 percent of the world stepper market, almost all in sales to American companies.

Steppers were in the news in 1989 and 1990 because Perkin-Elmer, which had been working on a new generation stepper with IBM, called it quits. Wishing to sell its semiconductor production equipment business, Perkin-Elmer found no takers. Perhaps American companies agreed with Perkin-Elmer Chairman Horace G. McDonell, who told security analysts: "As a company, we have to conclude that the situation is completely outside of our control. Competition with Japan, the tremendous pace of technological change, and the tremendous capital requirements of this business combine to create tremendous risks. Frankly, we feel we have better alternatives."[8]

With a sales pitch like that, it was no wonder Perkin-Elmer found it hard to sell the semiconductor equipment division. Nikon sniffed around, but a well-timed story in the *New York Times* (Dec. 10, 1989) aroused U.S. nationalism and scared the Japanese off. It took several more months, and the intervention of IBM, to engineer a sale—nearly a giveaway—to Silicon Valley Group, a small company previously specializing in mechanisms for transporting wafers along a production line. Perkin-Elmer had to keep 20 percent of the business in order to sell it; IBM took an undisclosed equity position and promised to buy substantial numbers of the new machines.

Looking Ahead

Somewhere between the 16M DRAM and the 64M DRAM may come a new level of production equipment and a new level of expense. Focusing light through masks and onto wafers may become nearly impossible when the mask pattern includes lines that are less than half a micron. Even at 1 micron, visible light is already too coarse to be blocked by such a fine line, so steppers flash short-wave ultraviolet light. To get below half a micron, even ultraviolet light may not be enough.

One solution is even shorter wavelengths, using X rays. This idea has been under development since 1972, awaiting the long-predicted day when light cannot do the trick. The combination of ever-more reliable steppers and ultraviolet light has put off that day—fortunately for Moore's Law, because X-ray printing has not been ready. Problems with X-ray printing include destruction of the masks by the powerful rays, but the real show-stopper has been the price of a good X-ray source. Synchrotrons generating X rays of the right wavelength and strength have proven hard to build, and even if they were available would probably drive the price of a stepper up above $15 million. Even IBM, which has worked on X-ray technology for more than a decade, finds the cost more than daunting. The normally secretive company invited other U.S. companies to join its X-ray development effort, though only Motorola signed up right away.

Another solution amounts to using a well-sharpened pencil instead of a printer to put patterns on chips. One example is electron-beam lithography, in which a beam of electrons is magnetically steered to place extremely thin lines on silicon. Of course, Gutenberg proved that printing was faster than handwriting, and chips made with electron beam lithography have been the 20th century equivalent of illuminated manuscripts. Electron beam machines have been used to make prototype chips and to make masks, the slides carrying chip patterns that optical steppers shine through to print chip patterns. But they haven't brought their high accuracy to mass production because they are too slow—processing at best five wafers an hour to an optical stepper's 30 per hour. Nor can their slow speed be overcome by numbers, because they cost too much—several million dollars each.

The developer of the latest electron beam machine, however, contends that intelligent use of his machine will not stand in the way of rapid mass production. Marty Lepselter, founder of Lepton Inc. in New Jersey, suggests that his machine be used along with optical steppers. Optical steppers would lay down most of the patterns for printing, but certain key layers of doping chemicals would be printed using the electron beam machine. In his sales pitch, Lepselter claims that a fabrication line capable of making 4 megabit DRAMs could, with the addition of his machine, make 64 megabit chips. The $6 million price tag on the Lepton machine would be justified by his promise, for it would bypass a whole chip generation, and delay the need for even more expensive X-ray steppers. At an even higher price, Lepselter envisions multiple beam machines that would use teamwork to achieve higher speeds.[9]

If the biggest Japanese and U.S. companies specializing in mass production don't sign on to Lepselter's idea, it stands a good chance of being tried by some upstart, in South Korean or Taiwan. And in any case, better electron beam machines will probably find a market in the growing sector of the industry that specializes in custom chips.

In addition to the design firms that proliferated in the 80s, a new family of chip foundries specializing in custom production are being set up at the start of the 90s. Those that specialize in the densest possible chips are using electron beam machines. But at a somewhat lower level of complexity on the chip, laser-etching is opening up another possibility.[10] Two companies, Lasarray and Lasa Industries, are reaching toward the ultimate custom chip machine—a design workstation linked to a miniproduction line, all on a rather large table top. The Strategic Defense Initiative Organization is promoting the idea that a Star Wars device developed at Los Alamos National Laboratory, the Free-Electron Laser, may power a better photoprinting device than an X-ray machine.

11
Price and Quantity

Lepselter's Law

There is another law, less well known than Moore's law, that should be called *Lepselter's Law*.[1] Also formulated with tongue in cheek, Lepselter's Law also turns out to be as true about integrated circuit pricing as Moore's Law is about chip density, because the two laws are two sides of the same coin.

Lepselter's Law says, in its complex form:

> The initial high price of a new DRAM declines rapidly with a rate much larger than $1 a year. The rate approaches $1 a year at a price level of about $3. This price level . . . corresponds to the peak volume of DRAM shipment as well as the maximum return on investment. We shall designate this important price level the *pi level* because the transcendental number pi has a value fairly close to 3. Beyond the pi level, the price continues to decline and eventually settles at a level corresponding to one half the pi level.

The process repeats itself with a new generation of DRAMs every three to four years, Lepselter adds, since the low cost of the current generation holds down the cost of the next generation to no more than four times the existing price per chip, usually less. In its simple form, Lepselter's Law says, "The cost per bit of memory chips will be halved every two years."

Lepselter, who spent most of his career at Bell Labs before taking his electron beam lithography research project out into a company of his own and trying to commercialize it, has a scientist's sense of humor. He would never name his rule Lepselter's Law;

he prefers the gentle jesting tone of "The Pi Rule," a pseudoscientific paper he wrote. Nevertheless, after a bit of prodding and adjusting for inflation, and ignoring the fact that nothing in life follows a smooth curve, his rule of thumb isn't too far off.

In March 1980 64K DRAMs sold for $28. The price had fallen to $8 by the end of 1981, it hit $5 in April 1982, and reached less than $2 by 1984. Between September 1984 and September 1985 the price of 256K DRAMs fell 93 percent to a lite more than $2. 1M DRAM prices fell more than 50 percent between the fourth quarter of 1988 and the first quarter of 1990, to about $5, as the 4M DRAM was just beginning to come into wide use.

There are fairly simple reasons for this, rooted in the production process. As we saw in our examination of Moore's Law, several hundred chips are made at a time on wafers of silicon. More than a dozen exacting production processes are conducted on the wafer to produce its chips. Sometimes a process is replicated hundreds of times for each wafer, while other times the entire wafer is subjected to the production process once, so that all the chips are treated simultaneously.

Early in the production cycle a wafer fab line is a place where high-priced engineers tear their hair out in bunches. Brand new production equipment machines often don't work according to expectations: ovens don't hit the right temperature; diffusion machines don't spread the same concentration of a gas over all the wafers; transport machines break down or damage wafers; steppers don't step precisely or make their exposures through unfocused lenses; the list of possible malfunctions seems endless. Gross malfunctions are followed by subtle maladjustments: Was the failure of one quarter of the memory cells in the 331st through 339th chips on wafers 200 through 210 caused by incomplete silicon dioxide deposition in the fourth stage? And if that was the cause, was there a hot spot in the oven or a stray breeze in the diffusion machine?

Whole wafers go bad in bunches and even a "good" wafer may produce only 5 percent or 10 percent good chips on a good day. The rest are trash. And all the tweaking and tinkering and fiddling with equipment is not taking place in a friendly atmosphere. Engineers from the semiconductor company blame production equipment; production equipment engineers blame the fab line workers and each other. And all of them are quite conscious that the price for the new chip they would like to make is currently quite high. The company that first produces the chip in large quantities will reap healthy profits. Many jobs and maybe even the whole company depend on making the fab line work.

Later in the production cycle—months later—the manufacturing engineers have learned how to use their production equipment better. The fab line now yields good chips at rates in excess of 50 percent. So, for the same cost of materials and equipment—and possibly less cost of labor—the fab line's production has risen 5 to 10 times in the space of a few months.

Economists have studied this process and concluded that the manufacture of integrated circuits is just about a perfect example of "learning economies." They have written equations that describe the learning process, which come down to one simple rule: managers who know from experience how fast the learning process takes place know in advance what their costs will be at any stage in the life cycle of a product.

Economists have also noted that manufacturing know-how can be protected, up to a point. Unlike a chip design secret, it can't be disclosed in a professional journal or to any customer with a microscope. And the profits from having the best manufacturing know-how stay at home as well, because the producer furthest along the learning curve is the producer with the lowest costs, and the highest profits.

Firstest with the Mostest

The result is that cutthroat competition pervades the semiconductor industry. The only way to proceed along the learning curve is to get started on production. And the way to proceed fastest along the learning curve is to ramp up production as fast as possible. Knowing that one's competitors know these facts produces a pell-mell scramble to be first to enter new markets, first to offer new products, first to go into volume production, and, finally, first to cut prices to stimulate demand. Multiply this by 10 companies struggling to enter a market, and a glut is the obvious result.

Now supply and demand in the market take over. In memory chips, the first company into volume production makes money, probably a lot of money; the second and third companies make some money; the fourth and fifth may break even; latecomers lose their shirts. But even latecomers don't stop producing, because the marginal cost—the cost of making one more chip—is so low that the latecomer loses less money producing than it would by shutting down.

Why, then, do firms keep playing in the DRAM market? They explain: one, the winner apparently does stand to make a lot of money and you can't win if you don't buy a ticket; and two, DRAMs are easy to make compared to other kinds of chips, so the production skills honed in the DRAM competition serve companies well when they come to introduce new generations of microprocessors or custom chips, for which the market may not be so competitive.

There may be a third answer: smart companies don't play in the DRAM market. Intel and Motorola, which dropped out of DRAMs in 1984, are the leading microprocessor companies. (Motorola, however, moved back into DRAMs in 1989 in partnership with Toshiba.) Both are moving rapidly into the business of constructing computers out of their chips. In 1989 Intel got only two thirds of its revenue from chips; one third came from computers and components such as printed circuit boards. The profit as a percent of sales from components and computers was less than from chips, but required much less capital investment. As a Goldman Sachs securities analyst, Rajiv Chaudri, put it, "Between the $200 microprocessor and the $5,000 box there is not a lot of technological value added. This is something that both opportunistically and strategically makes sense."

Other major U.S. semiconductor manufacturers have found other chips to make. Even Micron Technology, which was founded to build DRAMs, is moving into the production of add-on boards stuffed with its memory chips, instead of just selling chips to board makers. Such behavior is driven by the quest for profits, since profits are hard to come by in DRAMs.

Hundreds of other U.S. semiconductor companies don't make chips at all. They design chips and let other foundries, in the United States, Japan, or elsewhere in the Far East, use excess capacity on their fabrication lines to make the actual products. At the close of the 80s, for example, the fastest memory chip in the world was designed in Colorado, manufactured in Japan, and sold by a large U.S. chip house in California.

Today's Winner

Moore's Law says nothing about who will make DRAMs or any other chip. Lepselter's Law suggests that who will make DRAMs is subject to sudden change. Every generation of DRAMs saw companies fall by the wayside. Large companies, such as General Electric, RCA, Honeywell, Sylvania, and Philco-Ford failed to make the grade. Entrepreneurial companies from Silicon Valley failed by the dozen. And the combination, when a big company like United Technologies took over a successful semiconductor company like Mostek, produced some of the biggest failures of all.

In the mid-70s came a new wave of entrants. A shortage of 16K DRAMs in 1978–79 caused U.S. computer companies to turn to Japanese semiconductor companies for the first time. They were there to turn to because Japanese companies aggressively licensed integrated circuit technology and designs from U.S. firms. (Most American companies were content to use the royalty income as a cost-free income stream; though Texas Instruments held out for entry into the protected Japanese market, and indeed entered the 90s making most of its high-volume chips, such as DRAMs, in Japan.)

The 16K DRAM was the last memory chip competition American firms won. Toshiba introduced the 64K DRAM in 1980, six months ahead of the United States and Japanese competition. Japanese firms crowded into the U.S. market and captured nearly 80 percent of 64K DRAM sales.

The Japanese government had targeted the semiconductor industry as ideal for the industry of a country with few raw materials and an abundance of educated workers. The invasion of Japanese chip producers and the inability of U.S. semiconductor companies to penetrate the Japanese market produced one of the longest running and most difficult trade relationships between the two countries.

Section IV

THE HIGH-TECH FOOD CHAIN— SEMICONDUCTORS AND PROTECTION

A popular way of describing the electronics industry is with an appeal to ecology. In nature's food chain, elementary creatures such as algae and protozoa are food for higher order creatures, which are then food for still-higher creatures. Man, the creature atop the food chain, is prey for no animal. Yet man is dependent on the existence of lesser creatures, the food for the creatures he eats. In the electronic food chain, semiconductor production equipment and materials create integrated circuits, which are components of printed circuit boards, which are components of computers and electronic devices of all sorts. American man, at the top of the food chain, is dependent on the existence of small bits of electronics.

12

Chips and Quality

Hewlett-Packard blew the whistle on Silicon Valley. With a public declaration in 1980 that Japanese chips were better than American chips, Hewlett-Packard executives tried to change the American electronics industry.

Richard W. Anderson, general manager of the Data Systems Division, made a presentation in Washington; other Hewlett-Packard executives said much the same thing in California, Texas, and elsewhere. Anderson recalled that in 1977, in the early days just after several companies introduced the 16K DRAM, Hewlett-Packard could not get enough of them because American suppliers were having problems producing them in quantity.

> After much anguish, we decided to talk to a Japanese company who had been calling on us telling us of their memory for some time. And I would like to state at the outset we took a very cautious approach because we remembered well the impressions from post–World War II Japanese products; namely that they were cheap, low cost, and low quality. And so our engineers went through a very rigorous qualification program; and we were pleasantly surprised to find they qualified.[1]

Anderson recalled another pleasant surprise. "We had fewer failures in incoming inspection; we had fewer failures during the production cycle; we saw fewer failures of products in customers' hands." In 1979, when another supply crunch hit the American chipmakers, Hewlett-Packard went back to Japan and signed up two more Japanese suppliers. It was the same story: "excellent quality."

When Hewlett-Packard got down to business, it compiled performance records on 300,000 equivalent memory chips, half from three U.S. suppliers and half from three Japanese firms. None of the Japanese shipments was rejected at the loading dock, as some U.S. shipments were. Field failure rates for Japanese chips ranged from 0.019 percent per thousand hours for the worst firm to 0.010 percent for the best. The best American supplier's failure rate was 0.059 percent per thousand hours, and the worst was at 0.27 percent failures per thousand hours. A computer with memory chips from the worst American supplier was 27 times as likely to have a memory failure than a computer with memory from the best Japanese company.

Hewlett-Packard did not exactly rush right out and shout its findings from the rooftops; nor did the other computer companies that were experiencing similarly deficient quality in their American suppliers. After all, the quality of components contributes to the reliability of products and reliability is a competitive advantage. Clueing in the competition is not a great business tradition. Eventually, though, Hewlett-Packard announced its findings.

The First Stage Is Denial

U.S. semiconductor companies denied that they had a problem. Hewlett-Packard had a problem, they said. Either the company used the wrong test, or some test that the Japanese were prepared for, or the Japanese had fooled the Americans by shipping specially tested parts to targeted customers like Hewlett-Packard. Or perhaps the Japanese reserved their regular quality chips for the home market, while selling high-quality chips in the U.S. market at equivalent prices.

American semiconductor manufacturers spent the 80s conceding that the U.S. industry had a quality problem about two years earlier, a quality problem that was now fixed, so that their quality was equal to the Japanese quality. Unfortunately, they kept on making these statements through the 80s, conceding 1980's quality problems in 1982, 1981's quality gap in 1983, and so on. They were following a moving benchmark, matching Japanese standards of quality that had already passed them by.

The Japanese had other explanations. They left more space between chips on each wafer, which made for fewer chips on the wafer but made each one more likely to be a successful chip. They encapsulated the chip in a plastic package filled with an inert gas. They had diminished the problems of "soft errors" caused by alpha particle emissions from the package by coating the chip with a radiation-resistant layer.

Another explanation is that the Japanese companies were all selling to Nippon Telegraph and Telephone, which had extremely high requirements for reliability and directed research toward that goal in the programs it sponsored. In the United States, AT&T had similar requirements for high reliability, perhaps even higher since AT&T was developing technology for transoceanic cables and communications satellites. But AT&T designed its own high-reliability chips at Bell Labs and manufactured them in its own Western Electric facilities. None of its requirements were felt in the U.S. merchant semiconductor industry.

The Mil-Spec Trap

The quality demands of the U.S. military may have been another cause of low quality in the U.S. merchant chip industry. The military specified high reliability in a very military way. Chips for military purchase were required to be tested elaborately, in high temperatures and low temperatures, in high pressures and low pressures, high humidity and low humidity. The Defense Department wanted to be sure that everything it bought would work wherever a soldier, sailor, or airman might find himself—from Point Barrow, Alaska, to Riyadh, Saudi Arabia, from 1,000 feet under the ocean to 70,000 feet in the air. On the well-known military principle that a thing worth doing is worth overdoing, these "Mil-Spec" testing requirements were imposed on components that would spend their working lives in air-conditioned Pentagon basements as well as those destined for radars and radios in submarines, fighter jets, and tanks.

The chips thus tested and sold to the military were produced in exactly the same way as the untested chips sold to everybody else. The testing did not necessarily guarantee better performance.[2] Indeed, failure rates of tested chips in service were often no different than failure rates of untested chips. They differed only in price. Mil-Spec chips could run five times the price of other chips, depending on the price cuts imposed in the competitive civilian market that were ignored in the world of military contracts. More than one company fell victim to the temptation to sell the military chips that had not been tested. Officials could rationalize that there really was no difference, since there really was no difference. They found, however, that no company is without disgruntled employees, and that all that mattered was that the military thought there was a difference. Fines and a few dismissals of "responsible" officials would follow. The cavalier attitude toward quality, however, would remain.

The Deming Way

American firms pursued quality with testing, while the Japanese attitude toward quality was more fervent, and much more effective. Many Japanese industries had been converted by the American prophet of statistical process control, W. Edwards Deming. If ever there was a prophet without honor in his own country, it was Deming. From a Ph.D. in physics in 1928, he became a statistician, publishing a book, *On the Statistical Theory of Errors*, in 1934 and following it up with instructions, written and oral, for achieving high quality in any manufacturing concern that would listen to him.

Deming called for a system of "doing it right the first time," and using statistical analysis of carefully gathered data to determine every slip in the production process, as it would happen, before it would cause defects in the product. "By describing statistically exactly what is done, the method locates your problems and leads to innovations that solve them."[3]

The power of the Deming method is twofold: the quality of finished parts is enhanced and the cost of producing them is lower, despite the extra effort involved. Why? Because in a post-Deming factory there are virtually no defective parts sent back for reworking, almost no defective products scrapped or reworked, and almost no defective products sent back by customers. The avoidance of detailed inspection of every part and of the extra labor that follows defective production more than pays for the extra care taken in the original production process.

Another American statistical quality control expert, J.M. Juran, estimated in 1980 that 10 percent of the whole American economy was going to rework and waste.[4] "Higher quality costs less, because higher quality means that of every hundred units we start into production, more survive," Juran said. "It's something called the *yield*. The lower the yield, the lower the quality; the higher the yield, the higher the quality and the lower the costs."

For example, a pre-Deming factory typically sets a standard for a part, say a dimension of so much, plus or minus some deviation. Production is tested, and the machine that makes the part is taken out of service for adjustment when the finished product ceases to function because of a fault in the part. (Since this happens randomly, the factory line is often down for unscheduled maintenance, another source of higher costs.) Defects often arise, however, when two machines turn out parts that must match, but fail to match because their errors are in opposite directions, even though each was within tolerance. Such faults are hard to trace without the detailed statistical records on each machine that a post-Deming factory develops. Also, a post-Deming factory takes every machine down for scheduled maintenance often enough so that the production machines remain close to perfection. Statistics tell the managers how often is often enough.

Deming opposed quality control departments and quality control engineers, because "quality is everyone's job." His method requires that quality be embedded in the production process, not put on later like a coat of paint. But few American companies picked up his message. They were already the quality leaders of the world using older techniques. It was not until 1950, when Deming was invited to speak to the Industry Club of Japan, that he found a receptive audience. "Made in Japan" was then an international joke, a guarantee of a cheap price and equally cheap workmanship. Deming's methods, adopted widely in Japan, reversed the image entirely. By 1970, Japanese products in many industries were clearly equal in quality, even to the most prejudiced critic. In some areas, especially consumer electronics, there were Japanese brand names—Sony TVs for example—considered the top of the line in American stores. By 1980, "Made in Japan" was a guarantee of quality in steel, in cars, in consumer electronics, in integrated circuits.

Juran, who was also brought to Japan in 1950, recalled that of the 30 or 40 countries where he had given quality control courses, only in Japan did the top industrial executives attend his training. "There was a power vacuum in Japan at that time as a result of the dislocation of the war. They undertook to make a revolution in quality and the top leaders of the economy were also the leaders of the revolution."[5] In 1980, Juran predicted that it would take at least 10 years for Americans to catch up to Japanese quality. "I don't see any escape from that because of the inherent momentum there and the problems of trying to take something as big as the American economy or the European economies and trying to move them at a new pace. The inertia is so massive, and [so are] the problems. It took the Japanese 10 years to take that training through the hierarchy once they started." When American manufacturers argue they used the 80s well, the choices of their customers often suggest otherwise.

Made for Each Other

There is no line of work more amenable to the Deming principles than the fabrication of integrated circuits. Printing electronic devices onto microchips requires the fanatical attention to detail and the constant adjustment toward perfection of the Deming method. Dozens of independent processes must be precisely matched to create devices and connections instead of junk. Driving machines to their limits, and then improving them, is more productive than keeping them in operation within certain specified tolerances. Integrated circuit designs also must take "manufacturability" into consideration—a part that cannot be made reliably cannot be made reliable, and should be redesigned.

As integrated circuit production was automated more and more, it became more and more effectively controlled and pushed ahead by statistical quality control. Production equipment and its effective use came to drive advances in integrated circuits.

In the early 70s, the Japanese primarily used American-made semiconductor production equipment because it was the only such equipment in the world. That would change, in part because the Japanese found much American equipment could not be made to live up to their standards. Or, as frustrated American equipment makers said, the Japanese tried to make their machines do things they weren't designed to do. What was difficult to accept was that they succeeded. Japanese chip producers excelled at making the production equipment turn out a new generation of chips on the fabrication lines designed for the previous generation. The American method of building a whole new fabrication line for every new generation was less efficient than the exacting, tinkering methods of the Japanese. Chipmakers in both countries carefully guard the intricacies of their production processes, but equipment makers have been inside enough Japanese factories to tell convincing stories.

Sometimes the equipment makers were astonished to realize that they hardly recognized their own machines—Japanese production engineers had made so many modifications to squeeze out higher levels of performance. The smart Americans, of course, took careful notes and made their next generation of machines the way their customers had taught them, but a surprising number scoffed and ignored the proffered lesson until it was too late.

A Good Idea Is Not Enough

The congressional Office of Technology Assessment, in its book *Making Things Better*,[6] devoted some research to the uneasy relationship between U.S. production equipment manufacturers and their Japanese customers.

In 1977 a small Massachusetts company called GCA introduced a new technology in the photoprinting of circuit designs. The method was called direct-step-on-wafer, meaning that the machine stepped across the silicon wafer and made direct, or at least very close, contact with it to print an image of a single chip. People in the industry twisted the term around to call the machines wafer steppers. The new technology blew the old projection systems, made by Perkin-Elmer of Connecticut, right out of the water. In order to move from 16K DRAMs to 64K DRAMs, and in order to make comparable advances in the production of other chips, every factory had to have its wafer steppers.

GCA was one of the highest flying stocks of the late 70s. It won the acclaim Wall Street investors reserve for companies with unregulated monopolies, posting a price-earnings ratio in excess of 50 times earnings and a stock price that multiplied eightfold in two years. But GCA was riding for a fall. A Nikon stepper entered in 1981. Result: GCA's market share in Japan went from 95 percent in 1981 to 40 percent in 1982. Every year brought fewer sales, as Japanese chipmakers gave all their business to Japanese firms.

U.S. trade lobbyists often cite the GCA story, and similar stories in other segments of the semiconductor production equipment industry as proof that the Japanese don't fight fair. As many frustrated industry people have said, "They will buy an American product only if it's better than a Japanese one, and only as many as they have to. Then they will work with a Japanese supplier to tear down the American product and match it. And then, they buy Japanese, all the way."

That is a partial description of how Nikon beat GCA. As the Office of Technology Assessment relates, the Japanese Ministry of International Trade and Industry sponsored a project that brought five semiconductor producers together for research between 1976 and 1979. It included heavy emphasis on manufacturing processes. Toshiba, the company that had the most experience with GCA steppers, was selected to work with Nikon on a Japanese stepper.

"Toshiba set performance specifications but did not provide a design. Instead, Toshiba engineers reviewed all details of development, manufacture, and testing; provided technical help in design concepts, electronics and materials, and components selection; and in the process visited Nikon several times a week. The result was a stepper which, though not radically different from GCA's, gained the reputation of being more reliable."[7]

In a footnote, OTA reports, "According to U.S. industry sources, the GCA stepper has better focus and more precise alignment than the Nikon—but only when engineers set it up. The Nikon stepper is more robust and requires far less set-up time. It can run well day after day with little adjustment, and therefore is much superior in throughput (an important consideration for mass production of commodity chips)."

OTA insists that the close relationship between vendor and supplier was not the only reason for Nikon's success. "The nearly instant preference Japanese semiconductor firms gave to the Nikon stepper, combined with the large investments in new equipment that these firms made through the mid-80s, were critically important."

True enough, though some put more emphasis on the Japanese demand for reliability and GCA's apparent unwillingness or inability to improve its first model. "Spokesmen for GCA noted that their Japanese customers were more demanding than American firms, asking for more fine-tuning and changes in the equipment they bought. But they were also more helpful in making suggestions for improving the equipment."[8]

In emphasizing the large investments that Japanese companies made in production equipment in the mid-80s, OTA also points out that GCA continued to act as if its monopoly had not been broken. GCA based all its plans on selling 500 or 600 of the $1 million machines; but in 1985, GCA sold only about 100 and lost $94 million. The dashed expectations were also due to a cutback in capital investment by U.S. chipmakers, who were losing hundreds of millions of dollars in their own competitive battle with the Japanese; also GCA had problems getting delivery of Zeiss lenses from Germany, while Nikon made its own.

GCA was eventually sold for a song to General Signal. It now has about 20 percent of the stepper market in the United States and negligible share abroad.

Canon, the second Japanese producer of wafer steppers, entered the business on its own without the aid of a MITI project and now provides strong, even cutthroat, competition to Nikon in the home market. (The competition, of course, strengthens both firms.)

Listening to the Customer

Larry Hansen, head of the semiconductor equipment group at Varian Associates Inc., talked in 1987 about the difference between doing business with Japanese and American chipmakers and the difference between what the Japanese did with his equipment and what Americans did.[9] His story shows that there was a successful strategy GCA could have used to keep selling its complex stepper.

A Varian machine that performed a particular crucial step in chipmaking was more complex than the leading competitor's device, but had 70 percent higher potential capacity. According to Hansen, the Japanese were willing to buy Varian service contracts and work with Varian to keep the machines running at high output.

Going one step farther, said Hansen, Japanese customers typically worked with Varian in the Japanese factory to get the bugs out of a new piece of equipment, to be sure it would do what they wanted it to do. "In the United States, they throw the switch and if it doesn't work, it will be waiting for us on the loading dock," said Hansen. Varian caught on, and began to offer its newest technology to Japanese customers first. With that strategy, Varian has stayed in the semiconductor production equipment business and done reasonably well.

13

The Japanese in Chips

The Japanese Method

The Japanese semiconductor industry was on a level playing field with the U.S. industry by the late 70s, although the U.S. companies did not recognize their potent new competition. It was the American customers of Japanese firms that discovered the new equality when they gave up on backlogged U.S. suppliers and turned to Japan.

The Japanese companies had been active in transistors and integrated circuits from the earliest days of the pocket radio. A strong local market in radios, hi-fi equipment, and calculators generated income and competitive pressure among the Japanese companies. Scholars and businessmen have argued since then about what technology the Japanese imported and what they developed in their own research projects parallel to American lines of research. (This is the polite way of putting it: the debate often boils down to pro-American charges of theft and pro-Japanese defenses of independent development.) Either way, and probably both ways, the Japanese companies achieved a great deal. Then, in the mid-70s, two key Japanese government agencies intervened.

Nippon Telegraph and Telephone, then a government-owned communications monopoly overseen by the Ministry of Post and Telecommunications, created a research project in integrated circuit technology for communications, in which Nippon Electric Co., Hitachi, and Fujitsu were very active. These electrical equipment and electronics companies invested their own money, but

NTT promised future procurement contracts, diminishing the risk of the investment.

The Ministry of International Trade and Industry, perceived in the U.S. as the managing director of "Japan Inc.," put up real money: about $80 million in interest-free loans that would be repaid from royalty income and profits from technologies developed. Toshiba and Mitsubishi joined NEC, Hitachi, and Fujitsu in this project, and the five companies put up about $120 million.

Research in the two projects emphasized basic technology development, such as circuit design, fabrication of microstructures, and materials research. Engineers and scientists from the companies worked together on teams with counterparts from NTT and MITI. The companies worked together also on manufacturing processes, production equipment, testing, and packaging, although in these areas each company formed its own team and worked on its own methods, exchanging information through written reports and through meetings. The companies reported later that the projects were more successful than they had expected, because they avoided developing specific products. "The joint development of various alternative technologies in order to identify the most promising ones for further development proved to be a highly efficient use of resources."[1]

A team of Japanese and U.S. academics who studied this period observe that NTT and MITI served as substitutes for the U.S. Defense Department (as purchaser) and the technical universities of the United States (as independent developers of integrated circuit technology).

Other Japanese electronics companies were left out of the NTT and MITI development projects, and expressed their irritation and frustration. "Within Japan the oligopoly trend toward large manufacturers is becoming conspicuous," said one Japanese trade journal in 1975. "Second level makers have reduced their in-house production and are placing more weight on outside procurement. Outside makers will be supported as outside procurement increases. This furthers the trend toward oligopoly."[2]

In the long run, though, other Japanese companies, notably Oki Electric, Matsushita, Sony, and Minibea, established substantial positions in the Japanese semiconductor industry. But the big five merchant suppliers established in the 70s—Toshiba, Hitachi, NEC, Fujitsu, and Mitsubishi—remain the dominant players in the most competitive markets.

Whether they constitute an oligopoly or not is a matter of some dispute. Most observers in the United States see the coordinated research and development projects, the evident effort of MITI to manage the industry, and the similarities in behavior of each company. They conclude that they are seeing Japan Inc., an oligopoly combining in restraint of trade. But if these companies are operating a cartel, it's a strange one.

Japanese chip companies compete vigorously, even viciously, at home and abroad. Their drive for market share is a drive of their own company's market share, not the market share of Japan Inc., against U.S. Inc. Proof of their vigorous competition lies in the accelerating pace of development. Japanese companies race each other to bring out new generations of memory chips and faster than ever. If they were operating as a cartel, they would surely combine to slow down this pace and slow down price cutting so everybody could sit back and make a nice profit without so much effort.

The American Method

U.S. chip companies substantially cut back their capital spending during the recession of 1974–75. Looking for money, they had licensed designs and manufacturing techniques to Japanese firms. Production equipment was for sale. On the research and development side, the recession slowed down the 16K DRAM enough in the United States and speeded development up enough in Japan so that Japanese firms introduced the new memory chips in their market at about the same time as American firms did in the United States. On the production side, the investment cutback meant that fewer new fabrication lines were built in the United States, too few to satisfy the demand that would be generated in the economic upswing of 1977.

Japanese chip manufacturers are divisions of much larger electrical equipment and electronics companies, but such companies in the United States had not been successful players in the integrated circuit industry. GE, Sylvania, RCA, indeed most big U.S. firms had tried, but it took a bet-the-company attitude to compete in the early days of the U.S. integrated circuit industry. Big companies found it easier to buy chips from successful bettors than to put up bets themselves. Only IBM and AT&T developed significant manufacturing capacity in memory and other integrated circuits that they could have purchased on the outside. Other U.S. companies, from General Motors to Digital Equipment, built integrated circuits they could not buy or would not buy for competitive reasons, usually custom designs for key functions in their products. In Japan, however, the situation was reversed. And big companies such as Fujitsu, Toshiba, and Hitachi needed integrated circuits for their own consumption and chose to develop their own capacity. With no entrepreneurial competition in their home market, they then expanded production and became semiconductor merchants.

The Japanese companies eventually became competitors of the most successful semiconductor merchants in the United States, such as Texas Instruments, Intel, Advanced Micro Devices, Mostek, Fairchild, and National Semiconductor. These were still small companies, dependent on cash flow for their investment capital. When these small companies were doing well, their stocks shot up to stupendous prices. A downturn in business would burst the bubble. These companies were dependent on the swings of the market. Some rushed to the market to issue stock and to the bank to open lines of credit whenever the time was opportune. Others allowed founders or early backers to cash in first and were surprised to find that the stock market has a window of opportunity that often shuts when least expected.

Capital expenditures by the U.S. industry in the 70s reflected the stock market collapse of 1974 and the sluggish years that followed. Capital expenditures by the Japanese industry fell in 1974 but recovered and grew almost immediately.[3] When the 16K DRAM generation began in 1977, the U.S. industry was caught short of capacity, opening the U.S. market to the Japanese.

Pricing followed supply. It's not a condition peculiar to the semiconductor industry that in a period of tight supply and high demand, prices rise. The early days of the U.S. market for 16K DRAMs was a seller's market and the sellers were pricing accordingly. But in the Japanese market for 16K DRAMs there was no such shortage. Instead, these sellers were trying to woo new buyers. It's not a condition peculiar to the semiconductor industry that in a period of loose supply and low demand, prices fall.

The simultaneous operation of a buyer's market on one side of the Pacific and a seller's market on the other side lasted much longer than it would now. Today the markets would balance in less time than it takes to fly chips from Japan to San Francisco.

Then it took months for Japanese salesmen to convince their potential American customers that they had an alternative, months to qualify their products, months for the customers to be sure they had parts that were the same or better than the ones that U.S. companies could not ship for half a year. Eventually, the Japanese semiconductor companies did make significant inroads on the U.S. market, often at lower prices to boot.

Dumping

U.S. companies called this dumping. That opened a can of worms, and the worms have crawled through the semiconductor industry ever after. Congress first outlawed dumping in 1916 and tried to tighten the law every few years thereafter.[4] According to law, a foreign producer is dumping if it sells its product in the United States at less than its "fair value," or "foreign market value," which might be the home market price, the price in a third country, or "the costs of production, plus at least 10 percent for general expenses, plus at least 8 percent for profit." (Note the use of "at least.") The Department of Commerce decides which method to use. Also there is a clause in the law that requires disregarding home market or third country market sales made at less than the cost of production. Thus any dumping case turns on the foreigner's costs of production. Since that is probably a trade secret, it turns on the U.S. estimate of the foreigner's cost of production. So any formal dumping procedure is a very complex proceeding, but one that U.S. law stacks in favor of the injured U.S. producers.

The dumping law was not invoked in the case of 16K DRAMs; U.S. firms and the government officials who began to get interested in the semiconductor industry just muttered under their breath. Eventually about a dozen American companies made 16K DRAMs and the early personal computer market was so clearly taking off that even a company that had lost money in 16K DRAMs could see the potential profit in the next generation.

Unfortunately for those companies, Toshiba was first to introduce the 64K DRAM to the merchant market in 1980, six months ahead of the competition (IBM beat Toshiba by several months, but doesn't sell to the outside world). Other Japanese firms followed quickly and gained a clear head start on American producers. Instead of coming from behind to gain a 47 percent world market share, as Japanese firms did in the 16K generation, Japanese firms had the market to themselves long enough to establish a strong position, more than three quarters of the world market. Even against domestic competition, they held more than half the U.S. market. Half the U.S. firms were out of DRAMs by 1982.

"Japanese firms have set 64K DRAM prices so low as to raise suspicions of dumping," wrote Daniel Okimoto of Stanford University in 1982.[5] "Some American executives find it hard to believe that Japanese firms selling at such low prices could even break even." These Americans were badly hurt by the recession of 1981–82, which slowed the growth of their customers' demand for chips. They believed that the Japanese should have reacted to weak demand the way the Americans did, by cutting back production. Instead, the Japanese continued to produce and cut price instead.

There was a respite for memory chip makers in 1983 and 1984, when the boom in IBM personal computers and PC clones sent demand soaring. U.S. semiconductor companies won back some of their market and the reduction in the number of competitors made for profits for all. That actually raised a new issue—the issue of U.S. access to the Japanese market. The Semiconductor Industry Association demanded an end to overt Japanese government protection and what the SIA saw as the systematic refusal of Japanese companies to buy American chips. But before that could receive anything more than lip service, demand for chips in the United States slumped again in 1985 and 1986. Some analysts estimated that U.S. firms lost as much as $2 billion during the period. The Semiconductor Industry Association rolled market access in with its dumping charges, gave up all pretense at free trading, and pressured the U.S. government to do something.

A Thin Wire

The merchant market for memory chips runs under some pretty fast and loose rules that were set by U.S. entrepreneurs in the cutthroat days of the 70s. For example: many chip sales are handled through distributors because the chip makers want to deal in large lots and not sell a few dozen chips to every teenage inventor who comes down the street hoping to be the next Steve Jobs founding the next Apple on credit. But chip distributors learned, the hard way, that it's dangerous to have too much inventory on the shelf that could become obsolete at any moment. So they demanded the right to return merchandise to the manufacturer. Also, many big customers learned, the hard way, that the chip supplies could go from bust to boom almost overnight, leaving them stuck with no reliable source of supply. So they insisted on having at least two sources of supply for every chip they would design into their products. Then, whenever the market would overheat, they could double-order.

Such rules of the game mean that boom periods include an unknown quantity of orders that will vanish in the first weak period, plus an unknown quantity of sales to distributors that will come back to be undone. Chief financial officers at chip makers don't have an easy time. Experienced CFOs question everything. And semiconductor executives who have survived a couple of cycles have learned not to bet the company in an up year. On the other hand, investing cautiously leads to supply shortages in the future, which leads to another boom period, and the cycle gets tighter and tighter.

Trade Negotiating

All the ebbs and flows of the demand side of the market were pretty much ignored by the Japanese firms, who just produced and produced and priced to match demand. Analysts who estimated that U.S. firms lost $2 billion in 1985 and 1986 put Japanese losses at $3 billion to $5 billion. Clyde Prestowitz, then a Commerce Department official, began a campaign to declare dumping a strategic tool of the Japanese semiconductor industry. He was successful: in 1985 the Department of Commerce filed an antidumping case on its own initiative, the first time it had ever made its own case instead of waiting for an aggrieved party. The Semiconductor Industry Association also filed a trade case seeking a wedge to open the Japanese market to U.S. chips. And Micron Technology, a DRAM producer, also filed a dumping case. Prestowitz and other aggressive trade officials deftly played the three cases off within the U.S. trade bureaucracy as well as with the Japanese.

The Japanese government came to the negotiating table with the Department of Commerce under the threat of antidumping duties greater than 100 percent, according to the initial Commerce calculation of the difference between the Japanese costs and the price of Japanese memory chips in the U.S. The Commerce figure was a "constructed price," using estimated production costs based on U.S. production costs, plus overhead and profit. The price computation was stacked against Japan, because it used American assumptions of cost and overhead and a profit standard that was generous even by American standards. But it followed U.S. law.

"There was no evidence Japan maintained higher-than-world market prices for semiconductors in its internal market at the time of the dumping cases," recalled the economic adviser to the chairman of the U.S. International Trade Commission.[6] In other words, the Japanese firms were "dumping," so to speak, in their own market as well. Estimates of their total losses in this period range up toward $4 billion.

In the first half of 1986, U.S. and Japanese trade negotiators endured many bleary nights of argument over dumping and market access. Japanese argued that the Americans had misinterpreted the nature of the semiconductor market; Americans stood fast on the construction of American law. The U.S. side felt confident because of the threat the dumping duties held over the Japanese.

In the real world, however, Japanese firms were building on their success in 64K DRAMs to capture virtually all the world market for 256K DRAMs. Most American chip makers bitterly gave up on DRAMs. Texas Instruments stayed in the business; Micron Technology, a new company, proudly used the stock ticker symbol "DRAM" and viewed its mission as beating the Japanese in memory circuits. (When it could not accomplish this mission impossible, it changed its ticker symbol to "MCRN.") Other U.S. companies dropped DRAMS and found other goals. Their leaders said they continued to support the antidumping effort in memory chips as a means of intimidating the Japanese against using the same tactics in markets for other types of chips.

Forward Pricing

In a competitive market such as that for integrated circuits, where the quantity produced goes up with yield while production costs are almost unchanged, you must expect prices to fall rapidly. If you do expect prices to fall rapidly, it is natural, in a competitive market, to quote the lowest possible price—even lower than your current cost of production. This is called *forward pricing,* or *learning curve pricing,* a price that will allow you to make a profit based on the costs you expect to be incurring at the time of delivery.

The U.S. Department of Commerce flatly asserts that forward pricing cannot be countenanced under U.S. antidumping law.

"How can I as a regulator make a decision based on assumptions of future performance?" a Commerce Department official explained. "You just don't know who's going to saturate the market or when, and you can't allow years of dumping." Another official, sounding more like an economist, charged: "Forward pricing can only be viable over time in an oligopoly," meaning that a market has to be managed or forward pricers don't make any money. The Commerce officials naturally charge, therefore, that the Ministry of International Trade and Industry manages memory chip supplies on behalf of the Japanese industry.

The first remark highlights the way Commerce officials see themselves in the world. If you think of them as trade negotiators, sort of a State Department for business negotiations, you miss the most important part of their role. They see themselves as regulators overseeing the terms of trade—more comparable to the Interstate Commerce Commission or the Federal Communications Commission than to the State Department.

Congress ordered it to be that way, they say, though Congress writes laws that are left to bureaucrats to interpret. But even if true, does it make sense? If we have the Department of Commerce maintain an orderly marketplace in the ebb and flow of goods to these shores, we will miss the disorderly benefits of new products and low prices for them.

The second remark, about being impossible to do forward pricing except in an oligopoly, simply misses the point. Forward pricing is logical in an industry with rapidly declining per-unit costs, especially one in which the per-unit costs decline most rapidly when the greatest number of units is sold. A cartel is no more required for profits in the semiconductor industry than it is in any other manufacturing industry.

Creating a Cartel

In the fall of 1986, at the last hour before the 100 percent anti-dumping duty would go into effect, the United States and Japan came to an agreement. The Japanese agreed not to dump. To cure dumping, the U.S. Commerce Department would have access to the cost accounting of Japanese firms, and using that inside data, which they would keep secret, U.S. officials would set a "Fair Market Value" for each company's chips, a price that the firms would not undercut in either the U.S. or in third countries. Each firm would have its own "Fair Market Value" based on its own cost data. The actual number, and the data, would be kept a close secret. Perhaps four people in the Department of Commerce are privy to this data; their work cannot be analyzed or questioned by outsiders or other officials.

The Japanese also agreed that the 10 percent American market share in the Japanese market would rise to a 20 percent share. In return, the U.S. dumping cases were suspended. For a few months, nothing at all changed. The Japanese were apparently being advised by their Washington lobbyists that President Reagan, with his free-trade instincts, would not invoke the sanctions that would force the Japanese to comply. The Commerce Department, however, did have the last word. After a bureaucratic struggle for his soul, the president imposed $300 million worth of sanctions in March 1987.

The sanctions were not imposed on chips as such, but on end products using chips made by the five big Japanese chip makers, such as TVs and personal computers, for which there were other non-Japanese sources of supply. The government was at some pains to find Japanese products to punish without also punishing Americans. In what should have been a convincing display of the interdependent nature of trade, even those products that were targeted turned out to have American salesmen, distributors, transporters, and so forth, who suffered from the protective action of their own government.

When the Japanese finally did comply with the antidumping agreement, MITI managed the compliance by withholding export licenses from Japanese firms. MITI also administered the industry by issuing "forecasts" of supply and demand which often missed the mark in gauging demand but were never more than a few percentage points from perfect assessment of actual supply. The forecast was taken by the industry as a production order. Ironically, Texas Instruments of Japan toed the MITI line as obediently as the native Japanese firms.

Prices for semiconductor memory rose all over the world, as the agreement gave MITI the nod to form a Japanese-led chip cartel. The United States expressed its satisfaction by removing the extra duties related to chip dumping, though $165 million of duties levied as retaliation for lost sales of U.S. firms to Japan remained in force.

U.S. consumers of memory chips—the now-booming computer industry—were shocked and outraged. They had pretty much ignored the semiconductor industry complaints. They had pretty much ignored the Commerce Department's advisories to their trade associations. At most, the chip consumers had sympathized, agreeing in principle that it would be terrible for everybody if the Japanese were able to monopolize the chip market and jack up prices or restrict supply, but enjoying low prices in practice. Now, however, the chip users found their Silicon Valley neighbors and the government had jacked up prices and restricted supply. What was worse, their large Japanese competitors—and IBM, incidentally—were not subject to the same cost increases because they acquired their chips internally.

The first Fair Market Values pushed prices up 200 percent to 800 percent, according to the American Electronics Association, which has chip buyers and chip sellers among its members. The biggest price increases were tallied in the spot market, while long-term contracts rose less violently. This meant smaller companies, lacking resources to enter long-term contracts, suffered the most.

Some observers derided this as a silly state of affairs, in which the interests of U.S. chip manufacturers, a $20 billion a year industry, had been placed ahead of the interests of the $400 billion a year electronics industry. Some warned chip protection meant the export of the U.S. computer manufacturing industry. "Our survey of major users found more and more people saying they have to buy or manufacture in Asia," a Dataquest analyst, Gene Norett, reported. An American Electronics Association survey found the same thing. "Because of the pricing differential, about 85 percent of 200 respondents in our survey are opting for offshore purchase or assembly or they are just using chips from their backlog," an AEA spokesman said.

These warnings had a good grounding in economic theory but they were somewhat overblown. Even in vast quantities, DRAMs are not usually a critical determinant of the costs of computers and other final goods. DRAMs account for 10 percent of the parts and assembly cost of a personal computer, and a lesser percentage of the cost of more complex machines. Doubling the price of DRAMs could therefore raise the finished price of a personal computer by 10 percent—not insignificant in world competition but not critical in the short term. Most U.S. computer companies were able to wait out the price increase, even though Japanese firms did arrive with new personal computers stuffed with DRAMs, such as the ever-more-popular laptop and notebook PCs.

Not only did the semiconductor agreement push up memory prices in the United States, it also pushed up profits in Japan. Instead of losing as much as $4 billion in 1985–87, the Japanese integrated circuit producers earned $2 billion in 1988 and up to $4 billion in 1989. Even the economic adviser to the chairman of the U.S. International Trade Commission found the situation preposterous. "To the extent that any force has worked to produce monopoly profits in the semiconductor industry, it is the 1986 Semiconductor Agreement itself."[7]

Managing Free Trade

The trade policy of the United States in the postwar period has been to promote free trade in the form of lower tariffs while holding down imports with nontariff barriers. The U.S. government negotiated "voluntary restraint agreements" to keep out low-price foreign steel, and was surprised to find that the auto industry, dependent on steel, became less and less competitive. "Voluntary" restraint of Japanese auto imports followed.

Brookings Institution economist Kenneth Flamm joined the chorus of economists who have noted time and again that quotas are an unrewarding way to manage trade restraints: "Had it been in the national interest to force an increase in memory chip prices, it would not necessarily have had to benefit the Japanese chip makers. Simply adding a tariff or countervailing duty to the cost of Japanese chips, whether imported as components or incorporated into assembled equipment, would have diverted the profits from price increases into the U.S. Treasury, not onto Japanese balance sheets."[8]

The Commerce Department almost never follows this sound advice, which can be found in any economics textbook. Officials there prefer to use the threat of tariffs to negotiate restraints of trade. One reason may be to shift blame: Commerce officials blandly deny responsibility for the problems arising from the "voluntary" restraint of another nation. Another may be devotion to the protected United States industry: if the United States imposed tariffs, all the profits would, as Flamm noted, flow to the Treasury; under trade restraint or quotas some of the profits flow to the U.S. industry that gains market share or the freedom to raise prices.

A later round of Fair Market Values reduced allowable chip prices; also, entrepreneurs found ways around the system. In real life, chip prices were somewhat lower in Japan than in the United States. Prices were also lower in other Asian countries, despite the attempt to corral third country markets. Smuggling was an easy way to make some quick bucks: instead of going as freight, memory chip shipments rode first class in the luggage of "businessmen."

The lasting effects of the chip agreement were to enrich Japanese producers, allow Korean producers to get established, and to make it easier for Toshiba and NEC to gain market share in personal computers in the United States. American DRAM makers still have less than 5 percent of the world market.

Dealing with a Cartel

Japanese semiconductor producers quickly slowed production of 256K DRAMs, changing over to production of 1M DRAMs sooner than they would have otherwise done. Since yields are low at the beginning of the production cycle, this sharply curtailed the volume of memory chips available. By November 1987, the Commerce Department and even the Semiconductor Industry Association found themselves in the peculiar position of asking that the Japanese firms increase production. Without explicitly cutting a deal, the U.S. side lifted part of the tariffs imposed on the Japanese firms, and MITI raised its forecast of supply and demand.

By the end of 1987, the Department of Commerce had countenanced MITI's administration of a chip cartel and was trying to manipulate MITI to balance the conflicting interests of the American chip industry and its customers in the computer industry. Or, as one Commerce Department official explained in all seriousness, "We wanted to prevent dumping without having a larger economic impact."[9] In other words, to have our cake and eat it.

In 1988, demand for memory chips heated up again and the Japanese firms, with world market share in excess of 80 percent, made handsome profits. The Japanese press noted that the big semiconductor companies were not plowing their profits back into the memory chip business, that they were not going all out to produce and grab market share, that they were behaving with uncharacteristic restraint.[10]

A Different Path

One American firm swam against the Japanese tide in the 80s. At the start of the decade, Micron Technology, an Idaho chip design consulting firm, produced a design for a 64K DRAM that was half the size of some standard chips. Half the size meant twice as many chips could fit on a given wafer, and held out promise of cutting costs enough to be competitive, even with the Japanese. Bankrolled by J. R. Simplot, a potato producer, the company went into the memory chip business in 1982.

Micron has had its ups and downs. It has never been first to market, never enjoyed a dominant position in the business, but it has survived as the only 100 percent red-blooded American DRAM maker.

Micron is the prime exhibit for the efficacy of the Semiconductor Agreement with Japan. After losing money in 1983, 1985, 1986, and 1987, the company cleared healthy profits in 1988 and 1989. Just compare 1987, without the Semiconductor Agreement, with 1988, the first year the agreement operated. In 1987, Micron lost $22.9 million, or 94 cents a share, on sales of $91.1 million. (Even the drop in the exchange rate from over 250 yen to the dollar in 1985 to under 140 yen to the dollar in 1987 did not make Micron's business profitable. Only the chip agreement could do that.) In 1988, sales tripled to $300 million, profits were $118 million pretax, and final net was $3.38 a share.

But 1989 earnings were down a little, mostly because Micron invested heavily in a new fabrication line and other efforts to build up the business, while sales only grew 50 percent. Investors began to wonder if even the chip agreement could keep Micron healthy, and they noted that it would expire in 1991. Joe Parkinson, chairman of the board, genially acknowledged, "Most people think I'm dumb as a post to stay in DRAMs."[11]

"Most people" apparently includes other U.S. semiconductor companies. Texas Instruments is a highly competitive DRAM manufacturer, so much so that some competitors and trade warriors have attacked it for being too Japanese. But the chip agreement brought no other U.S. companies to reenter the DRAM market except Motorola, which produces Toshiba memory chips on Motorola production lines in the United States. Motorola tried to license IBM memory chip technology but talks were broken off in the fall of 1990.

Finding New Niches

In general, American firms shunned the DRAM market and tried to exploit niches where design was the determinant of profits. DRAM profits would still have been low and the threat of ruinous competition high, so they concentrated on the other markets— logic, erasable read-only memories, microprocessors, or custom chips. For a little while in 1988 it seemed that the semiconductor industry in the United States and Japan had matured.

Kenneth Flamm, however, noted that stasis in computer chips was bad for the computer industry, and bad for the United States economy. Follow his arithmetic: computers account for about 2 percent of gross national product, and the steady improvement in microchips is largely responsible for increasing computer price-performance by about 20 percent a year. So, 20 percent of 2 percent is 0.5 percent: improvements in microchips "translates into an improvement in the American standard of living in the range of 0.5 percent of GNP. This is an extraordinarily large number when compared to GNP growth rates of two or three percent a year."[12]

Fortunately for the United States and Japanese economies, the "cartelization" of the memory chip industry lasted only about a year. As yields improved and output rose, competition drove prices back down. In 1989 there was a new competitive factor: South Korean producers of memory chips, Samsung, Daewoo, and Hyundai, unfettered by the United States-Japan chip agreement, undercut prices in the United States and Japanese markets. The cartel had lasted just long enough to attract a new producer to the market.

14

An American Renaissance

Closing the Technology Gap

Besides fighting dumping and demanding to be given a share of the Japanese market for chips, the American semiconductor industry also tried to overcome its deficiencies in manufacturing. The industry formed the Semiconductor Research Corp. in 1981 to fund advanced research in design at American universities. Semiconductor companies joined with users in 1983 to form the Microelectronics and Computer Technology Corp. to do long-range research in computer architectures, computer-aided design, chip packaging, and similar fields of wide application in the industry.

SRC, located in Research Triangle, North Carolina, has been reasonably successful: the research program funded graduate students and the funding steered talented students into semiconductor research. SRC funding also steered universities into expanding their research facilities in microelectronics.

MCC, in Austin, Texas, is harder to judge. It is a relatively new industrial laboratory with a unique and difficult structure as a cooperative venture among competitive companies. Some of the member companies do not see much value in MCC, to judge from bitter comments of the staff. It seems hard for all companies to get past the "Not Invented Here" syndrome (a behavior pattern that rejects all outsiders' work) and MCC member companies seem unable to see a competitive advantage in technology that's delivered to several firms at once.

MCC has invented new ways of disseminating the technology it develops. For example, MCC researchers developed a way of making multichip modules by bonding chips to a substrate and using a laser to make or break connections among them. None of MCC's members wanted to make laser bonders—it wasn't that crucial to them—but many of them wanted to buy one. So MCC handed the technology to a laser company with the stipulation that the first 18 months of production would go only to MCC members.

Ideally, a research consortium like MCC should not develop its own projects and then try to leave them on its members' doorsteps like foundlings. Instead, it should work to be "hired," more or less, by its members to do specific projects. The difficulty is that the members are capable of doing research they know they want done. What they need is somebody doing the research they *didn't know* they wanted. Even Bell Labs, which has been dealing with this problem for nearly a century, still finds the transfer of laboratory technology to the hands of users to be a difficult trick.

A third industry consortium was more closely focused on the job of restoring manufacturing skills. Sematech (SEmiconductor MAnufacturing TECHnology) was organized in 1987 to advance semiconductor manufacturing technology in the United States. It has changed concepts several times, retaining only the central pillar—a grant of $100 million a year from the Defense Department.

Congress and the Defense Department agreed to put up the $100 million a year on the grounds that the semiconductor industry is vital to the national defense. This requires some consideration. The main argument is found in a "Report of the Defense Science Board's Task Force on Semiconductor Dependency," published in February 1987 through the office of the Under Secretary of Defense for Acquisition. This report was timed perfectly to link with the industry's promotion of joint research and development, perhaps not a coincidence since many of the people on the task force were industry people involved with the germination of Sematech.

The national security argument runs like this: The U.S. military strategy depends on technical superiority to counter the numerical superiority of the Soviet Army and Air Force. The Strategic Defense Initiative is only the latest example of the quest for qualitative superiority; others include Stealth aircraft, specialized radars, missile guidance systems, radar jammers protecting obsolete bombers, spy satellites, and a whole range of electronic warfare systems stretching back to the 50s. Since all these devices now contain integrated circuits, it follows that integrated circuit production must be a strategic industry. Since some integrated circuits used in some important weapons systems are available only from "foreign sources," it follows that those weapons systems are dependent on a source of supply the United States does not control.

Shintaro Ishihara, a Japanese member of Parliament who coauthored the book, *The Japan That Can Say No*, crystallized this argument for the Pentagon: "Should Japan decide to sell its chips to the Soviet Union instead, that would instantly alter the balance of military power." The book was a bestseller in Japan. Though it had not been published in the United States, the U.S. Defense Department had it translated and circulated among industrialists, members of Congress, and Washington journalists.

Ishihara, however, was talking through his hat. His comments were meant to bolster his countrymen in a sense of their growing importance in the world, but the specific idea that Japan could play a geopolitical card based on its chip industry is little more than fantasy. His comment betrayed ignorance of the international integrated circuit business and of the military industrial complex in the United States.

Set aside all questions of the diminishing Soviet threat, and set aside any possibility of U.S. retaliation in a foolish trade war between the United States and Japan. Consider only the practical implications of the Ishihara challenge:

Japanese chips find their way into U.S. military products for the same reason that they are used in U.S. computers and other products. They are available, reliable, and they are cheap. In the open market for chips, defense contractors have selected Japanese firms. The emphasis here should be on open market: the Japanese do not make custom chips strictly for U.S. military markets.

When the U.S. military wants special custom chips it turns to its usual defense suppliers. In the 80s, having decided that "Very High Speed Integrated Circuits" would be an essential component of new radars and electronic warfare devices, the Pentagon spent more than $200 million a year in a "VHSIC" program for firms like Rockwell, Westinghouse, General Electric, and others to develop the ability to make complex chips. By the time the program finished, they had that capability and they were using it to make custom chips for installation in the military electronic devices they were producing. In the same period, the semiconductor industry and computer industry, companies that mostly had not participated in the VHSIC program, also learned to build chips of similar complexity. As the 80s came to a close, very high-speed chips of roughly the same power and complexity as defense VHSIC chips were available in the commercial market at a far lower price. The Defense Department continued to buy high-cost chips from its traditional suppliers. It's apparently satisfied with this outcome, for in 1988 it started another gigabuck program called MMIC, for Microwave/millimeter wave Monolithic Integrated Circuits, to be used in radar and communications applications.

Ishihara also fails to understand that the Japanese semiconductor industry is as dependent on the U.S. market as the U.S. market is dependent on the Japanese semiconductor industry. Only a very large market, larger than the Japanese market or the U.S. market alone, can justify the high volume production that is needed for low cost and high quality. For the Japanese government to forbid Japanese chip companies to export chips to the United States would be against the best interests of the Japanese semiconductor producers, consumers, and ultimately their whole nation.

That Ishihara was not realistic did not stop the Pentagon from circulating his book and stirring up a huge fuss about semiconductors and national defense that was sufficient to carry the Congressional funding for Sematech.

A Way that Could Work

The original idea for Sematech was to have a joint fabrication facility building memory chips in high volume, then passing the manufacturing techniques back to the members for duplication in their own factories. Closer examination showed that would be too slow, even if the transfer of technology and know-how would go smoothly. (Companies often have found it hard to just pass know-how along from factory to factory within the same company.)

The next idea was that Sematech would be a joint manufacturing research center, at which engineers from the chip-making industry and engineers from the semiconductor production equipment industry could work together to develop the best manufacturing technology.

Robert Noyce, the coinventor of the integrated circuit, became chief executive officer of Sematech. His first year, 1988, was a year of hardware: getting moved in to a vacant warehouse in Austin, Texas, constructing and equipping a fabrication line, hiring staff, drawing up a plan of action, outlining projects. During that year, however, Noyce found that the challenge was greater than he had believed. There was a hardware problem—some critical semiconductor production equipment was no longer built in America and much U.S. equipment was not the world's best. And larger was a sort of software problem. After a career in the dog-eat-dog competition of the chip business, Noyce decided that dogs would have to stop eating other dogs. In particular, he decided that the chip makers would have to stop trying to exploit the production equipment manufacturers before all the equipment manufacturers were driven out of business.

"I came to the conclusion that we had to do something quick," Noyce recalled.[1] "We have prided ourselves on being a competitive society and that required that we develop arms-length transactions. That leads to requiring multiple suppliers, to writing specifications to cover any contingency." Noyce decided he was sick of lawyers and litigation, sick of hard-nosed beat-em-down negotiations between vendors and customers.

The U.S. semiconductor production equipment industry is highly fragmented, consisting of more than 150 companies in 30 or 40 specialized niches—making and oxidizing silicon wafers, photolithography, etching the printed patterns, doping and implanting foreign chemicals to determine the electrical characteristics of the patterns, testing, assembling chip packages, and so forth. Most of these companies occupy a few niches or only one, and in most of the niches there are several competitors. They sell to a limited market, vying to equip fabrication lines at no more than a dozen merchant semiconductor makers and perhaps another dozen computer companies that make their own chips. It has been easy for the chip makers to play the equipment makers—half of whom have sales of less than $10 million a year—off against each other. Survival of a supplier for a long time was not a problem, because two more always sprang up to take the place of any that fell. But even after that era came to an end, the adversarial behavior went on.

"In the traditional vendor-customer relationship you say, 'It doesn't meet specs, take it back!' This has made our economy grossly less efficient. We're trying now to call people suppliers rather than vendors," Noyce said hopefully. Under his leadership, Sematech began to try to build relationships instead of only building hardware. Sematech became a place where equipment makers and those who use the equipment could work side by side to make the equipment work better—exactly the kind of cooperative relationship that Japanese chip makers sponsored. Even when Sematech rejected a supplier's bid, somebody from the consortium would sit down with the bidder and explain why it was unsuccessful.

Sematech also became a preacher in the gospel of statistical quality control. "Everybody says, yeah, they're for it, but they don't know how to do it," said Keith Ericson, Sematech's vice president of supplier relations. "Our toughest job is to create an industrywide environment of partnering and continuous improvement."[2]

Sematech brought together 14 purchasing managers and tried to get them to agree on a single definition of quality control. Fortunately, the federal government had given them something to agree on. Modeled on Japan's Deming Prize, the Commerce Department established the Malcolm Baldridge Award (named for the late Commerce Secretary who served from 1981 to 1986). Motorola, a winner of the Baldridge Award in 1989, showed the way, by making entry in the Baldridge Award mandatory for its suppliers. Motorola's idea is that a firm that can qualify for the competition has at least a basic idea of how to do statistical quality control. "So now we are trying to make the specs meaningful for the semiconductor industry and get the members to all buy in," said Ericson.

"Japanese companies see their suppliers as the key to their success," he added. "They say American suppliers are unreliable, untrained, and inconsistent." Sematech's goal, Ericson said, is to get the chip makers to quit complaining and make their suppliers part of their team.

Did Sematech's role as an honest broker between the semiconductor industry and its equipment suppliers require the investment of $200 million a year by government and industry? The money goes for the purchase of current production equipment and joint development of a next generation, with a goal of having at least one viable U.S. vendor in each critical production technology. Sematech supposedly validates the vendor for the semiconductor companies so they have confidence in the equipment when the time comes to make their own purchases. For the equipment companies, Sematech provides realistic feedback about what's right or wrong with their tools and teaches a vendor how to work with its customers.

Avtar Oberai, who monitored the industry for Sematech, said Sematech is trying to break down the "arrogance" of successful suppliers, who have no interest in finding out about their shortcomings, and the "secretiveness" of semiconductor companies, who discover and fix a problem but don't tell the supplier in hopes that competitors using the same tool will have problems.

Sematech's cooperative approach held promise, but the consortium was shaken when Noyce died in June 1990. There was no other leader who could provide his triple role as leader, as symbol of the industry, and as salesman to Congress and the rest of the government. It would be easy for Sematech to go back to research and development in technology, instead of working to promote cooperation in the industry.

The Voice of Industry

Is Sematech, and its effort to accelerate the pace of technical development in the production equipment industry, really important? Does it matter if the semiconductor companies improve their manufacturing technology or change their cutthroat culture? Does the United States economy really require holding the lead in the production of integrated circuits?

The conventional answer was presented in November 1989 by the National Advisory Committee on Semiconductors. The chairman was Ian Ross, president of AT&T's Bell Laboratories. Members included chief executives of Martin Marietta, Motorola, Texas Instruments, National Semiconductor, Tandem Computers, Applied Materials, and the vice president for science and technology of IBM. From the government, members were the president's science adviser, a deputy secretary of commerce for technology, the director of the Energy Department's Office of Energy Research, the director of the National Science Foundation, and the under secretary of defense for acquisition. The executive director was William R. Bandy of the Defense Advanced Research Projects Agency.

"Continued deterioration of America's semiconductor industry poses an unacceptable threat to U.S. economic and national security," Chairman Ross wrote to President Bush on the delivery of the committee's report. "This report warns of a major threat to the United States, a threat that endangers American industry, workers, and strategic self-sufficiency. That threat is immediate and serious and warrants the attention of the highest councils of government."

Inside the report, the committee's arguments for the "vital national role" of the semiconductor industry amounted to little more than a restatement of the importance of integrated circuits.

Today's $50 billion world chip industry leverages a $750 billion global market in electronics products and 2.6 million jobs in the United States. This is more than double the number of jobs in the U.S. steel and auto industries combined. As products such as TVs, computers, antilock brakes, microwave ovens, and phone systems improve in performance and cost, demand for them increases. That increased demand prompts producers of these products to seek further advances from chip technology, pushing the industry forward toward further innovations. Such cycles of improved productivity and performance, and expanding demand for the products that take advantage of the improvements, create enormous economic and social gains.

The committee simply quoted the Defense Science Board's assertions on the subject of chips and defense:

The United States has historically been the technological leader in electronics. However, U.S. defense will soon depend on foreign sources for state-of-the-art technology in semiconductors. The Task Force views this as an unacceptable situation.

A little later comes the committee's only direct statement about the importance of a U.S. semiconductor industry. It is the food chain argument.

Progress in the semiconductor industry advances the technical capabilities of industries that are linked to chips in the production chain, from computers and telecommunications to new materials, and indirectly advances many other industries. The semiconductor industry promotes the development of ever purer chemicals and materials, more powerful computer-aided engineering and design and computer-integrated manufacturing, all of which find broad application in other industries. In addition, the products of the electronics industry are essential tools used to achieve the increased productivity, lower cost, and higher quality that are required from all U.S. manufacturing. Leadership in chips can result in leadership in many industries—a fact widely recognized by our major international competitors.

The Advisory Committee urged a wide range of steps for the government to take, aimed at restoring the health of the U.S. semiconductor industry and its suppliers. The big-ticket items included reforming tax laws to subsidize purchase of manufacturing equipment; creating a Consumer Electronics Capital Corporation to channel government funds and government-guaranteed borrowing into rejuvenation of a U.S. consumer electronics industry; closing off Japanese imports unless the Japanese open their chip market; spending about $300 million a year for Sematech and other efforts to develop new semiconductor production equipment; spending about $200 million a year for long-range development of integrated circuit technology; spending an untold sum (probably several hundred million a year) to have two corporations develop prototype X-ray lithography machines based on X-ray generating technology developed at the national laboratories.

Other Strategies

Accepting the oft-leveled charge that Japan, as a nation, is on a drive to dominate integrated circuits as a means of dominating the information industry of the 21st century, we still should consider whether there may not be other economic strategies—in fact, whether the United States, the nation leading the world in economic development, ought not to have a different strategy than Japan, a nation playing catch-up.

After World War II, the United States led the world toward increased trade and lower trade barriers. Even though exports were less than 5 percent of U.S. production (12 percent in 1989), and imports were less than 5 percent of U.S. consumption (18 percent in 1989), still the United States accounted for a sizable portion of world trade in 1950 and some U.S. industries were very much trade dependent, in one direction or the other.

Also, as President Reagan never tired of remembering, the Smoot-Hawley tariff of 1931, which raised U.S. tariffs on practically everything traded, pushed other countries to erect retaliatory trade barriers around the world and added to the depth and persistence of the Great Depression. The U.S. government, including most congressmen, feels a sort of guilt for letting Congress get out of control on that one and views it as the American mission to make trade easier and more profitable for all.

In a treaty framework called the General Agreement on Tariffs and Trade, the United States and the rest of the non-Communist world negotiated steadily lower tariffs between 1950 and 1970. Since then, attention of the U.S. government and the GATT have turned more toward nontariff barriers to trade and to trade subsidies, with mixed results. Some barriers have been lowered, others raised. The trade in semiconductors between the United States and Japan is a leading example of how politically difficult these issues can be:

The Japanese explicitly subsidized development of their semiconductor industry (after the U.S. government paid whatever price was necessary to develop semiconductor products needed for defense and the space program); they captured the market for a principal semiconductor product (which the U.S. companies abandoned in a quest for higher profits) by slashing prices through illegal dumping (which would not be illegal if the companies doing it were in California); and they have all along kept out American competition in their home market (in which we are unlikely to be competitive, while our own companies are not competitive in our own home market).

Economics 101

Goods and services can be had for a price that's agreeable to buyer and seller. Subsidization is just another way of paying for what you want. Instead of paying out of your purse to the seller, you elect people who will tax it out of your purse. There really is no difference between the American people electing politicians who want to send rockets to the moon and the Japanese people electing politicians who want to have a world-class semiconductor industry. Both are equally sensible; both produce a world-class semiconductor industry; both are equally reasonable substitutes for a fully functioning free market.

Prices are determined in competitive markets by the quantity of goods produced and the intensity of demand for the products, backed up by money in the pocket of the buyer. Profits are determined by the costs of production, but prices are not. This is a crucial point usually missed by trade manipulators and often missed by businessmen themselves: In a competitive market, the price is set by supply and demand. Whether the producer makes a profit or not depends on his costs. If the market price is lower than his costs, he loses money; if the price is higher, he makes money.

Much of business law, including trade law, makes a different assumption, that businesses set prices to cover the cost of production plus a profit. But the only places where this really holds true are where government sets the price based on the company's reported costs—for example, the electric, gas, and water public utilities, whose prices are set by state regulators.

(Even this substitute for a market itself operates by market forces in the longer term: regulators respond to consumer demands for more reliable electric service by allowing rate increases for new construction; they respond to consumer demands for lower rates by refusing to allow new construction or even refusing to allow higher rates for old construction now unneeded. It is, however, an inefficient substitute for a market because consumers are slow to demand political action and regulators are slow to hear them. It may take decades for regulators to notice that energy-intensive industries are not expanding in their state. Such inefficiencies are considered the price of regulation of monopolies, but opening monopolies to competition is rarely considered. Many heavily regulated industries actually follow prices determined in a supply-and-demand marketplace, despite the best efforts of regulators.)

The 1986 Semiconductor Agreement with Japan attempted to change the market for memory chips from a free market to a regulated market. It focused on costs, not prices, and tried to legislate profits for the U.S. semiconductor industry. Instead, it legislated profits for the Japanese semiconductor industry and higher costs for the U.S. computer and communications industries. It succeeded only briefly, because integrated circuits are too important, and production technology is too widely available for a true cartel to be formed without much more oppressive government enforcement. We can measure the true worth of the agreement and the efforts to subsidize the U.S. chip industry by observing the real behavior of businessmen asked to put their money where their mouths were.

A Joint Venture

In the spring of 1989, a joint committee of the Semiconductor Industry Association and the American Electronics Association tried to lead the U.S. electronics industry to the idea that everyone should row in the same boat. Chairmen of Motorola and Compaq put their names to a proposal for a joint venture of semiconductor makers and computer makers that would enter the DRAM business. "DRAMs are a fundamental building block for both commercial and military electronics products and systems. We must have a viable U.S. manufacturing presence," they said.

By June, seven companies—Advanced Micro Devices, Intel, LSI Logic, and National Semiconductor from the chip makers; IBM, Digital Equipment, and Hewlett-Packard from the computer makers—established U.S. Memories Inc. with a plan to use IBM's current 4M DRAM design and manufacturing methods. IBM also detailed a vice president, Sanford Kane, to serve as president and chief executive officer. Neither Motorola nor Compaq was one of the founding partners. Their pullback was an early warning that the whole idea was an economic muddle.

U.S. Memories went forward with great spirit. "By licensing IBM's advanced memory design, U.S. Memories will have the jump start needed to quickly come on line as a serious player," said Gordon Moore, chairman of Intel and of the Semiconductor Industry Association.

"The time is right for a collective memory manufacturing venture in the United States to improve America's market position in what is truly a critical technology," said Kane.

"U.S. Memories represents a viable reentry vehicle for America to add to its presence in the DRAM field," said Wilfred Corrigan, chairman of LSI Logic and chairman of the new venture. He also gave credit to the semiconductor trade agreement with Japan for opening a window of opportunity. "By enforcing the antidumping provisions of the Trade Agreement, the U.S. government has given the domestic industry the breathing room necessary to address the DRAM situation in both an enterprising and a creative manner."[3]

The Wall Street Journal proclaimed the new venture: "American computer companies are getting serious about battling the Japanese competition."[4]

Flop

Each of these statements proved false.

By licensing IBM technology and taking an IBM man on as CEO, U.S. Memories raised the suspicions of other companies. IBM had produced DRAMs for more than a decade at volumes calculated to represent IBM's own irreducible need in recession periods. In periods of higher demand, IBM bought chips on the open market from Japanese and U.S. suppliers. But as the suppliers saw it, the computer giant played them off against each other and was an unreliable customer. In addition, IBM's DRAMs were subtly different technically from those in the merchant market. Micron Technology, which also received a license from IBM, wound up producing both IBM chips and merchant market chips. Those who believed that IBM was calling the shots at U.S. Memories found it hard to believe that anybody else would really gain from participation. IBM reinforced that perception by insisting that its 4M DRAM technology would stand instead of hard cash for its capital contribution.

The time was not right for another memory manufacturer. Other suppliers of DRAMs from Japan, South Korea, the United States, and even Europe were rushing into production. Between the announcement of U.S. Memories in June and the end of 1989, 1M DRAM chip prices collapsed from $30 to $9 and were clearly headed lower as 4M chips entered the marketplace.

U.S. Memories did not look viable. Its business plan called for production to begin in 1991, 18 months at least behind the early, most profitable time in the 4M market, and quite possibly within months of the time its Japanese competitors would begin selling 16M DRAMs. U.S. Memories planned to invest $1 billion to win a

5 percent share of the $9.7 billion world DRAM market (1989 sales). Somehow Kane projected profits in 1992 on $340 million of revenue. Big losses seemed much more likely. If U.S. Memories could make a profit, it would be if its owners agreed to buy specific quantities of chips at specific prices, taking the loss that rightfully would belong to U.S. Memories. Potential investors preferred to take their chances on the open market.

The last remaining possible justification for U.S. Memories was as a form of market protection. As Kenneth Flamm of the Brookings Institution put it: "A money-losing entrant into the DRAM business, which is able to impose some competitive discipline on the actions of the other players, ought to be counted as a success from the perspective of those who purchase the product. . . . Thus the costs of financing reentry into DRAMs ought properly to be regarded as 'anticartel insurance' as much as an investment in an independently viable business."[5]

But there were few companies willing to put up the premium. In its postmortem on U.S. Memories, the trade paper *Electronic News* said:

> The key issue became the size of the up-front investment rather than fear of dependency on the Japanese. . . . For Control Data, Unisys, Data General, Wang, Prime, Sun Microsystems, who were all hemorrhaging [cash] while the fund-raisers were circulating, there could be no positive response. Even Hewlett-Packard, a founding member, wavered at the 11th hour on the cash issue."[6]

Who Needs It?

Other turn-downs came from personal computer makers Tandy, AST, Compaq, Apple, and Zenith. Apple, which was caught in a DRAM price crunch just a year before and which bought most of its DRAM supply from Toshiba and NEC, saw better uses for its money. The company was not short—it had nearly $750 million in cash reserves—it just saw no reason to pay to make what it could buy. "The U.S. Memories option doesn't fit into our priorities at this time," was the way a spokeswoman put it, adding explicitly, "There's no direct benefit to our customers."

Data General engineering director Don Lewine was quite direct on the same point. He told *Electronic News*, "When all was said and done, they were going to sell us a commodity part at commodity prices, and that just wasn't real exciting."[7]

Sun Microsystems enjoyed a comfort factor in a string of supply contracts for DRAMs which the workstation supplier had nailed down at acceptable forward pricing; hence, the company did not even bother to look at the consortium's business plan. James T. Decker, Sun's manager of strategic commodity procurement, said, "We don't see in the foreseeable future a disruption in the DRAM business. We are confident that there is no reason to worry about a shortage."[8]

Maverick T. J. Rodgers of Cypress Semiconductors was a thorn in the side of U.S. Memories. During the summer of 1989, when U.S. Memories was trolling for government money, Rodgers told a congressional committee the joint venture didn't even deserve antitrust immunity. "Free enterprise semiconductor companies already face enough unfair competition from Japan—"We don't need even more unfair competition from a U.S. government-backed combine. . . . They will become a company armed with antitrust immunity and subsidies competing with my company and the hundreds of other semiconductor companies in the U.S. that do not enjoy the luxury."[9] Rodgers said if IBM would give him the technology it gave U.S. Memories, he'd be producing DRAMs in a few months. (IBM eventually offered to sell him the technology, but at a price Rodgers considered extortionate.) His assessment: "If you applied the same venture capital criteria to U.S. Memories that are used with new-start semiconductor firms, they would have had to grow to a $5 billion operation in five years to show the return that investors want. Investors saw that simply wasn't possible and that did in U.S. Memories."[10]

Another factor was the new willingness of Japanese DRAM suppliers to sign long-term contracts with consumers. If long-term relationships are the hallmark of the Japanese way of doing business, then it made sense for Americans to find ways of turning that to their advantage. Another cheap alternative to a manufacturing consortium—DRAM futures—came from the Pacific Stock Exchange. Since memory chips are a commodity, like corn or wheat or pork bellies, it ought to be possible to take the contracts that buyers and sellers already enter into and trade them. The federal Commodities Futures Trading Commission was still chewing on the idea long after U.S. Memories faded, but the idea of handing the risk of large price swings over to speculators had its attractions.

The end came on January 12, 1990, when Kane asked representatives of 11 companies to make their pledges. Only Digital Equipment was willing to make a money commitment and IBM made its promise of technology and designs for the 4M DRAM. With the contributions of chip makers, there still wasn't even $150 million of the original $500 million equity the venture had sought. U.S. Memories became a memory.

The Chip Cartel Returns

In the next few days, Japanese semiconductor companies announced plans to cut back production of 1M DRAMs, raising the possibility that only the possibility of U.S. Memories' succeeding had kept the Japanese from acting like a memory chip cartel. As the *New York Times* reporter in Tokyo asked rhetorically: "Were the production cuts a collusive effort by Japanese manufacturers to keep prices up and profits high?" His answer: "Some Japanese companies say they had little choice but to cut production because otherwise they could again be charged with dumping low-priced chips in the United States."[11]

So there was the Semiconductor Agreement rearing its ugly head again, blocking American consumers from a source of low-priced memory chips. And it was not necessarily even a good thing for the Japanese companies, which had invested more than $7 billion in new production facilities in 1988 and 1989. They had brought themselves well beyond the point of dependency on the merchant market, consuming only 20 percent of their own production.[12] What were they supposed to do with their chips?

One big problem with antidumping laws is the underlying assumption that selling below cost is either irrational or predatory. There are times, economists and accountants agree, when it is sensible. The problem is that "cost" is such a slippery concept.

One accounting for cost, the one that antidumpers like to use, usually includes an allowance for capital, known as depreciation, plus an allowance for overhead and an allowance for profit. Another concept of cost considers only materials, energy, and direct labor, known as variable costs. The difference between these two extremes is the expense the firm incurs whether or not it operates, also known as fixed costs.

In the short run, a company may face market conditions and market prices that don't cover fully allocated costs, including capital, overhead, and profit, but more than cover variable costs. In other words, running the plant and paying the workers leaves some cash to make a contribution to fixed costs. It should be obvious, to anybody but a trade lawyer, that the firm will operate this way as long as it can because operating puts off the day when fixed costs consume the company.

Only when prices don't cover variable costs should a company consider ceasing production, and even then the company may struggle on for a while because management believes it can weather this setback for a time, or because it would incur penalties, by law or union contract, for shutting down.

At some point, making a profit in DRAMs in a competitive market becomes impossible. If $200 million is invested to produce three million DRAMs a month and if the selling price is $13 per chip, the producer receives $39 million a month revenues, easily covering his capital, labor, and other costs during the two to three years that the production line operates at full production. But if the selling price is $5, revenues are $15 million a month and our producer probably does not break even. At $2, revenues are $6 million a month and he loses his shirt.

If it takes $400 million to equip a production line in the 4M DRAM generation, $5 a chip will not produce a profit. It may take $8 a chip. And a $1 billion fab line, widely assumed to be the entry fee for the 64M DRAM, puts profits from a $13 chip into question. Still we know that Lepselter's Law has worked in the past, because a fab line once built eventually overproduces. And we know that the price of one generation of memory chips almost has to decline to less than four times the price of the previous generation in order to give buyers a lower price per bit. Otherwise they won't change over to the new product.

A solution is that all the firms in an industry get together and agree to cut production and raise prices enough to cover costs—a true cartel. The first six months of 1990 offered a chance to see if that was what the Japanese chip producers were able to do.

The Chip Cartel Collapses

In January it was Intel that was the price leader, selling 1M DRAMs made by the South Korean firm Samsung for $6. Micron Technology even raised the threat of a dumping action against the Koreans,[13] which rather contaminated the economic experiment.

In February, the trade press reported prices had ceased to drop, saying that some DRAM producers were shifting lines over to making 4M chips. There were widespread predictions of a shortage. But no shortage developed and prices actually fell below $6, especially prices from U.S. suppliers. Jim Feldman, an analyst at In-Stat, a Scottsdale, Arizona, firm that monitors the chip industry, predicted that the growth in demand for memory chips would not outpace the growth in supply for a couple of years, at least. He said the Japanese industry was suffering from about 25 percent overcapacity and prospects were for a great deal of new capacity to come on line.

"The prices were so high in '88 and '89 that it more than financed their 4-Meg development," he said. "We figure it cost them $5 to make their 1-Meg which they were selling for $30 spot and $25 on a contract."[14]

Another Path

U.S. Memories was the wrong answer for the wrong problem. American semiconductor companies were already reaching for other answers that recognized reality—entering joint ventures, partnerships, and other business deals with Japanese companies. This is a way to ease friction and build the market share of U.S. producers.

An excellent example is found at the upstart Japanese company NMB Semiconductor, a subsidiary of the unconventional ball-bearing manufacturer Minebea. NMB specializes in the manufacture of ultrafast DRAMs, but its designs come from Ramtron, a Colorado subsidiary of an Australian firm, and it sells through Intel.

There are hundreds of other joint undertakings between United States and Japanese semiconductor firms. A sample:

> Motorola and Toshiba struck a deal in 1986 to swap Motorola's lead in microprocessor design and manufacture for Toshiba's lead in memory. Motorola gained a source for DRAMs, which it now makes competitively in the United States, and access to the Japanese market for its microprocessors. Texas Instruments and Hitachi entered a deal for joint development of 16M DRAM designs; AT&T has arrangements with Mitsubishi and NEC.

Other deals have involved the efforts of Japanese companies outside the semiconductor industry to become players. Thus Kawasaki Steel financed a semiconductor plant in Japan for LSI Logic and Kobe Steel entered a joint venture to make chips in Japan for Texas Instruments.

IBM, America's largest DRAM producer, is a worldwide company with research and production in Japan and Europe equal to its facilities in the United States. But even the world's biggest computer company feels the need to cooperate: in 1990 IBM entered a joint research and development arrangement on 64M DRAMs with Siemens, Europe's largest DRAM producer. It was the first venture of its kind for each company.

International arrangements don't always go well, of course. Intel and NEC wrangled for years over what rights Intel gave away when it licensed NEC as a second source for microprocessors designed in the late 70s. Motorola and Hitachi nearly gridlocked in a similar dispute over microprocessor designs when a federal judge ruled in June 1990 that both sides' arguments had some merit and neither product should be sold. The two firms quickly reached a compromise, of course, which was probably what the judge had in mind.

Some observers are skeptical of the wave of joint ventures, recalling that with hindsight, it appears U.S. chip makers sold the family jewels—designs and manufacturing know-how—to Japan in the 70s. But in an international marketplace it is essential to build trusting, efficient relationships across the oceans.

Kenichi Ohmae, head of the Tokyo office of McKinsey & Co., remarks that Nippon Electric Co. could just as easily be called American Electric Co., and Texas Instruments deserves the name Nippon Instruments. Ohmae believes, and we should hope, that Japan and the United States are becoming economically and culturally more alike. Stock markets and property markets and business markets are all linked and cross-owned, he observes.

This process alarms many people in both countries, but it is the way both nations can prosper. A hopeful sign of the new attitudes that may be developing from the international cooperative agreements came in October 1990 when two U.S. industry groups representing computer companies and chip makers announced that they had agreed to scrap the Fair Market Value system when the U.S.-Japan Semiconductor Agreement expires at the end of 1991. The American groups also agreed to ask the U.S. government to keep up the pressure on Japan to buy more U.S. chips and to remain vigilant against Japanese dumping, so cooperation has a long way to go before we accept the reality of what Ohmae calls the borderless world.

Section V
THE FASTEST GUN

A supercomputer defines itself: it is the record holder, the speed champion, the most powerful computer in existence at the moment. The abacus was a supercomputer, therefore, and so was the slide rule invented by Leibnitz, and Babbidge's analytical engine. ENIAC, UNIVAC, and their descendants were supercomputers, too. Today's supercomputers evolved from them.

15

Supercomputers

Science and Business

Scientific computing, meaning the use of very large, very powerful machines to perform enormous numerical calculations, was all
the computing there was up to the late 50s. Then IBM developed
a different philosophy. Instead of doing what people could not
do, IBM computers were designed to displace human workers
from simple repetitive tasks. IBM computers would count things,
arrange things, store things, and, in general, use numbers in a
businesslike way. Payrolls, personnel records, bank transactions,
and the like were the material of IBM's computer business. IBM
developed hardware and software to handle these business tasks.

IBM was successful beyond all expectations. Its capacious
computers were just what American business needed. IBM and
its competitors became the computer industry. Scientific computing became a small backwater, merely a market niche. But a niche
is an opportunity, and the opportunities in scientific computing
have grown larger and larger. In the 90s, scientific computing is
rejoining, and may dominate, the computing industry.

The Future that Never Happened

The computer changed the world, but rather differently than people imagined in the early years after World War II. Stories about
machines that ruled the world were popular then. In one, "MUL-
TIVAC" reduced elections to a spooky computer poll, in which
direct questioning of one voter by the computer produced the

name of the next president of the United States. In another, the all-powerful central computer was tended by a priesthood, trained for many years to whistle a binary computer language.

Most early fiction about future computers missed the mark. The fictional computers of the imagination were physically huge; we know now that truly powerful computers must be small to be fast. The computers were programmed in mysterious ways; computer languages are actually getting easier to use. Fictional computers were centers of power, either on their own or as tools of a human authority; computers are actually democratizing our society.

Oddly, writers built few stories around computer designers. Backyard spaceship manufacturers—usually deft problem-solving engineers with a touch of social naivete—were the favorite heroes. Ironically, space travel spawned a gigantic bureaucracy; computer design, especially supercomputer design, has been the realm of the individual genius.

Building Supercomputers

Seymour Cray was the individual genius in scientific supercomputing and he happens to be a deft, problem-solving engineer with more than a touch of social naivete. He put his University of Minnesota training in mathematics and electrical engineering to work in the early 50s, when the Twin Cities was one of the few centers of what would later be called computer science. Cray went to work for Engineering Research Associates of St. Paul, a descendant of the Navy codebreaking projects of World War II. ERA was soon bought by Remington Rand, which also bought Univac. Cray, at age 31, was working for the leader in electronic computing and he soon became a leader in computer design at Univac.

But while the young computer designer was trying to design the best computer, the company he worked for was trying to build a business. To Cray and some of his associates, these goals were incompatible. They struck out on their own, founding a company in 1957 called Control Data to be the instrument of their dreams.

For Control Data's first product, Cray was able to design a computer using the cheapest parts available on the open market. First introduced in 1960, it made Control Data a leader in scientific computing.

Cray took his reward in the form of freedom. He turned his back on both the computer and the company. In 1962, he moved his research group out of Minneapolis to his old home town of Chippewa Falls, Wisconsin. For the next 10 years, he turned out new computer designs while his colleagues treated him like the goose that laid the golden eggs, leaving him strictly alone. His CDC 6600 and CDC 7600 were highly successful scientific computers. Eventually, however, Control Data Chairman William Norris looked down a different road than Cray, toward business computing and toward computer services. Cray was still only interested in fast scientific computing.

This time Cray hung out his own shingle—Cray Research Inc., emphasis on the research. Control Data gave him a warm handshake, big profits on his stock, and an investment in his new company. Several of his key associates stayed with him in Chippewa Falls.

Cray isolated himself as much as possible. He has given very few interviews since gaining complete control of his professional life. In 1978, *Science* magazine published the limited fruits of an interview.[1]

"There is not much to designing, really," Cray said unhelpfully. His standards are not ordinary: he had wanted to be a particle physicist but he couldn't handle the math. He said he didn't use a computer to keep track of his design, just faintly ruled graph paper with quarter-inch squares, of which he consumed about a pad a day while in the throes of design. As far as anyone could tell, Cray built a concept of the computer in his head, stressing simplicity and density, then drew it.

Financing Cray Research

Cray Research was endowed with patient capital. Cray founded the company in 1972, and produced nothing until 1976. Investors, though, are often patient with investments that they believe have a chance of a huge payoff. Cray's business plan called for him to recoup most of the costs of his four-year development project from the sale of a single CRAY-1.

The first CRAY-1 was sold to Los Alamos National Laboratories, where nuclear weapons designers needed all the computing power they could get. There are limits to what they could learn lighting off small bombs in deep holes in the earth under the restrictions of the nuclear test ban treaty; they wanted to make mathematical simulations of large nuclear explosions. Nuclear weapons are detonated by the explosion of several nonnuclear charges, which fling plutonium or enriched uranium together to create a critical mass for atomic fission, splitting apart the atoms of plutonium or uranium. In hydrogen bombs, the heat of the fission explosion then sets off a fusion reaction, in which atoms of hydrogen are fused to create helium. The timing and the effect of the detonating explosions are critical. The intensity of the bomb designers' desire to run reliable simulations can be seen in the fact that the biggest warheads on top of U.S. intercontinental missiles are too big to test under the limits of the test ban treaty and so are untested, except by computer simulation. (In 1988, it was a simulation on a new, more powerful computer that alerted weapons scientists to the possibility a fission warhead designed as an artillery shell might go off accidentally. Many hundreds of the warheads, designed in the mid-70s, were stockpiled in Europe.)[2]

Similar intense desires ran through other early customers of the $7.5 million CRAY-1. The National Security Agency had acquired the ability to tap a large fraction of international telephone calls, those carried by satellite. But the volume of traffic had grown too great to assign people to listen. The agency taped the traffic, developed computer programs for recognizing key patterns—along the lines of picking out the word for bomb in 50 different languages—and played the tapes through the fastest computers it could buy. The CRAY-1 was a godsend to NSA, and with an immense budget cloaked in secrecy, NSA was just the kind of customer Cray Research needed.

Even a hungry base of customers and Seymour Cray's record at Control Data did not give him unlimited access to cash to start Cray Research. He put up $500,000 of his own money, and raised about $1.6 million from a small group of friends.[3] After two years of design work, he was ready to bring in outsiders. First came Lehman Bros., Control Data, and New Court Securities; then several venture capital partnerships also put money into the company.

Total startup investment: about $8 million. The first sale of a computer, for about $7.5 million, did not quite put the company in the black, but it was close enough: Cray Research went public, raising $10 million.

Two things about this startup pattern were true then, but no longer.

1. Cray could say: "In venture capital, there are just a few significant firms interested in high technology. They all talk to each other, so if you convince one, you automatically get the others."[4] Today, there are dozens of venture capital firms specializing in high technology. And there are hundreds, probably thousands of would-be Seymour Crays in companies and universities. So venture capital seems scarcer than it did in those good old days.
2. The investors got a heavy share of the company, leaving Cray with an 11 percent interest. Founding scientists these days are treated more generously, and at times during the 80s, the hopeful technologist might be left with majority control of the company.

Cray said he wasn't really all that interested in mundane details—all he wanted was to be left alone to work. "I have no real interest in being a businessman," he said. At one level, he was discouraged by his inability to handle particle physics, so it was "back to the grind, start another computer company and eke out a living." But on another level he was on a power trip: "I plan to make some changes in the scientific computing field—like dominate it. As we grow, we will develop a structure, but that won't be my job. I will continue to devote myself to technical areas."

Cray Research made a spectacular $3.5 million profit in 1978 on revenues of $17.1 million from the sale of just four units. But that seems to have interested Cray only so far as the company took in all the money he could spend on research. He hired a businessman to manage the company and sell the computers. In 1979 and several times thereafter he stepped in to be sure that Cray Research stuck with only the goal of building the biggest and fastest scientific computers.

Speed for Speed's Sake

The manufacture of Cray supercomputers was proof of Cray's lack of interest in business. While Cray and a few assistants worked in a small lab near his home, CRAY-1s were assembled by hand in Chippewa Falls. A CRAY-1 required placement of 200,000 integrated circuits onto 1,662 printed circuit boards of 113 different types.[5] These were then crammed into the semicircular computer chassis. Every connecting wire was cut to a precise length and fitted by hand. The process took three months and then the computer had to be tested.

Cray Research continued assembling supercomputers in much the same way for years. Other computer companies developed or bought automated assembly methods and designed their computers to be assembled by machine. Cray Research adapted people to fit the Cray design, instead of the other way around.

In the early days, there were good reasons for this policy. CRAY-1s were four times faster than the competition because Cray did everything possible to shrink the computer to the smallest possible dimensions. Since he was designing a computer to be built from basic parts that anyone could acquire, he had to achieve speed with the cleverness of the way he put those parts together.

Cray saw that one of the limiting factors of the speed of a computer was the length of connections. Electrons travel in metal conductors at a small fraction of the speed of light. Fast computers are so fast that it starts to matter how long it takes for the information represented by electrons to move from one part of the computer to another. By the time he was finished, Cray had designed a computer that occupied 8 square feet of floor space, compared to competition spread out over 1600 square feet.

He chose integrated circuits that could be crammed onto the printed circuit boards more densely; he packed the boards as close together as possible. He did not care about servicing the computer any more than he had to. He was forced by physics to care about the immense heat all those circuits generated in a small enclosed space, but he took the hard way out by building freon cooling units into the structure of the chassis.

The Cray-1, and succeeding models, have been a trial for business and technical magazine art directors. They are small. They don't look very impressive. Computers were much more awesome when they weren't so powerful. (The Smithsonian Institution had this problem. The old computer exhibit at the Museum of American History included a Univac from the early 50s. Spread out over most of a good-sized room, the computer from the past looked futuristic, even though it had less power than the dull gray boxes that sit under IBM PCs.)

As important as the densely packed physical construction of Cray's computers is the way in which the designer excluded everything that was not crucial to the one goal of building a fast computer. General-purpose computers had (many still have) a large menu of precoded instructions for the manipulation of data. That kind of design speeds up a slow computer that must do many different tasks, because each different instruction does not have to be specified, step by step, in the program. But it slows down a fast computer that must do only a few tasks, over and over, because it adds a tedious step—selecting the correct instruction—over and over. (Cray's choice, now known as Reduced Instruction Set Computing, became fashionable in the late 80s in the design of microprocessors.)

The most important feature of Cray's design for speed was vector processing, in which the computer performs arithmetic processes with sets of numbers. For example, if required to add many pairs of numbers, a scalar processor draws a pair from memory, adds the two numbers, puts the result back in memory, and goes on to the next pair. But a vector processor draws many pairs from memory in long rows called vectors and adds the two vectors together. Vectors may be piled on each other, to make a few steps and quick work out of complicated tasks. Cray not only designed the computer programs but also arranged the hardware itself to handle this kind of calculation with maximum efficiency.

Skeptics said that made the CRAY-1 too specialized. There were some who said Cray could never sell more than a dozen supercomputers. In 1972, Cray and his associates figured the maximum market for supercomputers at no more than 100 machines. But as the 90s opened, Cray Research alone had produced and sold or leased nearly 300 machines—about half the world total. The company grew at 42 percent per year in the decade after going public in 1976.

Many of the most challenging scientific problems can be handled with vector processing. For example, aircraft design, weather prediction, and the study of nuclear explosions all are problems in simulation. Models are built expressing with equations the relationship among components, and then the computer substitutes variables and runs the same equations, over and over and over, so the scientist can see what happens. Ideally, every atom would have a set of equations expressing its relationship to every other atom; in practice, these fluid dynamics simulations lump together large quantities of molecules and assume that they behave as units. Faster, more powerful computers permit modelers to reduce the size of the groupings.

(Much of the argument over the validity of the computer models that predicted nuclear winter or global warming had to do with the size of the units in the models. Global climate models don't work on the molecular level, they deal with chunks of air several hundred kilometers on a side, and two to five kilometers thick. Unfortunately, the behavior of climate in real life apparently is determined by lots of interesting things happening on a smaller scale than the model can represent.)

Making Profits Out of Speed

John A. Rollwagen, a Minneapolis boy who went to MIT and Harvard Business School, was the man Cray hired to oversee the business side of Cray Research. Rollwagen said he had a fantasy of being the numbers and administrative man for a true genius, and it came true.[6] But he was more than a sorcerer's apprentice. He deftly worked around Cray's single-mindedness and built a business. Offering time-sharing introduced new customers; offering trade-ins allowed old customers to move up while giving new customers the chance to buy a used vehicle at a low price.

Eventually, Rollwagen did what Control Data had done. He set up Cray Labs for Cray "to take bold and risky steps and not have to worry about interference from the rest of the company,"[7] a move that also insulated the company from Seymour Cray. The company set up Cray Labs, which more properly should have been called Cray's Lab, in Colorado, catering to Cray's passion for skiing. Just as Cray had fled from Univac, then from Control Data to a CD lab in the woods, then from the CD lab to Cray Research, he now fled from Cray Research to a lab in the mountains.

Back in Chippewa Falls, other engineers adapted the CRAY-1 to use more advanced integrated circuits, producing the CRAY-1S, which could be constructed more rapidly, at lower cost.

Cray's work was also adapted by a new supercomputing star, Steve Chen, who came to Cray with experience at Burroughs and Floating Point Systems and produced the company's most successful model, the X-MP. What Chen did was harness several central processing units, each about as powerful as a CRAY-1, and cause them to work together, like four horses pulling a wagon. Arguably, this was not as creative as Seymour Cray's implementation of vector processing, but it was an inexpensive way of rearranging components to soup up performance. Chen's X-MP was introduced in 1983, fortuitous timing for Chen and Cray Research, because Seymour Cray was dividing his time between two new designs and both had fallen behind schedule. For a time, Cray Research sold only the X-MP, and no model that had been designed by Seymour Cray. Even when the CRAY-2 did come out in late 1984, it did not run all the same software as the CRAY-1. The X-MP was more compatible and in some models, with some applications, was even faster than the "real" CRAY-2.

Although the company tried to stress that no supercomputer is really the product of one designer, a Chen-Cray competition continued, and in the next generation, Chen was the hands-down winner. The first Y-MP was delivered in 1988; the CRAY-3 went into "preproduction" in 1986 but never emerged as a product. Instead, the company had to write off an inventory of components and Seymour Cray had to go back to the graph paper.

A reason Seymour Cray failed to deliver the CRAY-3 may have been that he abandoned the philosophy that succeeded so well with the Control Data machines and the CRAY-1. For the CRAY-3, he did not select readily available logic chips. Instead he went for a new technology, gallium arsenide semiconductors, that promised to be much faster but were also much harder to make. Gallium arsenide is a semiconductor material, like silicon. Doped as a conductor, it allows electrons to travel faster than they do in silicon. But gallium arsenide is a brittle material, hard to fabricate into integrated circuits. Cray's search for raw speed led him to gallium arsenide, but his suppliers were unable to make the fast, reliable, complex chips he required. Cray's new project also used different cooling, and a different internal architecture requiring different software.

The Hard Way

Seymour Cray used up all the easy ways he saw to make a computer go faster in two generations and then tried a hard way. With the CRAY-3, Seymour Cray spent years on new technology that, so far, has not been a success. Similarly, Rollwagen said that Chen wanted to incorporate five breakthrough technologies into his next-generation supercomputer. Chen used up all the easy ways he saw of powerful computers in two generations and then he tried a hard way.

Both designers also seemed to share a disinterest in the fate of their company, as long as enough money rolled in to support their lab work. And because the money quit rolling in, both designers are no longer with Cray Research. Chen left first, in 1988, because Rollwagen and the board of directors would not, or could not, fund his research. Chen set up a new company, Supercomputer Systems, in Eau Claire, Wisconsin, with funding from IBM. SSI is secure enough that it can afford to be arrogant. A call to the corporate headquarters won't even get you the name of the person who talks to outsiders, just a promise to tell that person that you called and that he will call back if he thinks it's appropriate. And when he does call back, it's only to say he has nothing to say. It's like the Grin & Bear It cartoon, where Sen. Snort says, "No comment, and that's off the record."

A year later, Cray Research also cut loose Seymour Cray. As it had when ending Chen's project, Cray Research declared it could not simultaneously pursue both Seymour Cray's Colorado-based development project and the Minneapolis-based corporate development of a completely different system.

In announcing that it would spin off Seymour Cray into a new company, Cray Research said it would "enhance the attractiveness of CRI in the capital markets while allowing CCC [the new Cray Computing Co.] the opportunity to attract capital."[8] A translation was not provided, but it seemed that the underlying aim was to make Cray Research's stock go up while allowing Seymour Cray to use his magic name to raise more equity capital. Cray Research promised to give Seymour Cray's new company, Cray Computer, about $100 million in loans over two years and will also hold about a 10 percent equity interest in the new creation. SEC documents disclosing the deal leave readers wondering about the ties that will continue to bind the two companies.

Neil Davenport, president of Cray Computer, says its financing should be enough to bring the new computer to the production stage. "If we succeed in building a prototype and demonstrate it and get orders, we will need money to build machines," he says, adding, "We don't need more money for R&D."[9] But there's no schedule, nor would it be credible if there were one. As recently as late 1988, Cray Research was projecting 1989 deliveries for the CRAY-3. Two rounds of delays followed. The CRAY-3 was a year or two away for six years.

The immediate impact of the spin-off, discernible from the pro forma financial statements, was to goose Cray Research's reported earnings per share by about $1 a share—20 percent of 1988 earnings and an even bigger share of the smaller 1989 profit. The longer term impact for shareholders depends on the companies' technological efforts, and on the true relationship between Cray and Cray. Morgan Stanley apparently earned its $750,000 investment banking fee by designing an arm's length competitive relationship between the two firms while leaving them joined at the hip financially through stock and debt relationships.

Officials of both companies say the spin-off is intended to create two separate viable companies. Each one, however, is only viable if its projects succeed. Cray Computer has to deliver a CRAY-3 in 1991. As Davenport says, "If we haven't done it by then we probably won't be able to do it." He adds, reflecting Seymour Cray's style, "There is no plan B."

Seymour Cray made an appearance at Cray Computer's first annual meeting, in May 1990, and the news was not good. He acknowledged that there was no supplier capable of building his gallium arsenide integrated circuits in quantity and no source of the ultrafast circuit-testing devices needed. Three suppliers,

GigaBit Logic, Rockwell, and Fujitsu, all had problems, he said. Fujitsu had only a small research facility devoted to gallium arsenide chips and Rockwell was too tied up with work for IBM, Cray said. Cray bought most of the assets of GigaBit Logic and hired about 25 employees, moving the machinery and people from California to Colorado to gain control of the gallium arsenide production process. The result was that Cray announced a six-month delay in production.

Back at the Ranch

While spinning off first Chen, then Cray, Cray Research retained a project called C-90. The designation implied, but did not promise, delivery in 1990. It was renamed the Y-MP/16 and put into "preproduction" in 1990. For the time being, variants of the last production design Steve Chen worked on are the lead Cray Research products. Projected capacity of the Y-MP/16 is about the same as what the company had previously advertised for the CRAY-3: about 2 gigaflops, or two billion Floating Point Operations Per Second, using 16 processing units.

Chen's Supercomputing Systems is supposed to leap over that. A few claims are made in public: it will have 64 processors and run at 100 gigaflops. Cray Research used to make projections about a CRAY-4 with capacity in that area, and it used to guess at delivery somewhere in the mid-90s. Now it talks about a "follow-on product." No details. Seymour Cray took the ideas for the CRAY-4 with him, but the only project worth working on at Cray Computer right now is getting the CRAY-3 out the door and sold. If that doesn't work, Cray Computer will be looking ahead only to the sheriff's arrival for a bankruptcy sale.

With the clarity of hindsight, we can see Cray Research made a major financial mistake in 1987. A share price of $134.75 marked the peak of an institutional boom in Cray stock. A secondary stock issue plus bonds could have raised the hundreds of millions of dollars Cray needed to support Seymour Cray, Steve Chen, and any other promising designers the company might have wanted to encourage. Cray's last financing, though, was a $115 million issue of convertible bonds in February 1986.

Many Americans, including enough investors to beat down the stock from its February 1987 high to its October 1990 low of $20, lost confidence in Cray. After 14 years of leadership in supercomputers, Cray Research is under pressure on several fronts. Fujitsu, Hitachi, NEC, and other Japanese companies, under the sponsorship of the Japanese government, are working furiously on new machines and new technologies. IBM has also become a significant presence in scientific computing, as have a large number of small companies started since 1984.

Perhaps a company the size of Cray Research, with nearly $1 billion a year revenue, is too small to stay competitive and too big to be quick and creative. It has refused to fund development of two new technologies, while proceeding on the least adventurous line of research. Cray Research's return on equity has been sinking since 1986, and 1989 marked its first-ever slump in earnings.

16

The Supercomputing Business

Commercial Supercomputers

Just as Cray took little interest in the business success of his companies, so the business success of Cray Research was not entirely due to the work of Seymour Cray. After he left Chippewa Falls for the greater isolation of Colorado, lesser lights at Cray Research worked on projects that would make his computers more useful. While he worked on his lifelong goal of pushing back the frontier of computing, the company developed new peripheral products, such as a Solid State Storage Device with an integrated circuit memory capacity of 8.1 billion data bits. To connect such an auxiliary memory to a Cray, engineers built data channels capable of transferring up to 20 billion bits per second. Another step toward making supercomputers practical was an input/output system using a set of minicomputers to manage the flow of information to and from slow-speed mass storage such as discs and tape. And finally, in the mid-80s, came the development that really made supercomputing accessible to scientists who are not also supercomputer experts: graphics workstations were harnessed to the supercomputer, making possible the representation of results as pictures. The human brain is very good at recognizing patterns in images, and not so good at recognizing patterns in columns of numbers.

These advances helped Cray Research sell supercomputers to private industry. Starting in the early 80s, revenues rose dramatically and profits followed.

From the dynamic modeling techniques developed for simulating nuclear testing came techniques simulating geological processes. Supercomputer modeling could duplicate the processes inside the earth that created pockets of petroleum. Thus supercomputers became crucial tools for deciding where to drill the next oil well.

Aerodynamic modeling became an essential part of aircraft design, largely on price. Once the programs were written, computer models became much cheaper than physical wind tunnel models. Even the supercomputer itself wasn't much more expensive than a wind tunnel, and it often gave more reliable data.

Automobile design followed aerodynamic modeling. Designers in search of fuel economy look to reduction of aerodynamic drag. They also look for weight reduction, and supercomputing could do stress analysis of metal parts, allowing engineers to shave the amount of material in a part without losing strength. Every major car company in the world owns at least one Cray supercomputer, largely because supercomputing reduces development and design time. In the same way, supercomputers have been used to design lighter, stronger beer cans that require less aluminum and other such sophisticated, yet mundane tasks. Further into the business stratosphere, supercomputers are used to create chemical and pharmaceutical designs on the molecular level.

Supercomputing Centers

The U.S. government continues to be the biggest supercomputer customer. Los Alamos National Laboratory has the largest concentration of supercomputers in the world—the equivalent of 60 CRAY-1s—and the other national weapons and research labs, plus NASA labs, aren't far behind. But in 1985, the U.S. government took a new tack in supercomputing, one that has already proved to be the most promising direction in the whole field. The National Science Foundation received money to set up five supercomputer centers around the country, in Ithaca, N.Y., Princeton, N.J., San Diego, Champaign-Urbana, Ill., and Pittsburgh. Three of these centers installed Crays. The one in Ithaca installed souped-up IBM general purpose computers and the one in Princeton installed Control Data machines. Unfortunately, Control Data gave up on supercomputers in 1989, and the NSF quit funding the Princeton Center. One could easily argue that the nation needs more centers, not fewer, but NSF now applies a budget of about $70 million a year to keeping the four remaining centers up to date. Each of the centers also raises money from corporations and other sources.[1]

The Cornell Theory Center in Ithaca serves more than 1,900 users from 125 institutions, who can work on two IBM 3090/600s, optimized for scientific calculations, and several parallel processing machines.

The National Center for Supercomputing Applications operated by the University of Illinois at Champaign-Urbana has more than 2,500 users from 82 institutions; it has a Cray X-MP, a CRAY-2, several smaller high performance computers, and more than 30 graphics workstations.

The Pittsburgh Supercomputing Center was the first non-federal laboratory to get a Cray Y-MP, in December 1988, though all the centers now are in line for them. The center also has an assortment of graphics hardware supporting the Y-MP. There are 27 universities affiliated with the center, which has 1,540 users.

The San Diego Supercomputing Center, operated by General Atomics on the campus of the University of California at San Diego, has a Cray X-MP and a Cray Y-MP, plus an assortment of workstations and smaller supercomputers. It has more than 2,700 users from 25 institutional consortium members and 48 industrial partners.

The John von Neumann Center at Princeton University, managed by a consortium of 13 institutions, will not receive any more NSF funds, and so its future is uncertain. The state of New Jersey had promised generous funding, but the center would need more money to replace its Control Data computers with the Crays it wants.

Other universities have established supercomputing centers without the NSF. Facilities exist at Purdue, University of Minnesota, Colorado State, Ohio State, University of Texas, Huntsville, Alabama, and Houston. Boeing Computer Corp., Computer Sciences Corp., and several other private companies offer time-sharing on supercomputers. In addition, the congressional Office of

Technology Assessment looked around the government at the end of 1988 and found 70 supercomputers installed at unclassified locations in federal labs.

The establishment of the national supercomputing centers was far more than a government subsidy for computer companies. The supercomputing centers also steadily expose researchers—in universities and in business—to the value of using a supercomputer. The San Diego Supercomputing Center, for example, had companies from Aerojet General to Walt Disney Studios collaborating on projects in many disciplines.[2]

The centers steadily educate programmers to the intricacies of writing programs for supercomputers. They create job opportunities and a training ground for computer scientists. Between 1985, the first year of NSF funding for supercomputer centers, and 1989, the number of Ph.D.s granted in computer science in the United States doubled, to more than 600. And, because the NSF is more interested in getting good research work done than in promoting a particular company, establishment of the centers means there are well-financed administrators constantly evaluating the offerings of the supercomputer industry. On the political side, spending all that money means that there are key congressmen interested in the success of the supercomputer centers. What they invest in, they want to see work, so that users will thank them with their support and their votes.

What's It Good For?

The supercomputer centers publish annual reports that demonstrate just how important supercomputing is coming to be. Here are some samples:

- Scientists examined a supernova that exploded in the Lesser Magellanic Cloud, a nearby galaxy. They developed computer models, based on theory, that would produce results similar to what was actually observed. One model, developed by Stanford Woosley of the University of California at Santa Cruz and Lick Observatory and Tom Weaver of the Lawrence Livermore National Laboratory, divides the supernova into about 300 zones, attempting to track the mate-

rials and fusion reactions inside the star according to
physical laws, and according to their guesses about the
physical processes inside an exploding star. Their model,
however, is one-dimensional, and the problem really wants
a three-dimensional model, because the spin of the ultra-
dense neutron star left after the supernova explosion has
turned out much faster than expected. "Which means—dare
I say it?—we'll need a bigger supercomputer," Woosley reported.

- A group led by Robert Wilhelmson of the University of Illinois represented a chunk of air over the Great Plains 50 kilometers on a side and 15 kilometers high. Their model divides this space into cubes half a kilometer on a side.
Programmed with equations to represent the physical laws
governing the behavior of gases, water, and ice in the atmosphere, the supercomputer runs solutions for every six seconds in the evolution of a severe thunderstorm. If the
modelers pick the right starting conditions, a realistic thunderstorm develops on the graphics workstation screen, although the computer takes about five hours to calculate
what nature takes less than an hour to do. By watching the
model storm happen or not happen, they learned something about why storms develop.[3]

- A model of airflow, emissions, weather patterns, and chemistry in the Los Angeles area required construction of
500,000 nonlinear equations but enabled Carnegie Mellon
University engineers to demonstrate that controls on auto
emissions would probably not be as effective a pollution-
control strategy as changing over to alcohol fuels. "When
you think about $30 billion a year spent on air pollution con-
trol, supercomputing is an absolute bargain," says Gregory
McRae of the departments of engineering and public policy.

- David Eisenberg of UCLA used a San Diego supercomputer
to solve the molecular structure of RuBisCO, an enzyme
produced in all green plants that is the catalyst for the step
in photosynthesis by which plants combine carbon dioxide
with sugar to form nutrients. The protein is a target for ge-
netic engineering because it might be redesigned to make
plants that convert light to energy more efficiently. Eisenberg and various students worked for 18 years to, in effect,

X-ray the crystalline structure of RuBisCO. The crystals were hard to grow, and worse, they weren't symmetrical. A supercomputer mapping program helped the biologists divide the asymmetric crystal into many small regions, allowing them to infer the electron densities of each region from the behavior of regions around them. After computing 125 regional maps, they could piece them together, use the new large map to refine the regional maps, and so on. It was a process of repetitive calculations, well suited to a supercomputer.[4]

- A group of oceanographers at Scripps Institute and University of California at San Diego studying currents are trying to give the ocean a sort of sonar CAT scan. Instead of using a tomographic computer to integrate many X-ray pictures, the way a CAT scan does, the oceanographers have used sound waves to take pictures of water movement in a slice from surface to ocean floor. Combining these slices produces a three-dimensional picture of the ocean and multiplying the combinations over time produces a moving picture. The supercomputer is indispensable for performing the calculations necessary to analyze each sound signal, getting rid of reflected signals and signal changes that are not related to water movement. Then combining them is an enormous task as well. "The tomographic reconstruction of currents and eddies is much more complicated than medical X-ray tomography," says Bruce Cornuelle of Scripps, "because the data are incomplete and inconsistent. And the patient [the ocean] won't lie still."[5]

- Political scientists at the University of Wisconsin and Stanford studied the voting patterns of U.S. senators, using a statistical technique called *cluster analysis*. This required that the votes of each senator on hundreds of bills be compared to the votes of each other senator. Then subsets, or clusters, were compared, and so on, until there was good statistical evidence for the existence of four coalitions from 1959 through 1983. Jacob Stampen and John Davis built on the nicknames that arose late in that period: Boll Weevil (for the mostly Southern Democrats who support a strong defense and government intervention in the economy) and Gypsy Moths (for the mostly Northern Republicans who are unlikely to support government intervention at home or abroad). They called the other two Yellow Jackets, for strong prodefense conservatives who oppose economic regulation, and Honey Bees, for liberals with the opposite inclinations. The study is probably just an opening gambit in a developing scholarly computer game.

Supercomputers have been used to model the disappearing ozone layer at the South Pole, the movement of continental plates, wear on ball bearings, the role of individual particles in the crystal lattice of superconducting materials, the behavior of neutron stars and black holes, the propagation of cracks as metals fracture, the structure of molecules in complex enzyme systems, the flow of blood through healthy and constricted arteries, the tendency of bones to grow into distorted shapes when stressed by artificial limbs, and, almost inevitably, the behavior of prices on the New York Stock Exchange.

The Era of Competition

Supercomputing is growing faster than Cray Research. The old definition—a supercomputer is a Cray, and a Cray is a supercomputer—is no longer true. There's competition.

Three big Japanese computer companies, NEC, Fujitsu, and Hitachi, produced supercomputers during the 80s, although their performance always lagged behind the current best from Cray. These companies sold no computers in the United States; just as in Japan, government agencies and government-supported universities never bought Crays.

Seymour Cray's old company, Control Data, was a U.S. competitor for Cray, but Control Data was always weaker, slower, and less effective, whether it competed in scientific computing with Cray or in business computing with IBM. In 1989, Control Data closed its supercomputing division, conceding that its best effort was at least two years behind Cray's technology. IBM had some success with adding vector processing capabilities to its top-of-the-line general purpose computers, but the world's biggest computer company seemed to be watching, waiting, and keeping abreast of the technology, rather than making a full competitive effort.

During the 80s, there were deliberate attempts to nurture competitors for Cray abroad.

The Japanese Ministry of International Trade and Industry announced in 1981 that it would manage two cooperative research projects, the Fifth Generation Computer Project and the National Superspeed Computer Project. The Fifth Generation project focused on artificial intelligence, a concept as elusive as the other kind of intelligence. It does not appear to have met its goal, although spending several hundred million dollars may have produced interesting work with a long-term payoff. The superspeed project had more concrete results. Fujitsu and Hitachi, two industrial giants comparable in spirit to General Electric in the United States, adapted general purpose IBM-compatible computers from their existing product line to do vector processing—much as IBM has done. Nippon Electric Co., another firm with a large involvement in many aspects of electric and electronic equipment, designed supercomputers with an architecture and operating systems entirely different from its competitors. The NEC model most recently announced, SX-3, claims processing speeds up to eight times faster than the Cray Y-MP. It was not scheduled for delivery until late 1990 but it had U.S competitors worried.

As in most computer technology development, Europe has lagged behind, although not in money spent. The British government invested 350 million pounds in supercomputing between 1983 and 1988, and then the program, called Alvey, was eliminated. The European Community created the European Strategic Programme for Research in Information Technology (Esprit), which is sucking up $3.9 billion for the "catch-up phase." The problem Europeans face is chiefly political, as implied by the construction of an English program title to produce a French acronym. Nevertheless, Esprit has produced several innovative computer architectures, and the EC plans to invest more than $4 billion in a "commercialization phase."[6]

Section VI
FORKS IN THE ROAD

The disappearance of Control Data, the turmoil in the land of Cray, and the surge of NEC, Fujitsu, and Hitachi have left many American officials and Washington illuminati with a case of super jitters about supercomputers.

17

National Resources

David and Goliath

When Control Data decided that there were better investment opportunities in the world than eternally playing second fiddle to Cray Research, important officials of the U.S. government panicked. Their fear was redoubled when Cray Research spun off Steven Chen and Seymour Cray with the claim that it could not afford to fund their supercomputer projects.

To the spooked officials, supercomputers are a national resource, like an oil well. They were afraid the Japanese would overwhelm Cray Research, now the only remaining American supercomputer company. Trade lobbyists, competitiveness gurus, industrial strategists, and economic warriors embraced supercomputers as "the keys to the technological mill."

Michael B. Smith, a former deputy U.S. trade representative who coined that phrase, went on: "This single U.S. producer, which manufactures only supercomputers, now faces—like David—the Goliath of Japan with its three producers of supercomputers, Hitachi, Fujitsu, and NEC, plus the probable entry into the field of a German and/or joint European Community supercomputer producer."[1]

In a letter to the *Washington Post* after Control Data gave up on supercomputers, Smith spoke favorably of the advice of a Japanese international trade and industry official, who told him and other Americans "there was no way U.S. producers of supercomputers could survive in today's international world unless either the U.S. government nationalized the U.S. companies or forced their merger with IBM, the only U.S. firm capable of meeting the Big Three head on."

This Japanese advice, although it ignored the history, the structure, and the inclinations of the people in the American computer industry, crystallized the difference between the U.S. and Japanese electronics industry. The Japanese industry is built on the model of General Electric—gigantic diversified firms with gigantic financial, physical, and human resources and a bureaucratized structure to manage them. The U.S. electronics industry is built on the milkweed seed model, in which there is no management of individual units. There is enormous competition among them and each unit's success is largely a matter of fortune.

John Rollwagen, chairman of Cray, put the distinction this way. "In the United States we have our antitrust mentality and we espouse 'small is beautiful.' In Japan, it appears that the notion of critical mass required to effect market-share oriented trade policies are de rigeur. That is, there are significantly less companies competing for the same market dollar and therefore, there is more market dollar available to fund enhanced R&D."

After reading this comment two or three times, meaning seems to emerge this way: Japan allows its companies to monopolize markets; thus Japanese companies are more profitable; thus Japanese companies have more money to spend on R&D to create new markets, which they will monopolize.

While making this argument, Rollwagen never used the word monopoly. That would be admitting defeat, for if there is one thing Japanese firms don't enjoy at home and abroad, it's monopoly. Hitachi, Fujitsu, NEC, NTT, Matsushita, Sony, etc., etc., etc. Stories of their tooth-and-nail competition are available in many books and articles about Japan. And in the United States you hardly need do more than walk into a computer store, hi-fi store, phone store, or TV store to see that the Japanese firms compete here with each other, with U.S. firms and with European, Korean, and Taiwanese firms. The profit margins of Japanese electronics firms are not anything to write to Wall Street about. If they have monopolies, where are the profits?

The idea that either a nationalized supercomputer industry or one run as a monopoly by IBM could prosper in the United States could appeal only to a trade bureaucrat or a dispirited business executive picking up the pieces after his last failure. However, some parts of the U.S. government may believe otherwise. The Defense Department funded the development of supercomputers in the 70s, shoveling money to Burroughs, GE, and others. But it was Seymour Cray, working without direct government funding, who became the national resource. Now competitors complain that Cray Research has been handed sole-source contracts with the Department of Commerce and Department of Defense. They suggest Cray is being coddled with favoritism and under-the-table protectionism.

Survival of the Fittest

Smith's Japanese official put heavy reliance on the financial resources of the big Japanese companies, which allegedly discounted supercomputer list prices by as much as 86 percent in order to get orders from Japanese public agencies. Smith went on to say that he "wouldn't care or dare to wager any money" on the ability of Cray to survive without government help. He did not consider the possibility that the survival of Cray Research as an individual firm, with or without government help, is not particularly important.

Smith's warning was just one note in a chorus of warnings and battle cries sounded during 1989. A sample of hoofbeats from the Paul Revere's ride of supercomputers:

- The Institute of Electrical and Electronics Engineers declared: "Supercomputers are an embodiment of this country's highest technology. . . . Yet, given their dependence on the eroding technology base of the United States, they are vulnerable to a focused strategy by other nations." Guess who? "The Japanese government coordinates the actions of Japanese firms in accord with long-range strategic goals—in this case the goal of becoming the dominant supplier of information technologies to the world."
- The U.S. Trade Representative's office, responding in part to the IEEE warning and similar ones from other parts of the U.S. electronics industry, put allegations of buy-Japanese protectionism in supercomputers at the top of the American "Super 301," a tough new provision of U.S. trade law mandating negotiation to open selected key markets and requiring retaliatory protection if the negotiations are not successful. Putting supercomputers on the list is at least

insouciant and possibly provocative, since the U.S. government maintains a virtual embargo on Japanese supercomputers. For example, the Department of Commerce in 1987 forced MIT not to buy a Japanese supercomputer, offered at a deep discount. After the Commerce officials made their wishes known, MIT looked at its federal funding, swallowed hard, and bought a Cray. That their action was exactly what American officials claim Japan unfairly does seemed to bother nobody except the odd Japanese supercomputer salesman.

- Sam Adams, an American supercomputer salesman for NEC, hasn't sold a unit since 1986. "It's a little difficult," he says, pointing to a rider on the last Defense budget authorization that says a Defense agency cannot install a supercomputer manufactured offshore without specific exception from the Secretary of Defense. "The lightning rod of attention tends to carry over into other departments like Energy and Commerce, where there's a feeling on the part of users that they would like to procure the best there is. But the politicians and bureaucrats have not let that happen as yet." He puts in a word for internationalism: "Supercomputing is a worldwide phenomenal need. Fusion and weather aren't U.S. problems."[2]
- NEC announced a new model called the SX-3 in the spring of 1989 that it claimed was more powerful than any competitor. While that claim was dubious, it was clearly in the same class as the best Cray machines. NEC sold two in Japan, one each in Germany, Brazil, and the Netherlands, none in the United States. "We came close to selling the SX-3 to a state university and a national research center," Tadashi Watanabe told the Japan Economic Journal. "But for unexplained reasons both deals fell through."[3] Fujitsu sold 25 of its best supercomputer in 1989 and 1990, none in the U.S. Hitachi officials said they weren't even trying to sell supercomputers in the U.S.

Super 301 negotiations were highly effective on the Japanese side of the Pacific. Cray Reserach won nine orders from Japanese customers in the first three quarters of 1990. That was more than 50% of the Japanese market for supercomputers and nearly a third of Cray's worldwide business during the period. Orders came from Nissan, Toshiba, Mitsubishi, Honda, and even a Japanese university, Tohoku University.

The university order was significant because the kernel of the Super 301 trade complaint was that the Japanese government was not allowing government-funded institutions to buy Cray supercomputers. The State Department documented that Japanese supercomputer companies had given discounts to universities that ranged up to 86%, and the Commerce Department claimed this was clearly an anticompetitive practice aimed at Cray. The Japanese responded that the Japanese companies were competing against each other for the prestige of placing their equipment and the product endorsement that acceptance of their computers implied.

As reported by Jiji Press in Japan, the Tohuku University order was stage-managed. NEC had previously supplied a high-speed computer to the university and had planned to bid on the new one. "NEC dropped its bid in view of the protracted U.S.-Japan squabble over supercomputer trade," Jiji said. The report suggested that Cray took advantage of the lack of competition: "Some observers said Cray could have offered a lower fee in consideration of the so-called academic discounts, a popular bidding practice among Japanese computer makers in dealing with universities."[4]

Naturally Cray had no interest in acting like a Japanese company while it had the weight of the U.S. government and the weight of the Japanese government negotiating for it, any more than it would have given a discount to MIT after the Commerce Department cleared away the competition there.

The Japanese, however, began to figure that managed trade can be a two-way street. *Japan Economic Journal* reported: "According to sources, the Japanese government wil likely brand supercomputer business practices in the U.S. as unfair, and demand that changes be made to give Japanese makers a more equal footing. One Japanese industrial observer says government negotiations are not the answer, and that 'cooperation with U.S. makers including Cray would be more effective.'"[5]

That sounded like an invitation to Cray to join an industry-led, government-sponsored cartel to carve up the world market in supercomputers. While that might be tempting to Cray and to the

Department of Commerce, it should serve as a warning to customers and consumers around the world.

Growing Competition

Underlying all the governmental concern about supercomputing is a definitional premise that supercomputing is Cray Research and Cray Research is supercomputing. Skeptical questions need to be asked: Does the world really turn on supercomputing? If so, does supercomputing really turn on Cray Research?

By revenue, the supercomputer industry represents 1 percent of the $200 billion-a-year world computer industry. There are about 400 supercomputers in the world, about 250 manufactured by Cray Research, and this includes many older models that can't claim to be the most super.

We could put the question this way: Will the fastest supercomputer be a product or a strategic asset? If it is a product in a marketplace, then anyone can buy the fastest supercomputer, to use as a tool to solve whatever tough questions are solvable by computer. Then it is a question of access to tools. Similarly, if someone develops an important solution, say to an environmental problem, will that be a closely guarded secret, or will the inventor race to sell his answer, in the form of a service?

Most people who have tackled this question believe that supercomputers can be exclusive tools, and that answers from supercomputers can be valuable secrets that can be closely guarded.

For example, Cray Chairman Rollwagen told a Senate subcommittee that Cray supercomputers are "the only truly offensive weapon in our economic race for global industrial leadership and continued national security."

Richard M. Cyert, president of Carnegie Mellon University, where computers are a way of life, said this: "On the global level, it's fundamental: whoever has the fastest supercomputers has the best chance to find answers to the tough questions facing all societies."

Such judgments ignore at least three key points:

1. There are many new supercomputers, with name plates like Convex, Alliant, Stardent, and Sun. Some carry price tags of under $100,000, though the most powerful cost several million dollars. In deference to the big Cray ma-

chines with their price tags from $5 million to $25 million, these are known as minisupercomputers, superminicomputers, departmental supercomputers, desktop supercomputers, and personal supercomputers. They don't have the voracious requirements for cooling and power that distinguish supercomputers and drive up their costs. But in terms of the jobs they do—and the business they have taken away from Cray supercomputers—these machines are super indeed.

2. There is a whole new class of supercomputers emerging from laboratories whose designers believe can challenge conventional super machines by the conventional Cray-type definition. These machines come in various guises from Thinking Machines Corp. and other start-ups, as well as from Intel and other well-established companies. They employ a very large number of relatively weak computer processors instead of one or a few very powerful processors. Designers of the new "massively parallel" machines broke with the entire development of computing. Even though the new machines require new programming and new ways of thinking, they are finding a surprising number of applications in science and business.

3. Perhaps most important of all, software is only hard to develop. It's easy to copy. Even if direct purchase or under-the-table copying could be made difficult, reverse engineering (copying principles and methods rather than lines of code) is still comparatively simple. Mathematical algorithms that compose the underlying structure of complex programs are the result of inspiration and perspiration (as Edison might have said), but once created, they can be incorporated in new programs. Programming tricks also are relatively easy to transport. Patents, copyrights, and export restrictions have little practical effect on software.

Supercomputing has become an industry, not a company, and the industry is changing rapidly. Cray Research and the Japanese alike are in danger of being out-marketed by aggressive companies with small machines on the one hand and out-engineered by visionary scientists with new technology on the other.

A supercomputer is no longer the biggest most expensive box, it is simply the computer that will do your number-crunching job at the lowest cost. The trend is simply this: problems that used to be thought unsolvable are being run on big machines, while the supercomputer problems of recent years are going on minicomputers, workstations, and PCs. If you ask what is a supercomputer, the right answer is: a machine that does supercomputing.

Power, Performance, and Price

"There are some problems you wouldn't attack without maximum throughput," says Tom Weber, director of the National Science Foundation's Advance Scientific Computing division. (Throughput is computerese for combining the concepts of speed and capacity.) But he also says many problems aren't actually limited by the speed and capacity of the machine used to run them. Problem-solving, instead, is more often limited by the ability of the scientist to load the machine with data, or by his ability to pay for time, or his ability to use existing programs or write new ones to analyze his data. And each user must compete and lobby for access to supercomputers, unless he or she owns one.

For example, a geologist whose institution has massive data on rock strata beneath the ocean floor had a government grant to use a government-funded supercomputer to try to structure the data and make sense out of the data. But all his data were on computer tapes, and the supercomputer center had no tape drives. Even if that obstacle could have been overcome, the time for running the problem would still have been stretched out by the time for the menial task of changing tape reels.

This scientist could not solve his real-world problem by speeding up the supercomputer. That's why Weber and many scientists dismiss the computer speed contest as manufacturers define it, in terms of millions of instructions per second (MIPS), or millions of floating point operations per second (MEGAFLOPS). "I don't even talk about machoflops," jokes Weber. "Is it a supercomputer if it's faster than a Cray and it takes two years to program?"

Or, as Robert J. Paluck, president and CEO of Convex Computer Corp., asks in his sales pitch, "How fast is the Concorde if you have to drive from Texas to New York in order to get aboard?"

Enter the minisupercomputer.

"We are doing in scientific computing what Digital Equipment did to IBM 20 years ago," says Paluck, whose company is the most successful maker of minisupercomputers. "We are bringing the machines closer to the users, closer to their control. If there are 200 people trying to share the fastest machine in the world, then it's not that fast. Users care about how fast the machine runs their application, and 20 people sharing a slower machine can get answers sooner."

Weber says he has given up on defining a supercomputer. "I actually talk about high-performance computing, in order to fudge the question," says this official who writes more than $50 million a year in government checks to support four supercomputer centers around the country.

A peculiarity of American business management, Paluck explains, also helps sell the minisupercomputer: companies that are big enough to own a supercomputer are so bureaucratized that they charge their own departments' budgets for time on the big machine. So department heads hold down supercomputer use.

"If you own your own minisupercomputer, time on it is 'free,'" Paluck tells department heads.

Critics of the National Science Foundation's Supercomputer Center program say that the four centers provide about 5,000 researchers with an average of one hour of supercomputer time per week. The same $50 million a year, if spent on minisupercomputers at many institutions, could give the 5,000 users about 40 hours of time per week, or about 10 times the computing power. The supercomputer centers are justified by the fact that they can solve some complex problems that would defeat lesser machines. Besides, they are not simply Cray subsidiaries; they are buying minisupercomputers, minicomputers, and graphics workstations as well. Some of the most important work done at the supercomputer centers may turn out to be learning to tie various high-performance computers together, as much as the actual research performed.

New Commercial Niches

The comparatively inexpensive high-performance computing that Convex offers is also creating new markets that Cray does not address. "By focusing on the engineers and scientists, we have designed machines to handle huge amounts of numeric data," says Paluck, whose salesmen are finding that many businesses aren't ready for a supercomputer but do have problems involving huge amounts of numeric data. For example, Northwest Airlines uses a Convex computer to solve problems in linear programming, a formerly abstract field of mathematics that is just the thing for arranging crew and aircraft assignments to efficiently satisfy the airline schedule. It's the kind of problem for which there are many solutions, each one so large that it is hard to compare to all the others. Linear programming selects efficient solutions, but the enormous number of computations necessary to find a good solution made it impractical to use without a supercomputer.

The Convex system looks at all possible crew pairings and develops a schedule to minimize crew costs and maximize flight schedules, says a Northwest official. It considers hotel and per diem expenses, salaries, holidays, qualifications, flying time limits, work rules, and so forth, matching personnel to Northwest's schedule of more than 1,300 flights a day. There are several hundred billion possible solutions and the computer must pick one of the efficient ones.

"Of course they had tried to run it on their mainframe, but it took too long," says Paluck. "They saw us at a trade show, they ran some tests and they decided it would pay for itself in three months."

Paluck and some other refugees from the old Mostek semiconductor company founded Convex with $5 million in venture capital money in 1982 and shipped their first commercial machine in 1985. Their second-generation machine, using denser, faster semiconductor logic chips, came out in 1988. Through 1989, the company had shipped about $500 million worth of computers to customers in 33 countries, including nearly 100 to Japan. Sales growth averaged 50 percent a year.

In the five years after the founding of Convex, the computer industry followed a well-worn pattern: more than two dozen companies sprang up, each planning to grab 20 percent of the new markets Convex was creating. By 1986, the new industry was consuming itself in price wars.

"In the mid-80s there was so much venture capital available that venture capitalists invested in dozens of companies that were coming after Convex," says Paluck, who says he has counted 19 such companies that are already out of business. "All these others that chased us in," continues Paluck, "didn't realize that in any of these niche businesses there's room for one or two specialists, plus IBM or DEC. Look at transactions processing, or workstations; it's the same thing."

Some of Convex's competitors had great technical prowess but lousy business sense; others overextended and lacked the financial strength to make it through bruising price wars. As veterans of the memory chip wars of the late 70s and early 80s, Paluck and his colleagues had some perspective: "Even though we were growing at 50 percent a year, we tried to be mature."

At bottom, Paluck says, the secret of Convex's success was simple: to be first, not to make any big mistake, and to have a second-generation product while others were still struggling to establish themselves. This last task, he says, is probably the hardest.

Convex stock has not been a high-flyer, largely because many investors expected that Digital Equipment would enter and capture the minisupercomputer market. Some also threw IBM, Cray, and other threats into the pot as well, and shied away from Convex.

In fact, DEC did announce a minisupercomputer—or a high-end superminicomputer, if you like—toward the end of 1989. It made Paluck very happy, he says. "Their product line on paper looks pretty similar to ours, which is good because, in the past, they've said to our potential customers, 'stick to general purpose computers.' But now they have endorsed our way of doing things."

So by validating scientific computing, Paluck expects that DEC will open new markets for Convex. "Even if they ship today, we have twice the price-performance," he says.

Paluck acknowledges that Convex has a substantial debt to the Japanese computer giant, Fujitsu. Convex buys custom semiconductor computer chips, using emitter-coupled logic and complementary metal-on-silicon technologies. Some are customized according to Convex designs, others are off-the-shelf Fujitsu products. "They have given us unique access to their technology for seven years," says Paluck. "In the C-1, our first family of computers, we used 1K-gate CMOS, and that was the first in the United States. In the C-2, our second product family, which came out in 1988, we are using their 10,000 gate ECL and 20K gate CMOS, and that was first in the world. We even beat Fujitsu itself."

After hearing so many computer industry people—and bureaucrats and defense strategists—fret about a Japanese lock on chip technology, Paluck is something entirely different: "It's like we are part of the family. They have given us access to their technology and we have been a beta site for them. [A beta site is a favored customer who gets early samples of products and tests them in actual service.] Several of our guys learned Japanese to enhance that relationship." Paluck also says Fujitsu has provided Convex manufacturing know-how that's "phenomenal," and the relationship with Fujitsu opened other doors in Japan. "There are more of our high-end products in Japan than in the United States. Our customers there include NTT and NEC, Nissan, Hitachi, and a wealth of others."

Paluck's conclusion: "The Japanese are very objective with regard to buying product. They will help their productivity with anybody's machines. They are as selfish and greedy and businesslike as anybody else." Spoken like a winner.

David as Goliath

After the shakeout in minisupercomputers of the late 80s concluded with Convex as a real winner—at least until the next generation of technology—the company took aim more directly at Cray Research. Convex spent two years increasing the size and power of its second-generation machines. The first model of the 90s matched the power of a low-end Cray, and, at $3 million, undercut its price substantially. The third generation was to include models selling up to $10 million for a direct attack on Cray's core market.

"All our customers consider Convex a real true supercomputer company," Paluck says. "We have been held to be a minisupercomputer company," he complains. "Supercomputers are perceived, especially by the U.S. government, to be Crays and Crays alone. But 50 percent of our deals are done against Cray. We've won transactions of $8 to $10 million against Cray by selling three machines." A recent Convex success was even in a government procurement: Convex sold the National Institutes of Health three computers for the Human Genome Project (an attempt to locate the functions of the millions of genes on human chromosomes).

"Cray is making the pols in Washington believe they are a national asset, and so a lot of government money is going to them," Paluck gripes. "But the numbers in open competition show Cray is not the only one."

Cray Research recently began to notice that it faced competition from below. The company announced an "entry-level" model using the Y-MP technology for a mere $3 million and a spokesman says there is a continuing effort to hold down the cost of cooling and power that drive away buyers on a budget. In early 1990, Cray paid $35 million for Supertek, a struggling manufacturer of minisupercomputers, but said it would be late in 1991 before Supertek could be moved to Minnesota, straightened out, and offer its first product.Cray sent conflicting signals in July 1990 when Marcello Crumicio, the president who fostered the move toward smaller machines, quit because of "conflicting management styles" with Chairman Rollwagen.

Meanwhile, Convex is in a somewhat similar position itself—it has competitors beneath it whose personal computers grew into powerful scientific workstations, which are now growing into desktop supercomputers.

"You can throw away the old definitions of supercomputing," acknowledges Paluck. "It's the same as mainframes, minis, and micros: there's the high end, the middle, and the low end of scientific computing."

Desktop supercomputers are transforming the outer edges of engineering the way the IBM-PC transformed accounting or financial analysis. There are dozens of companies in this realm; Data General just recently introduced a workstation costing $8,500 that runs at 17 million instructions per second, the speed of a supercomputer a decade ago. Sun Microsystems replied with a $5,000 machine, and the set of chips required to clone such a machine costs less than $1,000.

The development of a new generation of speedy microprocessors has unleashed unexpected levels of power for small machines. They feature Reduced Instruction Set Computing, a design philosophy that cuts to the minimum the number of different instructions a processor can execute. Since it has fewer choices, the processor runs faster, enough so that it can build complex tasks out of the simple commands. (Seymour Cray adopted a RISC philosophy back in the early 70s for the CRAY-1 before the acronym was invented.)

RISC and Hazard

Current RISC microprocessors—there are seven main families, each backed by at least one $1 billion corporation—run at speeds equivalent to top-end IBM mainframes and may soon outperform them. And although speed is not everything, there have been comparable advances in capacity. The microprocessors are also comparatively easy to yoke together in teams of a dozen, or even hundreds of units, using proven designs developed on slower units. These designs, called multicomputers, multiply the performance of the individual units.

Intel, the California microprocessor company, has a division in Oregon that assembles powerful new Intel microprocessors into multicomputers. In Los Angeles, Teradata Corp. puts Intel microprocessors into database managers. Back in Silicon Valley, the newly public MIPS Computer Systems Inc. does the same thing with its microprocessors, though its multicomputers wear Digital Equipment and Tandem nameplates. Sun, the highly successful workstation vendor, is building multicomputers too, and so is its less-successful competitor, Apollo, which is now a division of Hewlett-Packard.

The RISC revolution has such supercomputing potential that C. Gordon Bell, a computer designer at Stardent, (who was a leader in the development of minicomputers during an earlier career at Digital Equipment) suggests change in scientific computing will accelerate. The performance of microcomputers, he says, has been increasing at about 40 percent a year since they were invented, while the performance of minicomputers and mainframes has been increasing at about 14 percent. RISC technology, Bell believes, will increase the microcomputer's rate of improvement to 70 percent a year. If those growth rates continue long enough, obviously, the trend lines will cross, meaning the extinction of the mainframe and the minicomputer as separate industrial categories. All computers then would be microcomputers.

Even the supercomputer would be subject to this progression, if it is indeed possible. Remember that Seymour Cray took readily available components and built them into an architecture that was more densely packed. That reduced the travel time of electrons carrying the information within the supercomputer. Shrinking components and packing them densely should continue to pay off in speed, and the ultimate is to shrink and pack them on a single chip.

Bell questions now whether multicomputers are necessary. A microchip that runs at 50 million instructions per second is probably fast enough for most tasks, he says, and machines with such chips at their heart clearly will be available at popular prices within a few years.

David Nelson, who was chief technical officer at Apollo, made a trenchant observation in 1987.[6] He classified computers into seven tiers, each separated from the other by a factor of 10 in cost. All the tiers improve in performance by about 35 percent a year, so a tenfold improvement happens in about seven years. Thus by Nelson's Law, the IBM 370 mainframe cost about $1 million in 1970; the roughly equal Digital Equipment VAX minicomputer cost about $100,000 in 1977; the Apollo workstation, also roughly equal in power, appeared in 1984 for about $10,000. A personal computer costing about $1,000 for the same performance should be available in 1991.

18

New Tools

There are still many people focused on the challenge of the old definition—to beat Cray and build the fastest, most powerful computer in the world.

One of the most successful so far is W. Daniel Hillis, founder and chief scientist of Thinking Machines Inc., a Cambridge, Massachusetts, neighbor of Hillis's alma mater, MIT. The company's product, The Connection Machine, was designed in his Ph.D. thesis and is now the leading commercial example of massive parallelism in computer design. The idea goes far beyond the multicomputer. In massive parallelism, the designer takes many thousands of very simple processing chips and connects them so they can work together on very complicated problems. The Connection Machine with 65,000 processors is already the fastest computer in the world on problems that require manipulation of enormous amounts of data.

The Connection Machine handles up to 200 billion bytes (computer representations of letters or numbers) in a single run. It finds its uses in aerodynamic simulation for NASA and Lockheed, geophysical simulation for Mobil, and text searching for Dow Jones, among other things.

"A couple of years ago, I represented the lunatic fringe," says Hillis, in the off-hand, smart-alecky tone of a person who thinks he was right when the world was wrong.[1] "I was trying to convince people that massive parallel processing was useful for anything. They would say, 'Oh, this massive parallel stuff is crazy stuff, it'll never work.' Now what everybody says is, 'Well, yeah, it's probably important for a few things, and we're looking at it.' What I can say is we've been looking at it a long time and we still like what we see. This is in fact becoming the fastest technology."

It's also cheaper technology, using computer chips that are less sophisticated than those in a microwave oven or a VCR. Lockheed Aeronautical Systems Company's director of research and technology planning, Harry E. Plumblee Jr., reports a 16,000-processor Connection Machine had a 50 percent to 500 percent cost-performance advantage versus a Cray Y-MP on problems involving fluid dynamics, such as modeling airflow over a wing.[2] He says, moreover, that the Connection Machine software can be improved substantially, so that "a cost-performance increase to greater than 1,000 percent is expected."

Hillis says:

It's not using very specialized technology for high performance, it's using high volume technology, so it's very much more cost-effective. And it doesn't need special power or special cooling. It can be wheeled into a room and operated. The cost of this *machine* is very often less than the cost of putting in refrigeration equipment for a Cray.

Inside the Parallel Supercomputer

In modeling fluid flows, such as the movement of air in a storm, the scientist knows every piece of air is influenced by every piece of air around it. But on a sequential computer, like a Cray, the computer takes each piece of air, and figures out what that's going to do; then takes the next piece and the next piece, figures out what that one's going to do, and then that one, and then that one, one after another. It might well have billions of calculations to do like that, which is why weather forecasting takes so long on a computer, even a superfast one.

"The storm does it much faster than that," Hillis remarks. "Because in the storm, every piece of air is deciding simultaneously what it's going to do. On the Connection Machine, what you do is, for every piece of air you have a separate processor. Each processor decides what its piece of air is going to do and then talks to the processors around it to tell them what it's doing. The fine-grained parallel machine is much closer to the physics of the situation. That's why those examples run in parallel very well."

Dow Jones, publisher of *Barron's* and *The Wall Street Journal*, bought two Connection Machines for its Dow Jones News Retrieval Service. The Connection Machines serve a new way of looking up newspaper stories, called DowQuest.

The "old" News Retrieval system, in service more than a decade, must be interrogated with precisely typed commands. Woe to the user who types .cp hl,dd,so/doc = 1 − 9 instead of putting two periods at the beginning of the command. In addition to being fussy about syntax, News Retrieval also retrieves any story with the key words the user specifies. Its only standard is the key words; it makes no connections or judgments.

The DowQuest service interrogates the same data bases, searching for the same key words, but the computer builds the connections for the user. It comes up with stories that the user would not know to look for.

"DowQuest is my favorite service because it uses my machine," Hillis chuckles. "If you ask it for articles with stock market crash, it searches through and gets you lots of articles. Probably you're not interested in all those articles. If you're really interested in, say, the relationship of the Tokyo Exchange to the American Exchanges, you look down the list of articles and you see an article that looks interesting to you. You say article number 5, that's the kind of article I want. You don't have to tell the computer why, you just say I want it like that. Then the machine goes back and compares that article with every other article that's been done in the last year and finds similar articles. That means reading every article and counting word comparisons and things like that to find similar articles. It does it in a fraction of a second and brings them to you.

"An ordinary supercomputer would read through each article and count up a score, read through and count up a score, for each article, one by one. If it was a fast good computer, it could read an article in a few milliseconds, but would still do the job in a few hours. On the Connection Machine, each processor gets an article, so it's like handing out the articles to everybody in Yankee Stadium and having them each read one."

Hillis acknowledges, "The communication problem in the computer is also like handing out the articles to everybody in Yankee Stadium and getting the answers back from them. It takes a lot longer than reading the article." That's why the Connection Machine is called the Connection Machine: Hillis's real architectural breakthrough was in designing the network of connections among the processors. "This is the part of the machine we are just learning how to build," he says.

What It Lacks

The disadvantage for Thinking Machines is that conventional software for conventional computers won't run on a parallel machine. Many potential customers want only to keep on doing what they've been doing, with their old software, only faster. The Connection Machine requires them to rethink their problems and do something new.

"The programs that exist are not written in a way that is amenable to breaking problems down into thousands of little parts," says Hillis. "That is, the cost is that everybody has to completely change around the way they do programs. And it's not even obvious that that's possible for all programs. So the challenge, #1, is a software challenge, of understanding the algorithms [mathematical structures] that work on parallel machines and switching to those."

Hillis says, however, that many problems thought to be impossible to program on a massively parallel machine are turning out to be "fairly simple," at least by his standards of what's simple.

A key is Fortran, the 30-plus-year-old computer language that is the most widely used scientific computing language. Before Hillis, Cray also exploited a feature of Fortran in his vector processing machines. Although Fortran programs assume a conventional scalar computer, operating on one piece of data at a time, the language permits programmers to write subscripts and loops. Subscripts pull one piece of data at a time from a large database; loops change the subscripts so the program chews through the whole set of data, one item at a time. To vectorize a Fortran program for use on a Cray, a programmer "unrolls" the loops so that a whole vector of data items could be attacked at once. To parallelize a Fortran program for use on a Connection Machine, a programmer specifies an array of data items. The specifications of the array and the operation are broadcast in parallel to each Connection Machine processor, which performs it on the item it controls.

"We recognized that most users would not shift to parallel processing if they had to learn new computer languages to get there," says Theodore Tabloski, director of software development. Thinking Machines also has versions of a more modern language, C, and of the leading language for artificial intelligence applications, LISP.

Plumblee of Lockheed says it from the perspective of the user: "If you are willing to rethink the problem, have an open mind to the potential of nontraditional computer architectures and programming styles, and are willing to stand out in front and take some risks, you can successfully use such machines."

That may not sound like a ringing endorsement, but Plumblee also suggests that there's little choice. "The enormous advances in supercomputer processor power have begun to level off. This leveling can be attributed to physical limitations."

A Parallel Universe

Massive parallelism is not new, nor is it unique to Danny Hillis and Thinking Machines. It goes back to a machine called ILLIAC-IV, built at the University of Illinois in the late 60s. Goodyear (the tire company had an aerospace and defense division) built a parallel machine with 65,000 processors—the size of the biggest Connection Machine—for NASA in 1981. Lawrence Livermore Laboratory developed a series of machines that were absorbed into the Strategic Missile Defense program and the equally secret Navy antisubmarine warfare effort. Most of the other national weapons research labs also have put together their own parallel computers, tailored to work on their special problems.

DARPA, with a more than $100 million-a-year Strategic Computing Program, has also financed development of many parallel machines. It devoted several million dollars to Hillis and The Connection Machine, and recently upped the bet with a $12 million contract to develop Thinking Machines' next generation. The project is called TeraOp, for 1 trillion operations per second. DARPA originally set this goal only for highly specialized problem areas, but in 1988, the agency decided that parallel processing promised such performance levels in general purpose computing.

DARPA's budget for strategic computing rose from $50 million in 1984 to a peak of $136 million in 1988. It was $115 million in fiscal 1990, bringing total spending to $696 million. Thanks to DARPA and to the attractiveness of massive parallelism, companies and university labs from coast to coast are working on exotic computer architectures. In 1987, DARPA was funding 10 different architectures and an operating system to support them. One already out of the lab and in the commercial world is iWARP, a joint project of Intel and Carnegie Mellon University professor H.T. Kung.

Kung and GE developed the original Warp architecture (named for the warp speed at which the Starship Enterprise travels in the old Star Trek TV series) as a "systolic array," in which data from a main memory is pumped into an array of processing cells, the way blood from the heart is pumped into the body's cells. Intel shrunk each cell to a single chip. Researchers have used Warp architecture to explore new ways for computers to recognize speech, written characters, and images gathered by TV. It's also being used to track submarines on sonar and airplanes on radar.

IBM, which is larger than most governments, has at least six parallel architecture supercomputer projects underway, including its own try at a computer to operate at 1 trillion operations per second. One is used to design mainframes and is emphatically not for sale. Since 1989, IBM has been using a highly versatile parallel machine called RP-3 to simulate experimental computer architectures.

"Nobody knows how architectures are going to have to be designed to handle all sorts of problems," says an IBM research spokesman. "RP-3 can be reconfigured in software so you can have 64 processors, each with its own 4-meg memories or all the processors attached to one huge memory." Researchers are asking what is needed to do different jobs, and they are learning how to optimize computing power to the task.

"Out in the world," the IBM spokesman says, "people are building machines first and then finding what works on them. Here we are researching it from the other way around."

IBM is actually not alone in this endeavor. Indeed, most parallel architecture machines have been designed and built for one specific task. Examples include: AT&T specializes in graphics and in using linear programming for allocating resources; TRW, Caltech, and Applied Biosystems got together on a DNA analysis computer, using thousands of TRW pattern-recognition chips; an IBM-backed team of physicists has a computer designed to calculate the weight of a proton.

Flavors Technology, a New Hampshire company founded in 1985 by Richard Morley, inventor of programmable controllers for machine tools, is targeting factory automation with a supercomputer. Morley took his knowledge of the field, added powerful hardware, and created his own new programming language. His product, the Parallel Inference Machine, manages a library of rules for the operation of automatic machines in a factory. A sample rule: "If pump pressure > 3000#/inch then reduce flow and send notification to control room, else continue flow and respond with current pressure when queried by control room." Morley likes to say he is making it possible to program the job, instead of the computer.

More than a dozen new companies had entered the field of massively parallel computing by October 1990, when *The Wall Street Journal* observed, "The gold rush into massively parallel designs recalls the scramble in seasons past to invest in artificial intelligence and the minisupercomputer." Venture capitalists showered $15.5 million on MasPar Computer Corp. of Sunnyvale, California; $20 million on Active Memory Technology of Irvine, California; $28.7 million on Myrias Corp. of Edmonton, Alberta; and $36 million on Kendall Square Research Corp. of Waltham, Massachusetts. Teradata's database managers have reached such a scale that the company is sometimes considered the largest massively parallel computer company, with sales of $224 million in the fiscal year that ended June 30, 1990.

In October 1990, Cray Research joined the crowd. Chairman John Rollwagen reassigned senior researcher Steve Nelson from the Y-MP/16 project to development of massively parallel technology. "We aren't going to be dumping our other line for a long time," said Cray Research's Charles Grassl, but the comment marked the first time that someone from Cray ever admitted the possibility that Cray Research's basic line might ever have to be dumped.

Mechanical Brains

There is always one more level of computing. Beyond massive parallel architecture there are neural network computers. Loosely modeled on the human brain, neural net computers create their own connections from processor to processor. It is said they are trained, rather than programmed.

Nestor, Inc., of Providence, Rhode Island, is a leader in applying neural net designs to such tasks as pattern recognition and speech processing. "They learn by example," says Clay Collins of Nestor, who explains that makes them easier to program, especially for those sorts of tasks that don't have mechanical step-by-step methods. "We have a simple application: mortgage insurance underwriting. There are guidelines for determining loan qualities, but to write those types of guidelines into a computer in any useful amount of time, is so difficult. What we do gives a system that adapts as quickly as possible, that feeds back and improves over time."

Collins adds that medical diagnosis is an attractive area because there is such huge variability in readings, even from the same individual but especially from different individuals. Doctors make shrewd guesses based on experience; the neural net computer may be able to pick up the same talent.

David Is Goliath

We may speculate about the future: if to attain greater speed, computers must shrink and also be designed in a massively parallel way, perhaps even as neural nets, then the computer of the future may be a massively parallel computer on a chip. Instead of placing tiny devices like transistors on a chip to form a microprocessor, designers may be putting thousands of micro-microprocessors on a (fairly large) piece of silicon. And if Moore's Law, Lepselter's Law and Nelson's Law hold true, even a little bit, it seems almost certain that supercomputing power on a chip will become a sort of commodity, just the way memory power on a chip has become a commodity.

Supercomputers are like hammers—they are tools. We need to nurture carpenters—that is, people who use supercomputers. In an article in the magazine *Issues in Science and Technology*, Irving Wladawsky-Berger and Marjory S. Blumenthal warned that "high-performance computing has so far remained almost exclusively the province of an elite cadre of scientists at major university and federal research laboratories and within a few of our largest firms."[3] They stressed that the supercomputer centers funded by the National Science Foundation were nearly saturated with scientific projects. They pleaded for more centers, constructed as consulting enterprises that would provide supercomputing solutions for businesses.

This concern for bringing tools within the reach of those with a job to do may be a better new business niche than a task for government. It may be happening already. The spread of the mini-supercomputer and the desktop supercomputer is bringing high performance within reach of the masses—the engineering and technical masses, that is. But worrying about who builds the tool, and where, is self-defeating.

In the late 70s the state of Minnesota produced all the world's supercomputers, yet other parts of the country, even other parts of the world, prospered. This is one place where America's milk-weed-seed dispersal of business covers and double-covers all the bets, from massive parallelism to gallium arsenide computer chips. Today, and in the near future, a buyer's options for obtaining powerful scientific computing are much wider—encompassing at least three Japanese supercomputer manufacturers, one widely recognized U.S. manufacturer, and many others less well known. Computing is in good hands as long as it is in many hands.

Of course, when computing is in many hands, people have problems understanding the industry. Today it seems certain that Cray Research will fare well in the short run, for big pieces of the U.S. government are cherishing and protecting it as a national defense asset. That may spell a return to the high margin days of the mid-80s and could produce a rapid run-up of Cray Research stock. But over the longer term, it is clear that computing power will become a commodity by the end of the 90s, just as computer memory became a commodity during the 80s. Although companies will struggle to be the low-cost producer of computing power, based on new technologies or on manufacturing prowess, a buyer will purchase MIPS and Gigaflops the same way he orders megabytes of memory today.

The interesting question will not be who builds the hammer, but what the carpenter makes.

Section VII
MAKING CONNECTIONS

Computer networks yoke together the raw power of many computers and their users. Networks have already expanded the power of the computer many times over; more powerful computers linked with faster networks are likely to be the path to the future.

19

Creative Networks

In the beginning, there was the ARPANET.

At the dawn of the space age, the Advanced Research Project Agency needed computer power. Researchers working on government projects needed a better way to use computers than putting their card decks in the back of the station wagon late at night and hauling them over to the computer center to do a run.

ARPA funded the earliest development of time-sharing—a set of programs and hardware by which users could phone their friendly neighborhood computer and do their work from a remote terminal. To the research scientist, hungry for computing power, it was almost as good as putting a computer on his desk. (Each of today's best desktop computers has more power than all the computers of the 60s combined.)

An essential element of time-sharing was the development of packet-switching, which crams more information onto phone lines by allowing continuous, simultaneous use of a single line by many users. How? No conversation, whether voice or data, is actually continuous. There are many pauses. Speakers pause for breath, or to think; terminals require inputs and must pause to retrieve data from memory. Communication actually takes the form of a burst of transmission, followed by a relatively long pause. In its simplest form, a packet-switched network takes advantage of this pattern. Each node receives and resends packets of information, by grabbing the bursts of transmission, tagging them with a route, and sending them on toward their destination.

Think of a transcontinental freight train. Cars from all over the East are assembled in Virginia into a St. Louis-bound train. On arriving in St. Louis the next day, the train is disassembled by switch engines and new trains are made up from those cars and cars from trains that arrived from Atlanta, New Orleans, Chicago, Pittsburgh, and from local shippers around St. Louis. Those new trains are then sent to Seattle, San Francisco, Los Angeles, and other points West.

Each freight car is a packet; each train is a continuous communication; many cars delivered from Boston to San Francisco constitute a message. If you tapped a trunk line in a long distance packet-switched network, you would see a succession of packets with different origins and different destinations, sharing a single circuit.

Dial 1-800-COMPUTER

All this packet-switching and time-sharing is just a different way of using the telephone network. When the original computer networks were being worked out, there was one AT&T telephone network, handling voice communication by the analog technology invented by Alexander Graham Bell. It's analog because the electronic waves carrying telephone signals are analogous to sound waves in air—larger waves are louder, more frequent waves are higher pitched. Computers, however, communicate digitally, meaning that signals are encoded as numbers consisting of zeros and ones using binary arithmetic. Packet-switching works because digital signals can be crammed together much more tightly and easily than analog signals.

ARPANET was first, and its users pioneered communication by computer over ordinary phone lines. The time-sharing and packet-switching technology was not held as a secret, even though ARPANET was restricted to defense researchers.

Other computer networks were created rapidly, some supported by federal funds, others by groups of universities. The largest academic network is BITNET, which was founded in 1981 and now has more than 1,500 nodes, or access points. Some were amateur creations—in the sense that nobody paid for the after-midnight efforts of computer center operators and hackers.

Others were set up by private companies for internal communications. They had this in common: existing physical resources, primarily computers and phone lines, could be used more intensely at virtually no direct increase in physical cost. It was a huge increase in productivity, for nothing was lost and much was gained.

Digitizing the Telephone

Between the 60s and the 90s, the long distance telephone system itself was transformed from an analog voice system to a system that was largely digital and sometimes more heavily used for data than for voice. During the period, the telephone system was deregulated and dismembered. In the new competitive industry structure that followed the breakup of AT&T, companies sought to offer new services and to cut the cost of old ones with a passion never seen in the old Bell System. Fiber-optic cable, using tiny lasers to fire digital signals down glass fibers, offered immense capacity at costs that dropped faster than anybody had expected. The long-distance networks built by AT&T's competitors during the 80s were almost entirely fiber optic—and perforce almost entirely digital. AT&T, which began first but worked slowly, responded to the competition.

Time-sharing and packet-switching gave their users access to undreamed-of computing power, but the new communications technology had unforeseen consequences. Users had undreamed-of access to each other. Electronic mail was faster than the U.S. mail, yet more impersonal than a telephone call. People could write notes to each other and say what they wanted, without the emotional content carried by voice. There is a big difference between WRITING CAPITAL LETTERS at your wayward colleague (the E-Mail convention for yelling) and actually yelling at him in person. This emotional distance also let some people cross self-imposed boundaries. Researchers from different departments or different institutions, who would not have worked together in the flesh, could exchange ideas freely.

In the commercial world, this free exchange may be the most important benefit. Many researchers, especially programmers, say they have colleagues on the network who are competitors on the phone or in the flesh. They would never converse on any other medium but E-mail. This is not something they all talk about freely, especially to their supervisors, but networks are a liberating force for cooperation and general advancement.

Electronic mail was an unforeseen use and consequence of the ARPANET, rather the way the sexual liberation of young people in the Roaring Twenties and ever after was an unforeseen use and consequence of the automobile.

Robert Lucky, executive director of communications science research at Bell Labs, says E-mail "created a whole new medium of closeness. It built bridges that weren't there before. Cutting across hierarchies, it brought new kinds of scientific cooperation."

What's so great about E-mail? Well it's hard to define, but there must be something great about it, because it's addictive.

"It's the convenience, the speed, and the social nuances of the medium," Lucky explains. "Speed: an hour, not four days. Convenience: I just sit here and type a message on a terminal I'm using anyway. (Of course, maybe I'm strange—I never use my record player because the records are 10 feet away.) The social factor: letters have letterheads, they carry overtones of positions and place. E-mail is much more anonymous, it isn't heavy with trappings of power. People can get to me who would not think of calling or writing me as an executive of the corporation."[1]

While it may be impossible to put a price on open scientific discourse, the free exchange also covered programs and data. Somebody with a troublesome problem, who spent many hours cobbling together a computerized solution, would, in the moment of triumph, put his new program on the network, barely taking time to give it a whimsical name. A colleague with a similar problem could look at his programming, revamp it to fit his local computer, and get a job done in much less time. Practically every science graduate student in the United States since the 60s owes something to computer networking this way.

Networking on the Network

President Bush's science adviser, Allan Bromley, reported to a congressional subcommittee: "We thought that the overriding reason for a National Research Network was to provide access to supercomputing centers for the bulk of American university faculty and students who could not participate in research at the frontiers of high-performance computing. We then learned that an equally important reason is collaboration, the sharing of software and databases, and the natural association of geographically distributed but functional complementary individuals. . . . A third important justification . . . lies in the innovation and productivity provided by a common quality network, distributed computing configurations, the ability to wheel computing power around the country, and the ability to access a national system of databases."[2]

ARPA, now known as DARPA, for Defense Advance Research Projects Agency, became the invisible hand guiding the U.S. computer industry. One DARPA veteran compares the process to an experimental garden. DARPA gardeners nurtured certain varieties of thinking, certain ways of using computers. Money was their fertilizer—DARPA paid generously for certain types of research projects. Then researchers, like bees, carried successful ideas, like pollen, to other gardens. And those ideas were carried not in air but on the wires of the ARPA network.

DARPA people claim credit for directly nurturing half the computer scientists in the United States; the other half were influenced by DARPA one way or another, mostly over the network. For example, DARPA managers recognized early that the power of computers would be determined by the power of computer chips. Unwilling to let chipmakers dominate the design of chips ("It was like saying that only printing press owners could write books," one DARPA veteran recalls), DARPA funded development of chip design software. Graduate students could use the network to exchange designs and to send designs to manufacturers, where many student designs could be combined on a single wafer. That cut the cost of making real chips, for testing, out of student designs from perhaps $20,000 to around $200. And the result was that the pace of design innovation in the semiconductor industry at least doubled between 1975 and 1985.

A Simple Substitute

Anybody with a personal computer can get a taste of what scientific networking is like by logging onto the big information utilities. The two best are Compuserve and BIX. Compuserve is big and has something for everybody; BIX, short for Byte Information Exchange, is run by the McGraw-Hill computer magazine *Byte*, but has gone well beyond the magazine's focus on personal computing technology.

A cut-rate, personal form of networking is the computer bulletin board. Users call in one at a time, post messages and software, scan what others have left before them, then leave. In the 80s, thousands of seeming altruists bought hardware, software, and phone lines to set up bulletin board systems (BBS, in their jargon). These system operators, who like to be called sysops, aren't really altruists, because they plainly get a big ego boost, maybe a feeling of power, from running a good board. A good sysop keeps discussions organized but freewheeling, collects good public domain software and keeps the users interested enough to keep calling in. Economically, however, they don't even try to recoup the thousands of dollars they spend on bigger memory discs and faster computers.

The computer bulletin board is the communications equivalent of a commune—a lot of people share and enjoy the work of a willing few. The BBS world has become a distribution system for "freeware" and "shareware," which are alternative, countercultural ways of making a name for yourself as a programmer. Unknown programmers who can't sell their work (and a few genuine altruists who won't sell their work) put copies of their programs on bulletin boards for anyone to use. "Freeware" means no strings attached; "shareware" means the programmer would like you to pay him $20 or so if you like the program and use it. Some programmers say they make more money on a successful piece of shareware than from licensing their work to an established publisher for sale at the established high prices in stores.

BBS are so numerous that they specialize: in the Washington area there are several hundred, including BBS for investors, ecologists, geopolitical strategists, real estate agents, accountants, tax experts, Dungeons and Dragons gamers, sports buffs, and so on. An enthusiast could spend all day, every day sampling local bulletin boards and finding ones that are useful and congenial. Some do. Compuserve and BIX and their competitors raise a barrier to kids and the hoi-polloi by charging fees.

BBS have networks of their own: several leagues of sysops have created relay networks so that their bulletin boards share postings and software. And there are communications networks that cater to the BBS user and his personal computer. There's a niche in the phone market to offer low-cost flat-rate long distance service so home computer enthusiasts can while away the midnight hours calling bulletin boards in distant cities.

The Business Network

Some networks are corporate properties. The most profitable are probably the computer networks established by major airlines to link travel agents with airline reservation systems. The largest is SABRE, run by American Airlines' parent AMR Corp. Others are linked to United, Continental, Northwest, and Delta. In each, the airline virtually gives away the terminals to travel agents in order to capture their sales volume and service fees. For years, the airline parents programmed their computers to give preference to themselves whenever the supposedly independent travel agents booked flights on the system. Competitors' antitrust complaints put a stop to the most blatant forms of preference, but it still works out that the owner of a system seems to get a preponderance of the traffic booked on it. Profits from such systems are substantial; in a few cases the market value of a reservations system even exceeds the value of the airline owner.

Communications networks are also part of corporate support systems. Virtually all companies with operations in several locations use private computer networks to manage the flow of data among their offices; many large business sites have one or even several local area networks, linking the personal computers and terminals of individual workers. Some of these commercial networks are standardized products in both hardware and programming; others are custom-made.

As factory automation has grown to rely more on computer controls, so factory networks have been created to link "islands of automation" and coordinate their tasks. Virtually all factory networks are custom made, at great expense of money and time.

The Network Business

The biggest networks are the public telephone networks, which are the basic building blocks for all the private networks. Computer technology allows many private networks to share, invisibly, a single public network, without even having an impact on the direct customers of the public network. The private networks don't have to be, and usually aren't, even compatible with each other. Computer people say the private networks are "virtual" networks, meaning that the networks aren't there physically, yet all the machines on the network operate as if there were a physical network. It's virtually there. Packet switching, with its ability to shuffle different messages through the same physical connection, makes it possible to build private networks without stringing more cable.

Digitization is nearly complete at AT&T and entirely complete at competitors MCI and US Sprint. Local telephone service, however, is another story. The twisted pairs of copper wire connecting homes and older offices to the telephone network lack the capacity of fiber-optic cable. That presents a chicken and egg problem: there are no services for families that would make use of the high capacities of fiber optics because there are no fiber-optic connections to the home, and vice versa.

Other things stand in the way, as well. If there were a fiber-optic link to the home, the natural thing to carry on it would be television pictures. You can probably hear the screams of your local cable television company right now. A few congressmen have suggested letting telephone companies break the cable TV monopoly; it may be the hot issue of the 90s on Capitol Hill. Another thing that would be a natural is local advertising, especially classified advertising. The American Newspaper Publishers Association spends a sizable fraction of its efforts and lobbying budget on keeping the phone company out of Electronic Yellow Pages, a business that doesn't now exist, and never will if the publishers have their way.

These special interests, and any others that might perceive a competitive threat in the future, such as videotape rental outfits, rely on government regulation and the residue of popular contempt for Ma Bell to forestall the day that the local phone company becomes an effective competitor. Consumer advocates, opposing any investment that would drive up the cost of basic telephone service, are their willing allies.

In the comments of the International Communications Association and the Consumer Federation of America on a Commerce Department study of telecommunications, the consumer advocates asserted fiber-optic links to the home would be both a losing proposition *and* an unjust enrichment of yuppies at the expense of old folks and people in rural areas. In general, consumer advocates express more concern that someone may be forced to pay for a service he does not want than the possibility that someone else will have no access to a service for which he would pay handsomely. Consumer advocates have not yet recovered from decades of fighting the Ma Bell monopoly. They see phone companies as junior monopolies, not as new media competitors.

Thus consumer advocates urge regulators not to let the phone companies take a chance on building new businesses with optical fiber connections to the home or anything else, because they believe that the costs of failure would be passed to consumers, while the profits of success would be passed to shareholders. They ignore the fact that a successful new service enriches those who receive it.

Holding Back the Baby Bells

Regulation that grew out of the old Ma Bell regulated telephone monopoly prevents the public networks and the public telephone companies from offering all the services and entering all the businesses that even their current technology and physical plant might allow. Under the terms of the consent decree that broke up AT&T, the local phone companies (so-called Baby Bells, though they have revenues of $20 billion to $40 billion a year) were barred from offering data processing services as a part of the telephone network. U.S. District Judge Harold Greene, who oversees the consent decree, feared that the local telephone monopolies would have too much power if they tied services to their communications links.

Congressmen and FCC commissioners resent the overwhelming power that Judge Greene wields over the telephone industry, but neither the lawmakers nor the rule-writers have been able to agree on anything to replace him. Judge Greene is slowly weakening the constraints on the Bell Companies, as he judges the maturity of the competitive marketplace. For example, he allowed the phone companies to experiment with gateways, in which the companies offer connections for digital access to computer services provided by others. Though this is complicated and awkward, it's a beginning. It's made more meaningful by the Federal Communications Commission's demand for Open Network Architecture—access for new information businesses to the telephone network for computer services on the same physical, technical, and financial terms as for the telephone companies themselves.

Not all gateway experiments have been entirely satisfactory. A Southwestern Bell experiment in Houston closed, in part because people didn't pay their bills. If anything, the service—especially the games—was too popular, almost addictive, and Southwestern Bell's practice of charging by the minute nearly bankrupted some of its most enthusiastic customers. A competitor supplanted the phone company by offering similar services for a flat monthly fee.[3]

The next step is Integrated Service Digital Network, or ISDN, a technology that is supposed to convert the telephone network into a rudimentary digital network, even without rewiring homes and old offices. ISDN would be a weak competitor for cable TV, since it would have capacity for only a couple of television signals (maybe only one HDTV signal), a couple of data channels, and a voice channel.

But that might be enough to start a ball rolling. One can imagine—and the telephone companies have imagined it—offering switched video programming. That would be a service in which a viewer selects from a catalogue the movie or special program he wishes to watch. Then he picks the time he wants to watch or tape it and orders it sent to him over his ISDN phone line. The idea combines the stay-on-the-couch convenience of pay-per-view cable with the enormous selection and personal timing of the local video rental store. It would work even better if the phone companies had fiber-optic links to the home, but ISDN is manageable without the investment in rewiring. (New communities, however, will be getting fiber-optic phone lines as a pure matter of economics in the early 90s, as the cost of fiber cable falls below the cost of copper.)

In the 90s, the regulators, lawmakers, and the judicial system may agree to let the phone companies out of bondage. The bad news is that probably won't happen until today's vested interests—the newspaper publishers, cable companies, broadcasters, and all—are ready to compete. The good news is that technology is pushing all of them in the same direction—toward a unified network that combines phones, cable TV, and computer links. Getting there looks tough, but it will be easier than it looks. Many things are happening now to set it in motion.

20

Opening Hardware

Opening Networks

There is a big difference between the scientific networks and the PC bulletin board systems on the one hand and the corporate computer networks on the other. Those built by and for users can accept connection to a wide variety of computers built by many different manufacturers. Those built by consultants and computer companies for private industry are intended to work with greater efficiency. The cost has been the exclusion of most computer gear, except that specifically designed to work with the network. This is a cost incurred entirely by the customer; the supplier often sees it as an advantage to tie the customer to his equipment.

Building private networks that reliably connect computers of different manufacturers, using software from different authors, has been a black art at best and more often an expensive impossibility. The result, in many firms, was a high-tech tower that threatened to collapse in a rubble of babble. Computer users were beaten senseless by the failure of their computers to communicate.

Only occasionally, after great effort and at great cost, would the mainframe computer over here give up its raw material specifications to the minicomputer over there milling a part. And both would ignore the inquiries of an analytical engineer and his microcomputer trying to develop a cost report. On the typical U.S. factory floor, the problem became overwhelming before it was identified as a problem. A succession of plant managers bought automated equipment as it became available, from whatever vendor invented it, made the best sales pitch, or offered the best price. The result: "islands of automation" in which parts would be machined or assembled efficiently and then cast adrift.

Even in the office—where words and numbers seem to be simple compared to the orthography of engineering—word processors, accounting systems, sales and marketing, and inventory control systems frequently would work at cross purposes or not at all.

A new idea was needed, and in the late 80s, a new idea called Open Systems took root. Customers decided, rightly, that no single computer vendor, not even IBM, was big enough or good enough to supply the best and cheapest solution to every computer problem. But no computer company by itself would make its products compatible with those of its competitors. In fact, about all that some computer companies had going for them was their "installed base," meaning the number of customers they had captured and convinced that switching to another brand would be too expensive and disruptive.

General Motors was the biggest and loudest customer to scream about the frustration of incompatible computers, and Mike Kaminsky, a GM industrial engineer, was the first and loudest screamer in the company. "You need to communicate. In an assembly plant the type of engine changes the caster, the camber, the toe in, the toe out—everything in the suspension and tuning."[1] Automation of the car ordering system was coming along in the early 80s, but would have been more useful if an order from the dealer directly programmed computers to make needed changes along the assembly line. That was impossible, because the ordering, manufacturing, and inventory systems were all incompatible. And things that happen on the assembly line require communication back to the head end. Said Kaminsky: "If you start to get bad parts, you want to communicate back up the line that the part creation process is bad."

In a factory with 20 different brand names of unconnected automated equipment, communication of that sort was next to impossible. Kaminsky started working on the problem in 1980, trying to develop standards for computer communication at GM and trying to get GM's suppliers to adopt those standards.

After the U.S. government, GM is the largest purchaser of computer equipment in the world, so Kaminsky had some leverage—but not enough. It took four years to get a demonstration project going, to start to shove what Kaminsky called a Manufacturing

Automation Protocol down the throats of the computer industry. Eventually GM said that it would only buy new equipment that worked in MAP.

That was when computer makers realized they had a problem. GM's vendors swallowed hard, and in 1985, 17 companies got together to try to have more influence over what they would be forced to eat next. Virtually all were direct competitors somewhere in the computer-communications industry, but a 1984 federal law had exempted research and development consortia from federal antitrust laws. By calling their group Corporation for Open Systems (COS), and later by hiring a former chief of the Justice Department's Antitrust Division as general counsel, the competitors could cooperate to set standards for computer communication and enforce them.

The corporation was headed by Lincoln Faurer, a burly ex-general whose previous job had been head of the National Security Agency, which uses computers by the acre to crack codes and listen in on international communications. In five years, Faurer succeeded in turning a big part of the computer industry upside down. Working with nothing more than the determination of a few big customers, the Corporation for Open Systems forced computer companies to pay attention, to help write a workable communications standard and accept it.

COS hired its own engineering staff to create tests and test equipment to embody the COS standard. Any manufacturer now can hook his gear—so far, just certain types—up to the COS test equipment and run a series of test programs. If everything works smoothly, the manufacturer wins a COS certificate of "interoperability"—like an Underwriters Laboratory safety certificate or the Good Housekeeping Seal of Approval.

Interoperability isn't compatibility: all COS-certified computers don't work alike. Instead, no matter how they work inside, they send and receive all kinds of data in a common format.

Interoperability has not quite become a requirement, and it is far from universal. But it is what customers want, many have become sophisticated enough to demand it, and vendors not only offer it but brag about how compatible their products are. Leadership now depends more on basic issues of quality and price, and less, much less, on keeping customers in the old corral.

"The days of account control are fading," says Colin Chapman, a Data General executive caught up in the Open Systems movement. "We used to battle to control the account, now the accounts are demanding that we work together." Open systems, he adds, present an obvious marketing problem: "To be blunt, if we are all the same, then how are we different?" He answers: "Our job is to create different ways of doing things with the same documents and databases."[2]

It's hard to say who stands to win or lose in a world of open systems. IBM—the leader in so many areas of computing—could have a lot to lose as systems open. There is no bigger computer corral than what computer people call "the IBM world." Time and again IBM brushed off competitors by making technological advances in ways that were hard to copy quickly. And many times, the hard-to-copy features involved communications. Thus some prognosticators think interoperability means a huge opportunity for IBM's competitors. On the other hand, open systems means that IBM's competitors will build a lower fence in which to corral their longstanding customers. Changing to any other system will be less risky and less expensive, so customers are sure to abandon vendors that don't keep pace.

A Paradigm for Paradox

Open systems can't be both the means to IBM dominance and a golden opportunity for IBM's competitors—or can it? Faurer says, "Each is reasonable but neither is correct. What is correct is that the companies have decided to look for advantages over their competitors with real features instead of what networks their products connect to. They have concluded that an expanded market of open networks will get them more business than today's market of proprietary networks."

For another way of looking at the competitive issues, consider the automobile industry. Where once there were hundreds of small companies all making automobiles, now worldwide there are scarcely one dozen major firms. Yet underneath that surface of a mature industry dominated by industrial giants, there are thousands of other companies in vigorous competition, providing parts and supplies and service to the giants, the end users, and the customers. Even today, the company that builds a better brake pad will see the world beat a path to its door.

So it could be that as the computer industry matures, there will be fewer computer companies, but many more companies offering parts and supplies and service. Interoperability could be the key to expanding that part of the industry.

Standardization, the crucial issue about which compatibility revolves, is itself not too simple. It's coming, everybody agrees. Users demand it. But it can be a "boon or a bane" to an individual company. At a National Research Council symposium,[3] experts offered these contradictory lessons from IBM experience:

> Based on internally developed standards, the 360 System family of compatible computers cemented IBM's leadership position in the 60s, in the large international market for mainframes. The company's proprietary control of what became an industry standard gave it a clear advantage, and most other computer manufacturers directed their attention to market niches not filled by IBM mainframes.
>
> IBM chose a different tack when it made its relatively late but hurried entry into the personal computer market, revealing its microcomputer architecture to the rest of the industry and purchasing the machine's operating system from an outside vendor, Microsoft. The openness of the company's standard was effective in promoting the development of software and peripheral equipment by other firms, assuring that customers had ample support. The strategy made the IBM PC a marketing success. But within five years after the computer was introduced, cheaper PC 'clones,' most assembled in the Far East, claimed significant shares of the market. U.S. sales of imported clones in 1988 were up 50 percent over the previous year.

Boon or bane, indeed, but to whom? What we have here is a classic case of Charlie Wilson syndrome. (The former chairman of General Motors said, "What's good for General Motors is good for the country.")

The dominance of the System 360 enabled IBM to earn monopoly profits, but it was hardly good for the country, or for IBM customers in any country. It was not even entirely good for IBM. IBM used its near-monopoly position in mainframes to lock in its customers. As the Justice Department charged in its antitrust suit against IBM that ran throughout the 70s, the company deliberately slowed the pace of technological innovation during the 60s and early 70s, until its monopoly was broken by upstart minicomputer makers like Digital Equipment. (The suit dragged on for more than a decade, and was dropped at the beginning of the Reagan administration by new antitrust officials who decided that time and competition had overtaken the issues in the case.)

And the open architecture of the IBM PC may have been the greatest contribution the company ever made to the nation. Open architecture spawned an industry that IBM could not have created itself, and the worth of it should be measured by the enthusiasm with which customers accepted it and by the growth of software developers, add-on board manufacturers, and other cottage industries made possible by the openness of the IBM PC. Lots of personal computers had technology and features well ahead of the IBM PC—Apple and Commodore, to name but two—but IBM's open architecture gave customers more choice at lower prices. Interestingly, IBM seems to be failing in its attempt to create a new, closed architecture standard.

The question that is worth asking about standardization is whether adopting standards freezes technology, making it too hard to move on and up to better machines.

Mainframe technology did stagnate under the rule of IBM. A monopolist aims to maximize revenues. One way to do that is to extract as much profit as possible from a given product before moving on to its successor. IBM applied that strategy to its near-monopoly by sowing "fear, uncertainty, and doubt." When a competitor announced a product with more features or better performance or a lower price than an IBM product, IBM salesmen would warn customers that moving to the competitor would be very expensive, very difficult, and take a long time. And besides, the salesmen would say, IBM has a new product coming out soon that will beat the competition (on features or performance, rarely on price). FUD, the acronym for Fear, Uncertainty, and Doubt, became a computer industry buzzword, as did the reworking of the letters IBM to stand for "I've Been Misled."

The PC standard, on the other hand, was an open standard, arrived at not by a megalithic corporation, but by IBM engineers working in isolation from the rest of the company, with little regard to corporate strategy. And the engineers worked in partnership with Intel, the chipmaker that created the microprocessor at the heart of all PCs, and with Microsoft, the merchandiser of the DOS operating system software. The PC standard allowed Intel to develop more advanced versions of its microprocessor, each mostly compatible with the earlier generations, and allowed Microsoft to develop advanced versions of DOS more or less on schedule with changes in the hardware.

21

Opening Software

Operating Compatability

Hardware is only half the issue in computer compatibility. Taking data and handing it off to another computer is all very well, but it would be even better if the two computers agreed on a way to organize and manipulate data. Enter software compatibility.

The key issue is the operating system—the program that holds a computer together by defining the way it handles data. Operating systems have been the bleakest, most incompatible area of computing. Until recently, virtually all computer companies had their own operating systems and most big ones have several—all incompatible. Entering the 90s, though, the age of UNIX is upon us.

UNIX is an operating system first developed in 1969 at Bell Labs as a program to allow several users to work simultaneously on different files on a minicomputer. The programmers who wrote UNIX over a period of several years were not trying to create a commercial product; they were tinkering with ways of using minicomputers, which were then a new creation from a new company, Digital Equipment Corp. In its early days, DEC sold hardware without software, like selling paper and a typewriter instead of a book. The Bell Labs programmers were just trying to make the new gadget work for them. They borrowed useful programming concepts wherever they could find them, and invented what they could not find. They even created "C," a new computer language in which to write UNIX.

UNIX and C grew together and the Bell Labs people created a kind of programming subculture, almost a way of thinking about computers, at the same time that they developed their program. The key was the idea of a toolbox. People who needed a job done wrote software tools, which lived in the toolbox according to the rules of UNIX. Then the next programmer would build new tools with previously built tools, and so on. Imagine that the first programmer built a wooden box; the second built a handle, the third built small compartments, the fourth invented the hammer, the fifth the screwdriver, and the sixth the saw (and a new cubby in the toolbox to hold the saw). Now the first guy comes back and uses all the tools to build a workbench. UNIX came to have every feature imaginable, all available, and yet, all optional so as not to clutter up each individual toolbox.

In a series of interviews with the original UNIX programmers, science historian Michael S. Mahoney found one other important attribute that made UNIX successful: the manual.[1] The programmers insisted that there be a high quality, intelligible manual. They found, moreover, that insisting on a high quality manual produced high quality programming, because most of the evasions and obscurities in the instructions covered up evasions, obscurities, and blank spots in the programming.

"When you wrote down the uglies, you'd say, 'We can't put this in print,' and you'd take features out and put features in to make them easier to talk about," recalled Doug McIlroy, editor of the manual.

One of the UNIX tools is "UNIX to UNIX COPY PROGRAM," or UUCP. This allows any UNIX computer to phone any other UNIX computer in the world in its directory of computers and pass on information, such as electronic mail. This produces a state of anarchy that some find satisfying and others find horrifying. ARPANET restricted usage to legitimate defense-connected users working on government projects; BITNET (Because-It's-There Net), CSNET (Computer and Science Net), and NSFNET (National Science Foundation Net) have central managers and restrict usage to noncommercial use. UUCP isn't even a formal network, it has no manager, and only peer pressure decides what's appropriate to run on it.

Together, the mass of special networks that can communicate with each other, however clumsily and slowly, are called the internet. One measure of how widely the internet spreads came in November 1988, when a young computer scientist at Cornell released a worm program. The program was supposed to reside quietly in a computer, copy itself, transfer itself to any other computer that its host contacted, and repeat the process in the new computer. The author, Robert T. Morris, made a small mistake in programming, and the worm turned into a rabbit. It replicated wildly, forcing each host computer to spend all its time making and storing copies of the worm program. In a matter of hours it paralyzed more than 6,000 computers. Now that's anarchy!

On Your Desk

The personal computer revolution of the 80s had little to do with UNIX, except to provide an invidious comparison. The most successful personal computer—the IBM and its clones—had operating system and software philosophy supplied by Bill Gates and his Microsoft Corp. DOS, the operating system for the IBM-PC, was rigid, uncrackable, virtually unchangeable, while the PC hardware and working software were open. The user could plug in new boards, load new software, even buy a whole new computer from another manufacturer, knowing only that all the new stuff was compatible with rigid, invariable DOS, which he could not change and which even Microsoft changed but rarely. The result: programmers hated the PC because they ran up against arbitrary DOS rules; but customers were happy to buy reliable products that worked the first time.

The world of DOS and the world of UNIX are coming together with a crash in the early 90s. Reliability and uniformity are seen as virtues in themselves. As with hardware, users want software that works on various machines and cooperates with other systems.

The new generation of workstations and advanced computers, based on Reduced Instruction Set Computing chips, is bringing the day of true compatibility much closer. The people who developed Reduced Instruction Set Computing chips were UNIX-oriented scientists. Most RISC chips are tailored to run UNIX, so machines that employ RISC chips introduce UNIX along with their cheap computing power.

A very recent development in the world of UNIX may turn out to be the most important of all. Software engineers call it CASE, for Computer Aided Software Engineering, a play on the Computer Aided Design systems that revolutionized drafting and chip design in the 80s. Writing software has become as big a production bottleneck as making engineering drawings used to be. CASE engineers are trying to automate the process of writing software. It is complicated, to say the least, since programming remains as much an art form as an engineering discipline. Nevertheless, certain types of software, particularly those for modeling complex interactive systems, have been written nearly automatically, with the author-engineer specifying broad relationships and leaving the specific organization of bits and bytes to a CASE program.

UNIX in Real Life

By the mid-70s, UNIX had escaped from the labs. Legalistically, AT&T licensed it to all comers; realistically, UNIX became shareware. Use of UNIX spread rapidly in the research and academic communities with the Digital Equipment minicomputers for which UNIX was designed. UNIX became the standard operating system for computer students, and as computer students became computer scientists, they took UNIX with them into business.

But as UNIX spread, it mutated. The toolbox became a workbench, with six legs, or was it four, or eight? And were the slots for hammers on the left side or the right side? How many screwdrivers could be accommodated? Philips or slot head? Etc., etc., etc. Some versions of "full UNIX" grew to more than a million lines of program code, and they grew more and more incompatible. Still, each version shared basic UNIX virtues: easy use by several users, easy creation of new special programs, portability from one computer to another. Versions of UNIX were created for mainframes, supercomputers, and virtually every kind of hardware a computer scientist might encounter—especially engineering workstations, the high-powered personal computers that appeared in the 80s.

Microsoft has a UNIX, Sun Microsystems has a UNIX, IBM has a UNIX, AT&T, naturally, has a UNIX. They have competed to have their UNIX versions adopted widely, Meanwhile, other makers of the new generation of scientific personal computers, from engineering workstations to desktop supercomputers, have tried to adapt to as many versions of UNIX as possible. The result, as the 90s opened, was chaos, not the simple DOS-like ideal of uniform, reliable software. Even companies as well established as AT&T and IBM feared letting their competitors set UNIX standards.

In 1988, the answer seemed clear: follow the model of the Corporation for Open Systems and establish a software consortium to set a standard for UNIX. But it seemed like such a good idea that AT&T and Sun Microsystems established one consortium while IBM and Digital Equipment established another. The two have battled some and compromised some, but still are working more at cross purposes.

What's needed again is the intervention of customers. As UNIX becomes more widely used, and becomes more important to major computer users, the importance of compatibility, which is the user's concern, will undermine the importance of control, which is the manufacturer's desire. In the 90s, it ought to be possible to set up a new terminal, PC, workstation, or desktop supercomputer, on a local area network, connected in turn to a gateway for access to any of dozens of other networks, and know that if the vendor adhered to the standards as he claimed, the new piece of gear will work smoothly.

Some call this "digital dial tone," others prefer "Broadband Integrated Services Digital Network." W. Russell Neuman, director of the Communications Research Group at the Media Laboratory of MIT, defines it as "all of the advanced, high-resolution visual displays as well as voice, graphics, and data which a broadband network can carry." Neuman says that the concept requires that networks be designed with open architecture and that equipment—TV sets, phones, and computers of all types—must comply with an open architecture standard too.[2] Neuman believes the government should order open architecture, much as it ordered that all television sets be able to receive both VHF and UHF stations.

An Open Network of Computers

The United States needs—and private industry in the United States is rapidly building—an open structure for communications. Computer communication requires an open digital network, and all other forms of communication have reached the point where they can and will use it too. Access to computing power will be spread more widely, while becoming cheaper and easier to use.

Without the government's doing anything, it seems clear that technology and economics are driving the communications and computing systems of the country into a single industry and a single inexpensive, universal, digital, high-capacity network incorporating voice, pictures, and recording. Whether we continue to call it by its old separate names—the TV, the computer, the fax, the copier, the tape machine, the book, and so on—or whether we call it by some single 21st century name like the Matrix or the Net, it will be there. The remaining questions are when, how, and who.

As the 90s open, the United States government has a remarkable opportunity to answer when, how, and who, a chance to accelerate and guide the change to the single intelligent network. In late 1989, President Bush's Office of Science and Technology Policy put before Congress a proposal for spending $1.9 billion over five years on supercomputing and a national network connecting supercomputers at super data rates exceeding 3 billion bits per second, or 3 gigabits. It was the administration's answer to an earlier proposal by Sen. Albert Gore, the once and probably future Democratic presidential candidate.

The national research network would be the interstate highway system of the 90s, an infrastructure investment that could have the same wide and deep impact on our country that construction of the highway system did.

Allan Bromley, President Bush's science adviser, says, "It will provide a network to take best advantage of the nation's investment in computing, allow maximum access to advanced hardware and data bases, transmit the most useful information, maintain growth, and continually rejuvenate the computing capacity of the nation."[3]

Gore is a genuine enthusiast: "This network is the most important, most cost-effective investment that the Federal government can make in American science and technology," he declared at a hearing kicking off his bill.[4] "Like the interstate freeway system, the network is an infrastructure for the benefit of all Americans. And like the interstate freeway system, the network will require leadership by the Federal government."

The Administration's proposal includes a list of 20 "Grand Challenges," meaning the major projects of the 90s and the early 21st century that will require application of a network of supercomputers:

Prediction of weather, climate, and global change.
Challenges in materials science.
Semiconductor design.
Superconductivity.
Structural biology.
Design of drugs.
The human genome identification project.
Quantum chromodynamics.
Astronomy.
Transportation.

Vehicle signature.
Turbulence.
Vehicle dynamics.
Nuclear fusion.
Efficiency of combustion systems.
Enhanced oil and gas recovery.
Computational ocean science.
Machine speech.
Machine vision.
Undersea surveillance for antisubmarine warfare.

The relevance of high-powered scientific computing to them is not in doubt. The relevance of the supercomputing network is twofold. Supercomputers could be harnessed together to attack some of the largest problems. But perhaps more importantly, a supercomputer network would allow researchers to share graphic models and the data on which they are based. Most of the 20 Grand Challenges require supercomputing for some sort of visual representation or modeling; just as the networks of the 70s opened researchers to sharing computer programs and data, the National Research and Education Network should make a new level of scientific cooperation possible.

Robert Lucky, executive director of the Communications Sciences Research Division at Bell Labs, notes that the old saying that a picture is worth a thousand words is pretty close to the literal truth. "It requires almost exactly a thousand times the communications capacity to transmit pictures as spoken words. Network television signals, for example, are transmitted digitally in the telephone network at 45 million bits per second, as compared with the 64 thousand bit per second rate used for digital speech." High definition television pictures, though, are worth about 12 times as much as regular television. Without compression, HDTV requires about 1.3 billion bits per second. Even still pictures of high quality carry massive amounts of information, Lucky adds: "As we turn the pages of National Geographic, for example, we may be using the equivalent of hundreds of millions of bits per second."[5]

What's It Good For?

A high-speed, high-capacity network could do much more than link supercomputers and the scientists that use them. Bolt Beranek and Newman, a Massachusetts electronics design firm, listed the business applications of such a network. They included:

> Meeting with potential customers over closed circuit HDTV; computer tracking of product distribution; communication with customers for service; linking researchers from different locations to work on a project without moving them; allowing employees to 'telecommute,' living where they want without requiring the presence in an office; gaining quick access to data in distant locations; linking many plant and office locations under one management; creating companywide management of inventory and tools located in many different places; keeping track of changing government regulations; supporting the continuing education of employees; making strategic alliances and joint ventures easier to form.[6]

Technological history suggests, of course, that the most profitable uses of such computing power have yet to be invented.

BBN said that for itself, it looks forward to the day when semiconductor design tools, and the supercomputing power to run them quickly are available on a network. Even a $300 million-a-year company like BBN, whose main business depends more and more on the design of custom computer chips, can't afford the best design systems and software. The company also finds it hard to bear the cost of making only a few custom chips. A high-speed network could offer efficient, cost-effective connections to chip design companies and custom chip manufacturing companies.

It's an open question whether business will be allowed to use the National Research and Education Network, since government-funded networks have a tradition of excluding all but nonprofit users. In part, there's a certain academic distaste for business at work, and there's a more political fear of using government support to compete with unsubsidized business. These obstacles must be overcome.

The OSTP bill grabbed headlines in the fall of 1989, but the Bush administration did not follow through in its next budget proposal. The budget for fiscal 1991 made no mention of the supercomputing network.

Under pressure from Sen. Gore, Presidential Science Adviser Allan Bromley more or less swore that money for the NREN would be forthcoming in the fiscal 1992 budget. "I got into it too late for this budget cycle, but I believe I have an agreement with the OMB and in the next budget cycle we will be making some very concrete moves," Bromley said.[7] Gore and other senators, who have seen many middle-level officials make similar pledges that OMB never delivered on, were unimpressed. Sen. John D. Rockefeller IV urged Bromley to "give those guys in the White House a certain amount of time, then get out, go back to Yale, and teach somebody else to think straight."[8]

22

Opening Wallets

Fiscal Fine Print

The National Research and Education Network (NREN) represents an opportunity for American science and business alike, and one that need not cost anything like $1.9 billion. About $682 million of the OSTP bill was earmarked for purchase of supercomputers; another $667 million for supercomputing software development and $183 million supporting basic research projects. Only about $390 million of the president's proposal would actually go to building the new network.[1] While none of these goals are unworthy, they should probably be funded in reverse order—network first, research second, new software third, and new hardware last.

Supercomputers themselves are not in particularly short supply; government agencies and companies are buying hardware as rapidly as their budgets will allow. If a new national research and education network gave new users easy access, a fight for time on supercomputers might become a big problem, but the new users would also be a new revenue source. The network might accelerate the trend toward computer power utilities already being born in the National Science Foundation's supercomputing centers. Owning computing power might become a standalone business, like owning a farm or a factory, since the network would give the world a path to your door.

Software development, while an enormous stumbling block, has to be considered as either part of supercomputer procurement, in the case of operating systems and other basic programming, or as part of research, in the case of problem-solving application programs. While all scientists need money, buying new tools is different from finding ways to use tools intelligently and efficiently.

Intelligent, efficient use of the existing supply of supercomputers is the big problem. The network to connect them, to give people all over the country access to data and computing power, is what's important, followed by research support for those people who design and operate their research projects. Some insiders say that the $682 million for purchase of computers is meant as a hidden subsidy for Cray Research, although Bromley stresses the need to support massive parallelism and other non-Cray computer architectures. The OSTP bill offers no reassurance, for it sets no procurement policy and leaves purchasing decisions to existing agencies.

Today's Network Tomorrow

Much of the physical network for the National Research and Education Network already exists, in the form of fiber-optic cables in the nation's long distance telephone networks. And some early versions of the switching, routing, and operating systems are already working too.

The National Research and Education Network actually got started in 1986, as part of the National Science Foundation's establishment of national supercomputing centers. Each of the centers and some associated university groups built a regional network servicing the supercomputer centers, and in 1987, NSF put up $13.9 million to engineer a "backbone" linking them all. IBM supplied the packet switching and network management equipment and software; MCI supplied the physical long distance links.

The backbone quickly became the base of a national research network. Other networks from ARPANET on, became attached. ARPANET, in fact, ceased independent existence. NSFNET operates at 1.5 megabits per second. It was already experiencing growing pains in 1990 and was about to upgrade to 45 megabits per second.

Robert Lucky of Bell Labs makes the Daniel Boone case for pushing on further and faster:

The most important uses of a high-speed network are very likely to be uses that we have not yet identified or perhaps even imagined. In all past telecommunications history, users have been satisfied with the existing speed of transmission until they were given higher speeds— then and only then have new opportunities developed. Only in retrospect have the previous transmission rates looked inadequate. Investing in our national data network infrastructure is an investment in our future. It is like building a road into the wilderness. We must not be so shortsighted as to try to justify such an investment solely for today's uses; these uses grew around a lesser system.[2]

The next steps are crucial. At the moment, they appear to depend on interest-group politics. They depend more on a vision and on management than on money, though interest group politics is primarily about the distribution of money.

One task is to resolve the competing interests of AT&T, other long distance network companies, local telephone operating companies and, we hope, users of telecommunications and computing. Sampling their advice calls to mind the adage about the man with a hammer: to him, everything is a nail.

Regulation and Regulators

Alan Chynoweth, vice president of applied research at Bell Communications Research (known as Bellcore, it's the part of Bell Labs that went with the regional Bell Operating Companies after the AT&T breakup) says the breakup of AT&T required a decade of heavy work just to be sure that the seven operating companies and AT&T, plus the new competitive long-distance companies, could keep the telephone system operating as well as it had in the days when AT&T ran it all. That effort, he says, wasted valuable time, and continues to impede new network service.

"It is difficult to introduce a service that spans even one of the customer premises equipment-to-network or network-to-network interfaces, much less a nationwide service that will always span at least five separate entities," he complained to the House Telecommunications Subcommittee.[3] "The end result is that there has not been one major new national telecommunications service introduced in this country since the AT&T Consent Decree required equal access to existing services. The result is six years of no national service progress in a time of profound and rapid technological change."

Chynoweth's point is well taken, but it begs two questions. Would regulators have permitted new national services, or would they have held back while demand, cost, and price were carefully examined? Is it so terrible that most new capabilities are being introduced in private networks? As he points out, the private networks are virtually unregulated, allowing customized services, and the public networks provide facilities and access where needed.

Chynoweth finesses the first question, and the answer is unknowable, though cynicism where the FCC and the state public utility commissions are concerned is hardly unwarranted. As to the second, he gave the subcommittee the old AT&T monopoly perspective:

A balance has to be reached between the public and private networks. Too much defection to the private networks would disadvantage the majority of the public and small businesses who have to rely on a ubiquitous, state-of-the-art national network. The public network must have sufficient economic as well as technological strength for it to continue to provide leading edge information and communication service capabilities to all subscribers—residential, mobile, small, and large businesses and local, state, and federal governments.

Universal service is still the highest value in some circles. Although it may be somebody's business to worry about all those interests, it should not overhang the development of customized services for today's customers. Chynoweth's Ma Bell philosophy would give everybody what everybody needs, and let those with special needs take a back seat until special services can be offered through the public networks. Clearly this is in the interest of those who own public networks, but who else?

Bellcore has been working on wonderful new video and data services to be delivered through a national optical fiber network. Chynoweth talks of "telesophy," a coinage meaning "wisdom at a distance," in which a remote computer terminal could command retrieval of text and images from a "large" database, "such as the entire Library of Congress." Bellcore developed a new video conference system in an attempt—not entirely successful as yet—to make a participant feel that he's part of a meeting rather than a talking head among other talking heads on screens. Chynoweth warned that such things will not come without a national government policy to unite his fragmented industry.

Another Path

Others, mostly the Bell Companies' competitors, disagree. Dr. Sushil Munshi, vice president of technology planning at United Telecommunications, testified at the same hearing.

"Competition is driving technological change," he declared, giving United Telecom's US Sprint long distance network a pat on the back for providing the spur of competition. "US Sprint has had the unique advantage of designing and constructing its digital fiber-optic network as an integrated whole, incorporating absolutely state-of-the-art technology. . . . Our competitors, playing catch up, are now rushing to duplicate our ability to transport information."

Indeed, US Sprint, which switched over to its fiber-optic network in May 1988, is a shining example of what can be done with $3 billion. The new network has 23,000 route miles and more than 2 billion circuit miles. It connects to virtually every local telephone access area in the country. The system employs digital switches throughout. Circuits run at 1.2 billion bits per second. Its designers say the network capacity can be doubled or even quadrupled by upgrading the laser transmitters and receivers that pulse light down the fiber-optic circuits.

US Sprint also owns Telenet Communications Corp., which uses the new network for its Telenet Public Data Network, a packet switched data network that is the simplest way to gain access to distant information services. Telenet also has engineered more than 130 private data networks for corporate customers. All use the US Sprint system.

The US Sprint network is a great accomplishment, but it presents the company—and its competitors—with a capacity problem. Not only is there too much long distance capacity now, but the long distance carriers are building more fiber-optic lines and each fiber-optic line can increase in capacity as the technology advances. Therefore the goal of US Sprint is to tie as many new customers to the network as possible, especially high volume customers like supercomputer users. Naturally, US Sprint would like this to happen at the lowest possible cost to itself.

"Doubt remains over the near-term viability of the supercomputer networking marketplace," Munshi told the House Telecommunications Subcommittee. "The costs of connecting a research facility to a backbone network are high, requiring expensive on-premises equipment and costly fiber-optic links; for many institutions these costs may be prohibitive. While private industry is willing to absorb or defray some of these costs while developing experimental test-beds, neither US Sprint nor any other carrier can pick up these costs in large scale."

Enter Uncle Sugar: "If, through the development and implementation of the NREN, however, the government spurs demand by assisting research facilities in obtaining the required hardware and fiber-optic links, concerns regarding the market's future will dissipate, and industry will more readily invest the necessary research and technology."

Agreeing, Lucky of Bell Labs put the local phone companies and the long distance companies in perspective: "It is as if we had built superhighways between our cities, but no interchanges, or on-and-off ramps for access. [We also need] a motor vehicle code that tells everybody exactly what kinds of vehicles are allowed and how the roads are to be shared."[4]

David C. Walden, president of BBN Systems and Technologies Corp., a division of Bolt Beranek and Newman, also gave the subcommittee a more balanced picture. BBN was a prime contractor for the ARPANET and has developed large networks for government and private customers since then. The firm has also designed and built custom supercomputers for government clients.

A Graded Network

BBN takes the supercomputing network to the logical extreme. Walden told the legislators that providing large communication capacity to regional supercomputer centers is only a first step, to be followed by extension of the network to every place a user might be found. The minimum service, to homes, should handle high definition television pictures, with higher capacity service to small groups of users in schools and businesses. Large collections of people, in universities and big businesses, should have all the network capacity they need. And of course the network must be capacious enough to carry and route vast flows of information. The final goal Walden set was interoperability—that any individual using any machine on any private network should be able to communicate with anyone else as if they were on the same network.

Worthy goals. How are they to be achieved? Walden had some interesting ideas and warnings:

"The fewer constraints on funding administration the better." By this he did not mean just to throw money at the problem but he said the Congress should try to resist its usual impulse in large projects to send some money to every congressional district. "The proposed funds should be put in the hands of the best technology buyers in the government, people of great intelligence, judgment, and integrity, and these people should select the researchers or institutions with the best track records or the best proposals for research and development."

Walden suggested giving the network job to a cooperative industry association or to a quasi-governmental agency with no other function. Either sort of administrative setup would keep the network open to all—carriers, equipment suppliers, companies with private network, and users. The network agency should try to extend the national network to 10 percent of the households, institutions, and businesses in the country per year. This could not be done, he conceded, by building a network, only by coordinating the telecommunications facilities that are being built.

The development of HDTV, of cable TV, satellite TV, fax machines, personal computers, supercomputers, and intelligent networks must be coordinated so they can all work together, Walden said. "It is most important to do something now. Begin to move the country in the necessary direction. Do not wait for perfect solutions or complete coordination. Launch the sophisticated telecommunications infrastructure and let it evolve."

Going into Business

Lucky, at Bell Labs, had some practical advice about what to do now. On one level, he says, the key issue is pricing. How are you going to get this network built and paid for at a price that will attract users rather than repel them? The answer is that supercomputer users may establish the maximum capacity of the network, but other users must have access, at various prices.

"If the supercomputer user is the only user, then the total cost of the network will be carried by this one class of user." That won't work, because it will be too expensive. "If, on the other hand, a large number of users are able to access and use the high-capacity data highway, the cost of the network will be shared by a large number of users." That won't work either, because the large number of users will crowd out the supercomputer users, just as junk mail crowds the postal system and junk fax clogs the nation's fax machines.

"The ability to commercialize a gigabit network will be enhanced by creating a mass of lower traffic users who would purchase data services from the same highway but with priorities and prices that serve their needs," Lucky concludes, with a plea for government funding of research on this new way to operate a network.

The government, as it happens, is already funding related research. Los Alamos National Laboratory, the largest supercomputing center in the world, has been working on standards for an 800 megabit per second channel specification, compatible with the Open Systems Interconnect, to move high definition computer graphics around from supercomputers to graphic workstations. The biggest hardware challenge of such speeds is to develop switches that run fast enough to support the basic transmission speed. The biggest software challenge is to find ways of checking the data for errors while it's flowing, without slowing down transmission. Also, it's reported that Lawrence Livermore National Laboratory and the Navy antisubmarine warfare program have gigabit networks, but the contractor, Ancor Communications Inc. of Minnetonka, Minn., knows that loose lips sink ships. Any benefit from these military-funded networks will be indirect and may be a long time coming.

There is a dividing point here, between the people who want the federal government to build and operate and pay for a piece of the national infrastructure, like the interstate highway system of the 50s, and the people who want the federal government to set standards and step back out of the way, like the time zones and rail gauge set for the interstate railroad system of the 1880s. We will have to choose, and choose soon.

Section VIII
LIFE AS A NODE

If we choose to construct a national research, education, business, and entertainment network, or if such a network is a viable business, we will have access to immense quantities of data. How will we find it? How will we use it?

23
The Information Universe

Access to Tools

If information is stored in digital form—and within a decade few bits of information will not be stored in digital form—we should be able to get hold of it: computer data files from weather satellites, data files from daytime soap operas, data files from geologic core samples, data files from the cinematheque of films by Jean-Luc Goddard, data files from air pollution measuring stations in the Los Angeles basin, data files from programmers' and chefs' cookbooks, data files from radio astronomy, data files from every weekly business newspaper in the Southeastern United States, data files from everywhere about everything.

It's all zeros and ones, all binary digits. Practically all text being created today, including this book, exists as data files. Many pictures already exist as data files and by the time digital high definition television is widely used all new pictures will exist as data files. Starting in the 60s, most scientific measurements have been stored as data files.

We should be amazed and challenged by this prospect. Stewart Brand, the Whole Earth Catalogue founder who spent a year prowling around MIT's Media Lab, wrote in his book about the Media Lab, "Communication media are not just changing, they're changing into each other, and when they get together, they breed. Since the process self-accelerates and self-branches, there's no reason to expect a new stability any time soon."[1] In Brand's whimsical world view, this is an endorsement. He deplores stability and loves change and challenge for their own sake. More work-a-day people may have trouble with constant change.

Even Brand wonders. He encountered an entirely new problem of veracity when he entered the world of digital images. In a 1985 article for *Whole Earth Review*, he and coauthor Kevin Kelly reported that *National Geographic* had used digital retouching to move one of the Great Pyramids of Egypt so it would fit better on the cover. They found many examples in real-life journalism of image beautification and several examples of image blending. They created one for the *Whole Earth Review* cover—three flying saucers buzzing downtown San Francisco.

MIT engineers developed an "Electronic Darkroom" for Associated Press. SciTex and Hell offer electronic color systems for magazines. These systems scan photographs and slides and create high resolution digital video. Then, manipulating the data that represent the image manipulates the image. It's all HDTV now, and it can be trick photography.

A person who spends any part of his work day searching computer data bases for information will report that learning which data bases hold the information is one of his biggest challenges. Another is learning the search methods each database requires. A third, more subtle, is how to avoid playing in the database, overwhelming oneself by absorbing serendipitous but currently irrelevant information the database turns up. These are parts of a more basic challenge of learning how to recognize relevant information and what to do with information when you obtain it.

These challenges will become ever greater as the amount of data available increases. Space science provides an instructive example: More than 90 percent of the data from NASA earth observing satellites (not counting spy satellites) has been stored away unexamined in computer tape archives, and NASA plans to launch new satellites later in the 90s that will each collect more data in a single year than was stored between 1970 and 1990. The same problem exists with planetary exploration. Most of the pictures from the Voyager spacecraft flying by the outer planets and their moons were examined on the fly, with a few images selected for further study. The rest exist only as computer files. Yet in

August 1990 NASA put a radar surveillance satellite into orbit around the planet Venus that will generate images of that unknown planet for years.

Probably scientists choose the right images to examine, and are entirely justified in following the demands of their budgets not to publish all the other images. But this can only be true for the questions they are asking today. Tomorrow's questions may require yesterday's data. It gets worse: yesterday's data, if reexamined in the light of today's data, might generate tomorrow's questions.

A Mess in the Attic

Data storage presents a physical challenge—whose attic are we going to put this stuff in and how can we be sure that the data storage medium isn't fragile? Hollywood film studios stored movies and outtakes without regard to such questions for years. When old movies became valuable, the film had become brittle, the images had stuck together, the data could be retrieved only after immense labor.

Putting data files in the attic is nearly as bad as throwing them away. Data must be used to be useful. The tape archive occasionally serves its purpose, as when observers noticed that a hole in the ozone layer seemed to be opening over the South Pole. After extreme effort, the right tape files of satellite data were found in their archives, mounted on the right kind of tape drive (hard to find years later), and the hole in the ozone layer proved to be an expanding problem that had been going on for years.

Storage technology is advancing about as fast as our ability to gather data. Magnetic tapes have given way to magnetic disks, which are giving way to optical disks. Each generation allows greater storage density and allows quicker access to randomly selected bits of data than the previous generation. Music lovers know this from experience: finding a particular song on a tape cassette requires running through the whole cassette until that song is found. Even at fast forward, this is annoyingly slow, and to find the actual passage of music, one must play the tape at near normal speed. Finding a particular song on a phonograph disk is merely a matter of reading the label, counting the bands, and dropping the needle in the right place. And on a compact disk player, one punches the track number and the computer does the rest.

Unfortunately, our use of mechanical data storage technology such as tapes and disks is only just barely keeping up with the production of data. There's no time and no money for going back and putting all the old tape files on optical disks, to say nothing of books, scientific journals, and photographs. With enough staff and budget, though, the Library of Congress—books, pictures, magazines, journals, film, videotape, everything—could be reduced to a collection of compact disks mounted in a giant juke box that would fit in the average elementary school library. And those disks could be easily reproduced so that every school could be the equivalent of the national repository of information. Today the Library of Congress, tomorrow the libraries of the world.

It can be done. Gradually it will be done. It could be done soon if we agree that the government should take the next 10 years to digitize every bit of information in the United States. Using translatable formats that would not foreclose access to the information when the next data storage technology replaces the optical disk, the job might be done in time to put the knowledge of the world on the network.

And even if putting yesterday's information into computer-retrievable form is a huge job, it becomes less important to all but historians the longer we keep storing current information. Current information is overwhelming enough.

Managing Information

While information storage is becoming cheap, classification is still very expensive. Making use of data presents a management challenge far bigger than the mere physical storage of data. Before we even can ask where the data is that we want, we must ask what we want to know.

There are tales about the Princes of Serendip, who went on exploratory voyages, seeking wildly improbable things. They never came back with what they sought, but with far better things they had never imagined, and thus could never search for. And that is how serendipity—the acquisition of useful knowledge by accident—got its name. Network users may face a more difficult problem: the employment of knowledge in a useful way.

W. Russell Neuman of MIT's Media Lab has a view of a data and communications network.

> We are all familiar with the primitive forms of telephone transactions for the residential customer. We see a product advertised on late-night television and order it by phone with a credit card, or perhaps order an item from a direct-mail catalogue by touch-tone phone. Sometimes it proves to be convenient and productive. Sometimes not. The irony of these primitive versions of transactional services is that they carry with them all of the limiting and negative features of the advertising-based mass media, that is, all the information at hand is supplied by the seller. One sees the advertising stimulus and has only the options to resist or respond. What intelligent, two-way systems permit is the instantaneous inquiry of other information resources by the consumer while the transaction is in progress. Is the firm reliable? Is the product well-designed? Is it offered elsewhere at a lower price?
>
> Imagine that a new washing machine is needed. You may have the good intentions of going down to the library to look up washing machines in *Consumer Reports* or asking neighbors about what brands are reliable, but who has the time? So you end up at Sears again buying what an 'expert' salesman tells you you need.
>
> Imagine instead the user of an advanced transactional network. You indicate to the system what qualities you are looking for in features, reliability, and price for your new washing machine. Independent information providers, not a salesman in a toupee, provide all the information from independent testing and evaluation. Will the new machine fit in that tiny space in the laundry room? Will it be necessary for you to crawl around on your hands and knees with a tape measure? No, you identify the old model you had, and the data base informs you that the new one will fit in the same space.
>
> Then you remember that you would prefer to purchase an appliance that is American designed and manufactured rather than imported or just assembled in this country. Given this new information, the system suggests a few new options. You make your choice. Where can you get it? The system tells you that this model is available at several local outlets, the price at each, how many are in stock, how

far each store is from your home, and that the road is under construction near one particular store. You may order your new appliance
delivered or take a look for yourself at the most convenient retail outlet.[2]

Whew! Do you get the feeling that something is missing in this
picture? Who taught this consumer—who doesn't have the time
to check *Consumer Reports*—how to interrogate a couple of dozen
different databases, extracting information like prices and inventory that many retailers do not divulge to anyone who is not actually in the store waving cash or a credit card. If the consumer had
to accomplish all this at a PC keyboard, it would give a new meaning to the Yellow Pages ad phrase "Let your fingers do the walk-
ing." Even though a home computing and communications terminal that would take verbal instruction is probably not far off, there
is an immense amount of computing power and artificial intelligence implicit in Neuman's vision.

Another such vision, whistled up by Apple Computer Chairman John Sculley, is even more overwhelming in its assumption
of computing power. In a promotional video called "Knowledge
Navigator," produced to accompany a speech Sculley gave in late
1987, we meet a university professor of the early 21st century and
we watch him manage a slice of his day using a piece of equipment about the size of a notebook. When he unfolds it and plugs
it in, the notebook proves to be a high-resolution display screen.
He talks to it, of course, ordering up odd statistical displays such
as a map illustrating the distribution of rainfall in the Amazon
forest. And it talks to him. A talking head named Phil—the
Knowledge Navigator—occupies one window in the corner of
the large display, offering him suggestions about other possible
displays, reminding him of the names of other experts in the
field, interrupting him with news bulletins, fielding calls from his
mother, serving up a voicemail report from an overseas research
team, reporting on the results of the routine calls it has made for
him.

Phil "lives" in a machine that is connected to computers and
databases around the world. As an artificial intelligence, he represents who knows how many gigaflops of computing power and
terabytes (thousands of gigabytes) of computer memory, located
in the professor's notebook and in the national data and commu-

nications network. Can Phil be made real? We know that gig-aflops and terabytes on microchips are getting cheaper. Once installed in the network, programmers will gain access to and take advantage of all the computing power they can. Artificial intelligence, once the zone of sophisticated programmers seeking rather unsuccessfully to mimic the processes of the human brain, is becoming the province of superfast computing. And a superfast computer network will bring artificial intelligence to every node on the network.

The Rest of the Day

Neuman's supercharged consumer and Apple's professor with the Knowledge Navigator are two visions of a new life, as a node on a computer network. But when we look at these visions, we are amazed only by what we see. We should be trying to imagine what we don't see: What are these folks doing with the time and brainpower their machine is saving them?

The last time you bought a major appliance, the task easily consumed more than one evening after work, or a good chunk of a precious weekend day. If you have an office job, handling routine but unique tasks such as scheduling your meetings and documenting things you already know, probably consumes more of your time than you'd like to admit. Neuman's consumer buys his washing machine in less time than it takes you to pick a cable TV channel. Apple's professor studies his lecture topic, arranges a guest lecturer, settles his administrative affairs, and has his computer brush off his mother in less time than it would have taken you just to check your phone messages.

The early 20th century round of labor-saving devices moved about half the population of the United States off the farm and into the city. The post–World War II round of labor-saving devices moved about half the nation's mothers out of the kitchen and into the work force. Whom will we move where with the next round of labor-saving devices?

We know information workers have less and less reason for being clustered in an office. Most of their work is done on a telephone or a personal computer, and most of the rest, such as opening the mail, is either unnecessary or could be done anywhere. People stay in the office, however, to schmooze and exchange off-the-record comments or to attend meetings. Or people are made to stay in the office so that supervisors can be sure they are working. A computing and communications network, particularly one in which each terminal has a Knowledge Navigator, could eliminate these reasons.

Workers can gather around terminals that can compute and communicate in several different ways at once while reading the mail and attending a meeting. Just imagine using a Nexis/Lexis terminal for your research while Cable News Network is on a muted TV in the corner, and you talk on the phone to your buddy or your boss and wait for your computer to recalculate some monster spreadsheet. Put it all on the same high definition display fed by a fiber-optic cable and you can have 4 or 24 hours of hell at home, instead of 8 or 12 hours of high stress interleaved with boredom at the office.

As for the workers whose presence is required for the sake of discipline, many are already monitored electronically rather than visually. Workers in word processing centers use terminals that report the number of keystrokes they make per hour. Telephone sales people use terminals that report the number and duration of calls they make. On a broadband high speed digital network, your terminal could be your supervisor, as well as your friend, your television, your research assistant, your computer, your secretary, your playing field, your opponent, your newspaper, your colleague, your checkbook, your errand boy, and your telephone.

Life as a Node

Your terminal could become your life. And it could be exciting. The late Ithiel de Sola Pool was an enthusiast:

> The technologies used for self-expression, human intercourse, and recording of knowledge are in an unprecedented flux. A panoply of electronic devices puts at everyone's hand capacities far beyond anything that the printing press could offer. Machines that think, that bring great libraries into anybody's study, that allow discourse among persons half a world apart, are expanders of human culture. They allow people to do anything that could be done with communication tools of the past, and many more things too.[3]

Now, what do we do with the communication tools of today?

Passive couch potatoes merely view life—news and entertainment—going by on a TV screen. The denizens of Plato's cave could not be sure that the flickering images they saw were true representations of reality. Couch potatoes neither know nor care whether the images they view reflect reality.

Life as a node, in, of, or at a terminal connected by a network to vast quantities of data, offers an infinitely varied passive experience. And more: life as a node may also appeal to active spirits because they would participate in, and shape, "virtual reality." (Virtual is computerese for "substitute indistinguishable from the real thing.")

At a price of several million dollars, virtual reality is available today. Pilots train on flight simulators whose differences from reality can be ignored. Judging from heart rates and war stories, a crash in some flight simulators feels like real death.

At home, virtual reality began with Flight Simulator, the inexpensive PC program. It has moved up a notch to Mattel's Power Glove for Nintendo karate and boxing games. Instead of pushing a joy stick around, the player points his fingers and moves his hand to control the game. Strain gauges inside the glove register finger positions; the whole glove emits ultrasonic clicks received by three sensors on the monitor so the glove computer can triangulate on the position of the player's hand. Computer-aided designers, who need some kind of three-dimensional pencil, can move up from the $100 Power Glove to an $8,000 Data Glove, which reads disruptions in a magnetic field it generates, or a $15,000 Dextrous Hand Master, an electronic exo-skeleton that adds precision to the Data Glove technology.[4]

From the power glove to a broadband body suit is a matter of programming and tailoring and money. Spending enough of each should make it possible for a computer to take all its instructions from body movements instead of from crude interfaces like keyboards, joysticks, and mice. The maker of the DataGlove, VPL Research of Redwood City, California, is at work on a DataSuit intended to be an input device for computer animation.

As for output, VPL also offers goggles with video screens. The left eye receives an image and the right eye receives an offset image, so that the brain is fooled into perceiving the image in three dimensions. It's merely a digital, visual version of stereo headphones or of the 3-D movies popular in the 50s that sent the left eye an image through a red filter and the right eye an offset image through a blue filter. The goggles from VPL, however, also shift the image according to movements of the user's head, creating the illusion of a shifting field of vision.[5]

What does all this do for us? One possibility is that it gives us a $500,000 mechanized acid trip. Indeed, Jaron Lanier, a founder of VPL, told a *Wall Street Journal* reporter that he expects to see a movement to ban the technology. Lanier also said he expects to revolutionize pornography.[6]

Timothy Leary apparently did not burn out entirely during the acid years. He has resurfaced in Los Angeles as a futurist, computer evangelist, and consultant (his company is called Futique), expecting the computer to provide new altered states of mind. He predicts that sales of entertainment hardware and software will become far bigger business than sales of computer gear to business.

"Most digital engineers and most managers of the computer industry are not aware that we live in a cyberculture surrounded by limitless deposits of information which can be digitized and tapped by the individual equipped with cybergear," Leary proclaimed in an interview with David Sheff.[7]

Leary has been overdosing on the science fiction novels of William Gibson, in which data cowboys roam the virtual range of cyberspace. They experience data as metaphorically physical structures, mining it, blowing it up, being crushed by it. The books are good science fiction, though a poor guide to virtual reality.

"In the cyber world, you'll be having competitions, love affairs, exchanges, chess matches, debates, research projects; you'll be skiing down whatever mountain with all these wonderful people and everybody will be communicating with a global language of icons. Literacy will be as quaint as baby talk."

Leary actually hasn't been reading enough science fiction. Authors have been exploring more effective interfaces with the computer for a long time. Jerry Pournelle equipped his business executives and secret agents with an implanted device like a two-way hearing aid. The user whispered to herself and the computer replied with all the data she needed to pull off a business coup. Samuel R. Delany imagined a space ship with a crew plugged into the controls by nerve implants.

If these are worth imagining, why not go for the optic nerve— even the pleasure center of the brain? Larry Niven had a series of characters become addicted to direct electric stimulation of the brain. That seems too unfocused for real life, even though we know it works on laboratory rats, but imagine something that directly stimulates the pleasure center and shows you programs and allows you to communicate. That could bring new meaning to the term "couch potato." Will we need nursing homes for people to experience the plug-in life style?

Leary is optimistic, but he was optimistic about LSD. He thinks:

> Producers are not going to flood passive viewers with finished products. This is very important. Each individual will be intercommunicating with the entire universe of data, funneled through our comlinks with each other. There will be input from as many sources and as many people as he wants. He'll scramble and chop it up and use a bit of it or nothing and he'll share it with his friends. The 14-year-old kid in San Francisco will have five flirtatious love affairs going simultaneously—with a beautiful actress in Berlin, some girl in Brazil, virtual love affairs, virtual friendships, virtual competitions.

Leary is still Leary. A better bet is that life won't change very much for most of us, although there will be some people who zonk all the way into virtual life.

Right now there are lots of people coming as close as they can with keyboards and screens—you can meet them on any computer bulletin board. People who want to argue about politics without destroying friendships, who want to congregate without closeness, number in the millions and bulletin boards are made for them. They construct personalities and experiment with social interaction. This includes the virtual love affairs—people talk dirty to each other on Compuserve, possibly with more enthusiasm than they do calling a telephone sex line.

Hypertext

Virtual reality may be the preferred state for some, but there will still be many who are appalled rather than thrilled by Leary's prediction that literacy will be as quaint as baby talk. They will need some other, more literate, means to apprehend vast stores of data.

A candidate is "hypertext," a concept that goes back 50 years and is no less bewildering today. Hypertext—the term was coined in 1964 by computer evangelist Ted Nelson—is nonlinear writing, in which every idea is linked in many directions. You read along on a computer and you can pursue what interests you and then come back and move on. If this were a hypertext, you would be able to retrieve a full biography of Ted Nelson, read articles by him, get a definition of evangelist and an explanation of the non-religious, ironic usage here, and, of course, explore the term hypertext, simply by highlighting the words of interest and pushing the right command key.

Nelson says of it simply that "Everyone needs it in every field for everything."[8] It would help if it existed. Nelson says it will be in a perfectly automated form that would create the links from a given word in the text to every other text in the world, then slim down the number of choices to a manageable excellent dozen or so. Automated hypertext, in other words, would be like a wonderful librarian, who helps the perplexed student find just the right chapter in just the right book for his grade level. Automated hypertext would be a true "knowledge navigator."

The simplest example of hypertext is contextual help, which in some computer programs provides an appropriate screen of advice from many possible screens, depending on the operations and data the user has on the screen at the moment. A spreadsheet user who presses the help key when about to enter a formula should get a screen reminding him how formulas work.

Contemporary hypertext is found at Apple Computer, which packages Hypercard with every Macintosh computer. This program combines the simplicity of a 3 × 5 cardfile with the multi-level connectivity of a computer database and it seems to have acquired a fanatical following. But judging from articles written about hypertext in regular linear media, it has to be experienced to be appreciated.[9]

With luck, hypertext will mature at the same time that the national information network expands. We will need something to cope with all that information.

24

How America Can Win the Technology Race

There is no shortage of advice on technology policy. What all the policy mavens need is an editor. The advice in this chapter has been culled and edited from many sources. Ingredients are harvested from the well-simmered stew of government, the quick-thinking competitiveness of private industry, and the wide-ranging improbabilities of academia.

Sources are diverse and duplicative. Most of these ideas, in fact, have several sources. Some may not appreciate their ideas being found in the company of other ideas on this list, but anonymity of original source should soften such blows.

Reform Education

Education is one of those things, like baseball and cars, on which everyone is an expert. American education has produced generational waves of protest and reform since the founding of the Republic. Since the mid-80s, we have been going through a paroxysm of concern. We create commissions which survey the scene, recoil in horror, and urge the creation of more commissions.

"More and more young people emerge from high school ready neither for college nor for work. This predicament becomes more acute as the knowledge base continues its rapid expansion, the number of traditional jobs shrinks, and new jobs demand greater sophistication and precision." This 1983 summary from the National Commission of Excellence in Education[1] is still widely quoted despite an unemployment rate that shrunk in succeeding years.

There is one advantage of the American educational system compared to that of other countries that is usually overlooked: it is open and easy to reenter. It is true that the high school dropout rate is unreasonably high. And it is true that too many who finish high school are not educated, not even literate. And it is true that vocational schools and technical high schools are often warehouses for discipline problems and usually fail to prepare students for a trade. But when the system fails these students, or when the students fail the system, they are not lost forever. Remedial education is available with government financial support in the public school system, in private trade schools, in local community colleges, in state universities, in the military, in private industry—wherever motivated students seek it. As many as half the dropouts eventually attain at least the equivalent of a high school education.[2]

Instead of concentrating solely on public schools to solve the problem that companies have hiring accurate, well-spoken clerical workers straight out of high school, educational reformers ought also to redouble the national effort to present opportunities for advancement to people in dead-end jobs. There is no incentive to education stronger than a few years at the bottom of the economic ladder.

We also must recognize that good students are as important as those who are failing. Requiring unmotivated, hopeless, and helpless students to stay in crippled schools where they ruin the chance of others to be educated is self-defeating. Disruptive students need to be bounced out of mainstream classes as soon as they present a problem, so that those students who are not problems can have the opportunities they are trying to earn. If that leaves only a few students in mainstream schools, so much the better for them. Currently, we use geography for this purpose, callously setting some school districts apart as asylums for the ineducable. Parents unfortunate enough to live in such districts while actually caring about education are supposed to care enough to send their children to private school or move. We can do better than this frivolous system.

The 80s also saw a rising concern about American higher education. Even the best measure of the excellence of American education—the high demand for an American education shown by foreign students—has been taken as a sign of a problem. The

number of Ph.D. degrees awarded to foreigners is rising rapidly
and the National Research Council reports that since 1983, more
foreigners than Americans receive American doctorates in engineering each year. One third of doctorates in physical sciences go
to foreigners.[3] As for Americans, 18 percent of high school sopho-
mores indicate an interest in a career in natural sciences or engineering. Then 8.5 percent actually earn bachelor's degrees in
these subjects; 1.5 percent go on to graduate school; 1.1 percent
earn master's degrees and 0.2 percent earn Ph.D.s.[4]

There have been proposals to provide incentives for Americans
to study science and engineering, including efforts to find candi-
dates for engineering courses among women and minorities.
Making such proposals is a major sideline of the National Science
Foundation, the American Association for the Advancement of
Science, the Institute of Electrical and Electronic Engineers, and
similar professional organizations. But there are two all-too-sim-
ple reasons for the low interest in science and engineering.

The first is that these subjects are simply harder than liberal
arts subjects. A fascinating debate raged in the letters column of
the Proceedings of the Naval Institute in 1990 on the relative importance of engineering and humanities in the curriculum of the
U.S. Naval Academy.

"Every technical problem has a discrete, derivable answer,"
wrote Lt. Jeffrey E. McFadden in a prize essay. "But to master the
fine art of leadership, one must learn to operate in the 'grey
areas,' a skill rarely called for in technical problem solving." More
mature officers scolded McFadden for thinking of leadership as
something that comes out of a political science class or a book.
Then Midshipman Second Class Brett Howe let the cat out of the
bag: that the classes of 1987 through 1989 had graduated more
officers with humanities degrees than with engineering degrees.
He explained: "It is not unusual to see a midshipman switch from
mechanical engineering because his grades are unsatisfactory and
go into political science where he can earn higher grades. . . .
Although everyone is required to take certain technical courses,
nontechnical majors take watered-down classes. The diluted
courses allow for only the most rudimentary technical background. Also, nontechnical majors are notorious for doing worse
in their required technical courses."

The U.S. Naval Academy has a long engineering tradition. It

was a serious departure some years ago to allow nontechnical majors at all, and it was a change justified by the inability of the school to recruit excellent students.

That points to the second reason why so few students choose technical courses of study: science and engineering careers do not usually lead to the top, unless the technical person starts at the top by founding his own company. Scientists and engineers are not the highest paid workers, nor do they usually win promotion to executive ranks, even in companies that are dependent on their talents. Auto companies, computer companies, and most large industrial firms that were founded by engineers are now operated by managers who were humanities majors as undergraduates and went on to law school or business school.

Any technologist who can grasp the principles of the labor market should ask himself why this is so. He might also ask why so many technologically excellent companies in the United States have failed because of poor management, and why, in those that survive, so many technical founders have had to cede power to professional managers.

If the United States is running short of engineers and scientists, there may be something wrong with the way American companies use them. Or the country may actually have enough technologists. These two possibilities can explain why the rewards of a technical education do not seem to repay the effort necessary to acquire one.

In any case, there are simple solutions to the supply of technical graduates.

The low-cost solution is the one we are using now in a limited way: import them. Rewarding foreign recipients of U.S. science and engineering degrees with a sheepskin *and U.S. citizenship* would alleviate any shortage. The value of our economic and social liberty can be paid without cost to those who lack it.

A higher cost solution would be to offer 10,000 American students free-ride scholarships to science and engineering schools without regard to financial need, based only on grades and achievement tests. The cost would be less than a billion dollars, and would stir many parents to take more of an interest in their children's course of education. A similar system has produced highly motivated football and basketball players and should work for technically minded students as well.

The highest cost solution is the drastic overhaul of the elementary and secondary system that is so dear to the heart of every educational reformer. As many as 80 percent of American students receive so little effective science and math education that they are unlikely to be eligible for a technical college education. This will require money, large quantities of money spent on teachers' salaries to attract highly qualified new teachers, to motivate well-qualified teachers who find attractive offers outside the profession, to buy off organized objections to firing unqualified teachers, and to purchase teachers' services for a longer school year. Some of this money may be recaptured from administrative bureaucracies, but most of it will have to come from taxpayers. Many states have been making what seem to them to be large and expensive efforts to improve their school systems; much more will be required.

Adopt the Metric System

Burma, Liberia, and the United States have not adopted the metric system. All three countries thus operate under a handicap in competing in world markets, and the residents of all three countries have an equivalent problem using some products from abroad.

The United States began a changeover with most of the rest of the English-speaking world in the early 60s, but it stalled for two reasons.

One reason was, of course, that humans hate to change habits of thinking. Our system of government is extremely responsive to people who don't want to change, so Congress simply refused to put up the money or make the rules that would have finished the job.

The other reason was that the American market was such a large part of the world market, and the American production system such a large part of world output, that the United States economy simply did not have to obey the rules that were set for everybody else. Even our experience in the 60s and 70s with attempting to manage the dollar to our benefit (inflating the supply of dollars while expecting all other nations to continue to accept it as good as gold) did not disabuse us of the idea that the United States is an economic fortress.

Changing over to the metric system—for real this time—could improve our thinking as well as the competitive status of some of our manufacturing companies. The change should be presented to the American people as a necessary part of "winning the technology race of the 90s." If that teaches the American people that the United States is part of a world economic system, it will be a lesson more important than the conversion tables.

Simplify the Tax Code

The U.S. tax code is a monument to the concept of social engineering—a paper monument with the rigidity and mass of a monument made of granite. If a majority of congressmen once believed that some activity was deserving of help, chances are that activity enjoys a tax preference. As fashions in policy have changed, virtually every economic activity has qualified. Conservatives and liberals alike have succumbed to the temptation to use the tax code to create a great society, or an opportunity society.

Simplicity would work wonders. Instead of trying to create tax breaks, Congress should concentrate on lowering all taxes. Collecting taxes evenly, from butchers and computer programmers and day care workers and carpenters and drug companies and lawyers, would allow people to make more sensible economic choices. And, as anyone who watched the tax reform debate of 1985 and 1986—and the budget summit fiasco of 1990—ought to know, far too many citizens distrust the tax system because it is so unequally applied.

Spokesmen for high-tech industries have led the way in complaining that the cost of capital in the United States is too high. They have sought tax breaks for capital investment. Indeed, U.S. interest rates after inflation were among the highest in the industrialized world during the 80s. But the high price of capital also brought high returns to capital investment in the United States.

Fix the FISC

U.S. macroeconomic policy is much debated, but in the wrong terms. Our leaders bicker over what spending, borrowing, taxing, and money-creating policies will best tune the economy for prosperity. These policies are beyond our power. Bad luck, as much as anything, produced the stagflation of the 70s, while the policies that were designed to overcome it lacked power. Good luck, as much as anything, produced the low inflation and steady growth of the 80s, while the policies that economists believed should have wrecked the economy lacked power.

Instead of trying to overcome oil shocks or promote investment, we should devise a fiscal policy that allows for rapid adjustment to change. In general, this would be a policy that sustains the value of the dollar, allows prices and interest rates to move rapidly up and down in response to new developments, and renounces the practice of building in economic incentives and punishments. In particular, this would be a pay-as-you-go fiscal policy and a monetary policy that stresses inflation-fighting.

Invest Wisely

Government, business, and individuals have to live in the future they build. Investment in productive capacity is the way we build a future. Government invests in national defense and the social safety net; business invests in equipment and technology; individuals invest in their own productivity. All these functions overlap, of course, and much of economic life consists of capturing the maximum benefits from one's investments.

Investment is leaky—all the benefits never stay with the person or institution making the investment. A government social program paid for by all only benefits those who need it; business discoveries can be adapted and exploited by other companies that did not invest in the original ground-breaking research; the increased ability to produce that a person with special education acquires must be shared in a corporation or institution to produce the maximum economic return.

If the total returns to investment are greater than the individual returns, then the officials, executives, and individuals deciding on investments will pass up some that would benefit society as a whole. What can we do about that?

The usual answer is that government should provide investment incentives, and there we go down the whole slippery slope of messing about in the economy all over again. There is another answer: straightforward subsidy, otherwise known as charity.

We can perform our charity directly and democratically, by giving to those causes that call to us most powerfully. Or we can perform our charity indirectly, by paying taxes our elected representatives use to finance causes that call to us collectively. Either way, we should try to remember that charity can and should be an economically efficient allocation of resources, a means of overcoming the shortfall of investment.

A society whose members choose to invest, individually or collectively, an extra 10 percent of their wealth or their effort, should find more than adequate total returns to that investment.

The National Research and Education Network may be an example of a charitable investment, ranking with contributions to college scholarship funds, purchase of environmentally sensitive wetlands, and contributing to a church or a candidate for office. It stands at least as good a chance of producing a direct financial return to the contributor in his lifetime.

Promote Competition

Antitrust heads the list of regulatory reform on many a lobbyist's policy menu. In the 80s, Congress took a great deal of this advice, carving out safe harbors from the antitrust laws for joint ventures and collaborations in research. As the 90s opened, many companies, particularly in the high-tech industries, were back in seeking antitrust exemptions for joint ventures in manufacturing. "Courts would be required to balance a venture's procompetitive benefits against its possible anticompetitive effects," said the congressional Democrats' High Technology Agenda in the summer of 1990. Other proposals simply allow U.S. firms to band together to attempt to reach economies of scale that would allow them to compete successfully with imports. U.S. Memories was to be a sort of pilot program for an American manufacturing consortium.

If competition means anything, it means risk. The U.S. government should steer clear of antitrust changes that enhance the security of American firms from the threat of foreign competition. Accepting risk carries the possibility of large rewards, and the shareholders of a foreign company that accepts the risk of developing a U.S. market should receive those rewards.

A more useful antitrust change may be to subject joint ventures of U.S. and foreign companies to the same sort of regulatory skepticism that domestic joint ventures and mergers receive. The question of whether the business combination would dominate a national or regional market should not be ignored if one partner is from out of the country.

Product liability is a regulatory area that has received little attention in the arena of international competitiveness, but our national sport of civil litigation is draining our economic strength. States and the federal court system need to find ways to limit awards to true damages, leaving punitive damages to criminal actions. Standards of liability need to be changed so that only true responsibility brings civil liability. And we need a method for consumers to undertake an informed, binding waiver of their right to sue. Nobody who buys a light plane, for example, should do so without understanding the risks of private flight. And the purchaser having understood those risks, no purchaser's survivors should be allowed to sue the manufacturer of the airplane because it crashed.

Open Trade

There is no such thing as a level playing field in international trade. In trading any product, there are always advantages on one side or the other. Problems immediately arise in what to do about this. Those who require fairness eventually will try to close their markets. If there will always be advantages, they will not always be ours. It is the mark of an ignoramus or a cynic to call for fair trade or a level playing field.

Those who want to manage trade say that unfairness can be overcome by a simple business deal: if you open your market, we won't close ours. "Do you want free trade or more trade?" asks Clyde Prestowitz, a former Commerce Department trade negotiator who now runs his own think tank in Washington.[5]

Those who are interested in the best goods at the lowest prices offer the classical analysis of Adam Smith and David Ricardo: Free trade adds to the wealth of the country that embraces it, even if its trading partners do not. This is economically obvious and yet politically unacceptable. The most common reply is, "Yes, but . . . "

If imported microchips are higher quality or lower priced, the computer companies that buy them will have an advantage when they turn around to sell their computers in competition with manufacturers who bought in the domestic market. Yes, but what about the domestic chip companies that could not compete? Yes, but what about the foreign computer companies who will also have an advantage? Yes, but what about all the other industries up and down the electronic food chain that will also be competed out of existence? Yes, but what about the high prices our companies will have to pay when the last domestic producer is driven out of business?

The domestic chip companies that could not compete will have to find new, more profitable niches, or the capital and labor that they can no longer support will go back out into the market and find more profitable employment.

The foreign computer companies may repeat the process, and again it may happen up and down the food chain until something in the domestic system responds to the stimulus.

The high prices that are said to be on the way never seem to arrive, because prices are determined more by consumer demand than by suppliers' fiat. Conspiracies to fix prices create their own incentive for participants to discount or for new entrants to compete.

The country, like Japan, that closes its market to imports suffers in consequence. Japanese tourists receive an object lesson each time they visit Hawaii or Hong Kong and see lower prices not only for foreign goods but for goods made *in their own country*. Bill Emmott, former Tokyo bureau chief for *The Economist*, notes in his book, *The Sun Also Sets*, that Japanese retailers are also getting the message, "beginning to dodge Japan's costly and inefficient distribution system by buying abroad directly."[6]

When the advantage of imports seems to be caused by subsidies, targeting, and industrial development policies in the exporting nation, we should consider this to be a transfer of the exporting nation's wealth from their pockets to ours. Such policies manifest weakness: other industries and taxpayers in the exporting countries are being robbed to support the export industry.

Just because Japan has enjoyed economic growth while supporting export industries is no reason to conclude that supporting those industries caused Japan's economic growth. France, Germany, and other nations of the European community provide a more telling object lesson. There the tangle of export subsidies has become a political and economic noose that threatens to suffocate healthy industries along with the sick ones.

Redefine Business Identity

Firms are important to Americans if they employ Americans, sell to Americans, compete with Americans, attract investment from Americans, or invest in American enterprises. Their country of incorporation is not particularly relevant and we should not treat firms arriving to operate in the United States any differently than we treat firms born in the U.S.A. They should follow the same regulations and disciplines; they should enjoy the same freedoms. The sole question should be: Would we treat a firm from the other side of the United States this way? If a Massachusetts company took over an Indiana television manufacturing operation, we would ask only if the takeover created a near-monopoly and the potential for abuse of market power. We should continue to ask only that, and not demand to see the buyer's passport.

A line of economists stretching back to Ricardo and Smith and forward to Robert Reich in 1990 have concluded that this is a policy prescription that enriches the nation that follows it. That Japan does not follow it should not lead us to the conclusion that we should retaliate by harming ourselves. The U.S. government's efforts to open the Japanese market have been attempts to improve the sales of American corporations, but they have done more to improve the lives of Japanese consumers, who enjoy access to cheaper beef, cigarettes, fruit, and many other products. When negotiations fail, when Japan or some other country refuses to open its market, we only harm our own consumers by raising our own barriers to Japanese chips and cars, or European steel and sugar. We even hurt our born-in-the-U.S.A. companies by depriving them of the toughest competition they need to thrive.

Jettison the FCC

The Federal Communications Commission regulates the form and the content of U.S. electronic communications. It is a great success—at holding back the development of technology, at forming cartels of economic and political power, and at restricting expression.

The FCC's rule over content has always been questionable. The First Amendment guarantees of freedom of speech and freedom of the press obviously cover speech and expression carried by electrons as well as by ink. Nevertheless, the FCC forbids obscenity, regulates the number and kind of commercials that may be broadcast, limits the amount of network programming that may be broadcast in prime time, sets aside channels for non-profit operation, promotes diversity in programming, decides who may produce and own shows, and promotes station owner-ship by minorities. Ultimately the FCC decides who will be al-lowed to broadcast and what they will say, using what technolo-gies, for what purpose. That the FCC has not abused these powers much speaks well for American liberty but should not reassure us that the powers should be so concentrated.

All of these powers that the FCC has assumed are produced by one seemingly necessary power to allocate scarce room on the radio spectrum. The FCC is first of all a traffic cop assigned to be sure that radio stations don't interfere with one another. Two sta-tions broadcasting on the same frequency ensure that neither one can be heard. The FCC therefore reviews electronic devices to avoid interference. It sets rules for the positioning of transmitters. Most importantly, it assigns frequencies and sets rules for their use.

In a political attempt to be fair, the FCC tried to be nice about awarding frequencies. Some bands were set aside for amateur ra-dio stations, some for radio telephones, some for police, fire, ma-rine, aviation, pagers. The allocations were set up before World War II and leave little room for adjustment. To put a new technol-ogy like cellular telephones on the air required years of deep thought and experimentation. And the allocation system left some users, notably commercial radio and television broadcast-ers, with too few channels to accommodate all who would like to broadcast. Naturally, the FCC then decided which broadcasters to license. Trying to pick an assortment that will serve the public interest, it fell into politics.

The sorry tale of FCC frequency and licensing, however, is most frustrating because it always was unnecessary. Allocating the electromagnetic spectrum could have been left to anarchy or to auction.

The government could have turned its back on radio broadcast-ing and let the owners of transmitters work out their own eco-nomic arrangements. As A. J. Liebling said, freedom of the press belongs to anyone who owns one. The rough justice of radio—that when two stations interfere neither one can be heard, might well have provided enough incentive for broadcasters to make their own rules.

No government in the world, however, has that much faith in its citizens. The rule of the FCC was uncommonly loose: most countries considered radio too powerful to be put in private hands at all. Still, the U.S. government could have avoided any rule over content by auctioning off broadcast channels every few years rather than licensing permanent ownership during good behavior. We could do it tomorrow, and we should.

We can expect that the government would retain some choice channels for itself, and for nonprofit or low-profit uses that seem good to the officials of the moment. We won't get rid of that sort of thing in any republic except Plato's, nor should we want to. Political patronage is a sort of market too, trading in a different sort of coin and providing an outlet for those who have no economic market power. But auctioning use of most of the radio spectrum would make it possible to change use of the radio spectrum much more quickly. New technology and new ideas compete successfully for capital in an auction market; the same idea would work for other scarce resources.

Terrestrial radio transmission eventually should become the province of short-range personal communication—cellular telephones and whatever similar technologies may follow. The geostationary orbit is a more convenient location for the mass media's broadcast transmitters; interactive high speed information networks require so much capacity that they are better suited to fiber-optic cable.

Open up the Wires

Since the mid-80s, new cable television systems have offered at least 60 channels and many operators strung double wires to provide 120 channels.

Satellite broadcasting, now employed to distribute national networks to local cable operators and backyard dish antennas, will take the next step in the mid-90s with direct broadcasting to small antennas in homes. New satellite networks may bring another 120 channels to anyone who wants them.

Telephone companies would like to join the fray. Stringing fiber-optic cable to new homes is almost as cheap today as stringing copper wire, and the only thing that the telephone company can sell to the home is a telephone connection for voice or data. Fiber-optic cables, however, could add another 120 video channels in direct competition with cable television and satellite broadcasting.

Telephone companies currently are barred from the entertainment and information businesses by the rules governing the breakup of the AT&T monopoly. The cable TV and the newspaper industry have combined to keep the phone companies down and out of competition.

During the 90s it will become obvious that there is no longer any such thing as scarcity in the electronic media and no longer any chance of monopoly power. Just as network television broadcasting lost its monopoly, so cable television will not be the only high-capacity pathway to American homes. Satellites and fiberoptic telephone cables can provide nearly infinite capacity. There will be room enough for mass media distributed from a single source to many receivers, and for switched media, distributed from many points to many receivers.

The government could hasten that day by removing the shackles it has placed on the telephone companies. In the process, we would discover that much of the national high-speed computer network can be built on a sound business basis.

Let Standards Develop Naturally

Technical standards are a blessing and a curse. Once set, a standard should allow many manufacturers to follow the same specifications so that their products can operate together. This promotes competition, driving down prices and enhancing the importance of service and reliability. The other side of the coin is that standards freeze technology. A leap forward in performance may require abandoning the old incompatible standard. If we want high definition television, we will have to buy new TV sets.

Occasionally a single manufacturer sets and successfully defends a proprietary standard for some product that is so popular that potential competitors cannot successfully enter the market. But this happens less frequently and does less damage than many people appreciate. IBM's model 360 set such a standard for hardware and software. Intel's original microcomputer for the IBM PC set another. But in the rapidly changing world of computer technology, a barrier to entry often becomes a barrier to progress. IBM customers were so wedded to the 360 architecture that the company could not move into minicomputers without great difficulty.

It took six years of software development and three generations of Intel microcomputers for the IBM PC to catch up with the graphic interface standard that made the Apple Macintosh successful. Drawing on that experience, Apple wants to see more exclusionary standards operate in the United States. Lawrence G. Tesler of Apple put it quite frankly in a National Academy of Sciences colloquium:

> Japan and Korea do very well when they can find something that has been standardized, or create a standard and then leverage that to reduce costs, reduce prices, and gain market share and take the market away. . . . One thing that we have done is very carefully protect the insides of our computer, both the operating systems software and the hardware designs, so that they cannot be copied. We are very bothered by the fact that there are moves in the industry to try to standardize on those sorts of things, because we think . . . that is basically giving away the show to the competition from the Far East.[7]

It's an interesting theory, but one that will not succeed. Now that equivalent features are available, customers' demand for open systems will prevail over Apple's closed hand.

Raj Reddy, a professor of computer science at Carnegie Mellon University, argued for the importance of software over hardware. He said that closed architectures and operating systems make it hard to transfer application programs from one system to another, wasting the high-value effort of scarce programmers. "We should be standardizing routine things, including operating systems, and trying to use our creativity at higher levels."[8]

Be Cautious about Government Acquisition

The government is more successful when it sets out to buy things it needs than when it hires pure research for some vaguely defined goal. The classic example is the digital computer itself. The armed services needed to break codes, aim artillery shells, and design nuclear weapons. It hired researchers to build machines for those purposes. That some of the researchers later went into private industry to exploit the ideas they developed on the government dime was normal. That the ideas could be turned into useful commercial products was good luck, not planning.

When the Defense Department spent the 80s on a project to develop very high speed integrated circuits (VHSIC) it followed the wrong path. Instead of offering to pay a few thousand dollars per unit for chips of a certain impossible performance level, the VHSIC office went through a laborious multistage contract process, defining and refining the tools that would have to be invented and the technologies that would have to be applied. It

hired defense contractors to do the research, and to create production facilities for certain chips that would be incorporated into
new radars and other equipment, themselves designed in con-
junction with the VHSIC program.

After the expenditure of more than $100 million a year for 10
years, several defense contractors were able to make high-speed
computing chips in small quantities, tailor-made for sophisticated
defense gear. Meanwhile, on the outside, companies in the
United States and Japan had developed computing chips of comparable speed for mass production, at no cost to the government.
Defense contractors, however, find it more profitable to design
new custom VHSIC chips rather than to incorporate cheap chips
available at their local electronic distributor.

The government should not do research for the sake of American competitiveness—probably no one should. Funding researchers, though, is a different story. Science usually follows the
path of least resistance: picking the next lock, opening the next
door, unwrapping the next layer, digging the hole a little deeper.
Thus scientists acquire a feel for the things they want to work on,
in order to receive the positive reinforcement of success. The government is well suited to passing out money for the material and
labor of research, and it's well suited to resisting the lure of immediate profit. Money for university researchers may not always be
money well spent but it stands a good chance.

Don't Neglect Profits

The best indication of whether a technology is ready to come to
market is whether somebody thinks there's a profit to be made in
it. If that person exists, very little can effectively stand in his way.
If that person does not exist, few forces can drag the technology
out of the laboratory.

The loss of DRAM production to the Japanese is usually de-
plored as proof that the U.S. chip industry is becoming uncom-
petitive. The story is told as illustration that the cost of capital is
too high, or that the Japanese overproduce and dump in the
United States. While these things are true, the loss of DRAM production is most critically an illustration of the refusal of intelligent
American businessmen to sustain a loss for no reason.

Intel Vice Chairman Gordon Moore recalls that his company
had worked out the design and manufacturing methods for a
1Meg DRAM by mid-1985. That was a little too late to justify a

$400 million investment, especially in a market that already had too many producers. "Had we made the DRAM investment, we would be a much weaker company today," Moore told a colloquium of the Computer Science and Research Technology Board of the National Research Council.

"For a company to go into a business like that with the idea of making money frankly seems like a real folly," said Moore. "It is going to take something more than the usual market motivations to get a significant reentry in the United States."[9]

That "something more" has not yet been discovered. Various substitutes, which usually reduce to government subsidies and guarantees, have been offered, but they are fool's gold compared to real profits earned in a competitive marketplace.

Leave Commodities to Farmers

The United States spends from $10 billion to $30 billion a year on agricultural subsidies. The two biggest farm support programs are for wheat and corn. These products are textbook examples of commodities. They are mass produced, easily stored, indistinguishable units that are used to produce goods (bread and beef) for sale to the consumer. Why do we find it necessary to subsidize and stabilize production of these goods? Some would answer that it's not necessary. But if there's a good reason, it is to assure a comfortable level of overproduction, so that prices are stable and shortages rarely occur. What this does is lift the risks of bad weather and blight from the farmers, the bread bakers, and the cattle raisers while the taxpayers assume the risks of good weather and bumper crops. To hold the cost of the program down, the government then limits the acreage that can be planted, in a program always derided as paying the farmers to *not* grow wheat.

Is that what we want for a microchip market? Do we want a system that removes risk and shelters chip producers from boom and bust? Do we want a system that grades the playing field so level that everybody in the computer and telecommunications industry knows his cost for key components years in advance? Not if we want rapid technological progress, it isn't. The boom and bust economy in the computer and telecommunications industry increases the risk. The increased risk increases the rewards to winners. The high rewards to winners attract the high rollers who bring untried products to markets they hope to create.

Don't Mess with Markets

With the Persian Gulf crisis in the summer of 1990, there were renewed calls for America to achieve "energy independence." That idea played well in the 70s, but we should understand by now that there is no such thing as economic independence in an open international economy. Consider oil: if the United States produced enough oil to meet its needs, would that be sufficient to hold gasoline prices below the world price? Not without specific government action. In an open world economy with open commodity markets, U.S. oil producers sell to the highest bidder, foreign or domestic. Domestic prices quickly reach equilibrium with world prices.

With government action, such as price controls, there would be consequences, such as export smuggling, black market profiteering, and refusals to produce. As we should have learned in the 70s while sitting in long gas station lines, the supply disruptions would be worse than the price hikes.

Government action does succeed in holding domestic prices above world prices, using such methods as trade embargoes, quotas, and tariffs, but this is a strange, self-defeating form of independence.

Winning the Technology Race

There is no more important issue facing the United States in the 90s than winning the technology race. It is possible that more oil shocks and a recession may rock the delicately balanced U.S. Treasury, so that we spend the 90s trying to pay our bills. But even then, if we have to pay our bills we will have to use taxes, and that burden will not be so great if there are more profits and more income to tax. Stagnation is at least as debilitating as inflation in the weary combination of economic stagflation.

How we try to win is more important than whether we beat the competition. The United States can avoid economic stagnation by seeking economic efficiency. That means working at our most productive employment, whether that's teaching students to write new software, delivering the Chinese food that software writers eat, or running the software on workstations to analyze a fast-moving hostile takeover.

These 21st century service occupations lack respect and emotional resonance to many of us who live in the 20th century. But that does not make them less important than contemporary employment on an automobile assembly line, in a newspaper print shop, or at a Silicon Valley chip foundry.

It's a 20th century thing to divide the economy into manufacturing and service. Many of us believe manufacturing is good, productive, the prize in the race, because it produces stuff you can hold in your hand. But if we can reach a new level of maturity suited to the industries of the 21st century, we may understand that all economic activity is service: satisfying the needs of the customer.

The service occupations—and the inventiveness they demand—will be gaining in status over 20th century jobs, just as those manufacturing jobs grew in status, importance, and profit over 19th century extractive work such as mining and farming.

The adaptive process is likely to be insidious. You won't need to be expert in information, computing, and network technologies to live and function in the 21st century anymore than your grandmother needed to understand the chemistry of gasoline refining to live and function in the 20th century. On the other hand, if your grandmother was an up-and-coming woman who wanted to make something of herself in the new century, she needed to become comfortable with the energy, communications, and transportation technologies that transformed the world of her childhood. We will have to do the same for ourselves, and try to see to it that our children are ready to face an even greater pace of change.

Of course, when we speak of confronting the 21st century, we are kidding ourselves. We are speaking here of the 90s, leading into the first decade of the 21st century, perhaps to be known as the 'Oughts, or the 'Noughts, or the 'Zeros, or the 'Nulls. Most of the trends that will dominate the 21st century are as unknown to us as those of the 31st century. They will be established by people who are not born, based on technologies we cannot foresee. Let us not stand in their way.

Resilience

Americans have a substantial capacity for absorbing change and moving with the times. As Lewis Branscomb, director of the technology policy center at Harvard, observed at one of Sen. Albert Gore's subcommittee hearings, "We are beginning to notice that Nature rewards 'resilience' rather than strength or specialization."[10]

He says crises are nonlinear, meaning that they arrive at unpredicted times and present unpredicted challenges. Thus, he declares, "robust adaptability" is the only long-term successful strategy.

Donald N. Langenberg, chancellor of the University of Illinois and recent president of the American Association for the Advancement of Science, agreed: "The resilience of a species depends on its diversity. This nation's strength is in its ethnic, cultural, governmental (etc.) diversity. Even the diversity of having 50 states is an advantage. The object is to increase our options."[11]

The object is to increase our options.

So what is this technology race we are trying to help America to win? Is it a straight-line sprint on a race track, from these starting blocks to that tape 100 meters away? Hardly.

If the object is to increase our options, then the race course looks rather different. Imagine that we are in a deep valley, surrounded by mountains. No matter which way we go, we have to climb.

Notes

Notes

Notes

Chapter 1

1. Michael Abramowitz, "Broadcasters Woo with Crisper Shots," *Washington Post*, January 4, 1987, p. H1.

2. The basic technical information summarized here is presented in much greater detail by Robert Hoskins, "Advanced Television Systems," a paper written for the *IEEE Transactions on Consumer Electronics* 34, no. 1 (February 1988).

3. Bureau of the Census, *Statistical Abstract of the United States, 1990* (Washington, 1990), table 914, 1989 data.

4. Ibid., table 389, 1988 data.

5. Interview, June 1990.

6. "MUSE 6, PSI Drop Out," *Communications Daily*, June 4, 1990, p. 2.

7. Hearing before the Subcommittee on Telecommunications and Finance, October 8, 1987, Serial 100–188, GPO.

8. Interview, March 1989.

Chapter 2

1. This summary of HDTV technologies is based on a longer exposition by Barry Whalen and Mark Eaton of Microelectronics and Computer Technology Corp., an Austin, Texas, research consortium owned by 19 American high-tech companies, in a July 1989 letter to Sen. John Glenn.

2. "Economic Potential of Advanced Television Products," a study by Larry F. Darby, Darby Associates, as a consultant to the National Telecommunications and Information Administration, April 7, 1988.

3. "High Definition Television, Economic Analysis of Impact," by the ATV Task Force Economic Impact Team, AEA, November 1988.

4. Testimony to the Senate Commerce Committee, quoted in *Science*, May 19, 1989.

5. Congressional Budget Office, *The Scope of the HDTV Market* (Washington D.C.: Government Printing Office, June 1989), p. 6.

6. Reischauer statement to Senate Government Affairs Committee, August 1, 1989, p. 7.

Chapter 3

1. Hearing of the Subcommittee on Science and Technology, Senate Commerce, Science, and Transportation Committee, September 27–28, 1989.

2. Hearings of the Subcommittee on Telecommunciations and Finance, House Energy and Commerce Committee, October 8, 1987, p. 404.

Chapter 4

1. National Science Foundation report: "1989 Patterns of R&D Resources."

2. U.S. Congress, Office of Technology Assessment, *Making Things Better* (Washington, D.C.: GPO, February 1990), pp. 19–20, 28–30, and 184–95.

3. Ibid., p. 63.

4. James D. Watkins, "Commercialization of Technology," speech to associates of California Institute of Technology, October 5, 1990.

5. "Supercollider's Rising Cost Provokes Opposition," *New York Times*, May 29, 1990, C1.

6. Ibid.

7. *Science*, May 4, 1990, p. 541.

8. OTA, *Making Things Better*, p. 197.

Chapter 5

1. GAO, "The Research Tax Credit Has Stimulated Some Additional Research Spending," GGD-114, September 1989.

2. Federal Budget, FY 1991, p. A–71.

3. The data comes from the budget of the U.S. Government, FY 1991, p. A–49 ff.

4. GAO, "Value-Added Tax Issues for U.S. Tax Policymakers," GGD-89-125BR, September 1989.

5. "Tax Reform for Fairness, Simplicity, and Economic Growth," also known as Treasury I, November 1984.

6. William Farley, "How to Make Raising Money Cheaper," *New York Times*, December 24, 1989, section 3, p. 2.

7. Hearing of House Judiciary Committee's Subcommittee on Economic and Commercial Law, September 28, 1989.

8. Robert A. Blecker, "Are Americans on a Consumption Binge? The Evidence Reconsidered," pamphlet published by Economic Policy Institute, Washington, D.C., April 1990.

9. Testimony March 5, 1990, as reprinted in an American Council for Capital Formation broadside.

10. Maggie Mahar, "Paper Dragons," *Barron's*, August 27, 1990, p. 16.

Chapter 6

1. Hatsopoulos, "High Cost of Capital Revisited," a paper presented at the NAE Symposium, April 5, 1990.

2. Ibid.

3. William Farley "How To Make Raising Money Cheaper," *New York Times*, December 24, 1989, section 3, p. 2.

4. Statistical Abstract, table 1392.

5. March 20, 1990, speech at the Institute of International Economics, and subsequent interview. Reich also lays out these ideas in a *Harvard Business Review* article in the January-February 1990 issue.

6. "International Productitivy Service," *International Productivity Journal*, Spring 1990.

7. Bill Cunningham, "Don't Blame U.S. Uncompetitiveness on Wages," *The Wall Street Journal*, November 29, 1989, p. A-14.

8. See William J. Baumol, Sue Anne Batey Blackman, and Edward N. Wolff, *Productivity and American Leadership* (Cambridge, Mass.: MIT Press, 1989).

Chapter 7

1. Michael Porter, *The Competitive Advantage of Nations* (New York: The Free Press, 1990), p. 724.

Chapter 8

1. In this treatment of the early days of computer technology, I have summarized what I learned from the Smithsonian Institution's marvelous presentation, and from Kenneth Flamm, In *Creating the*

Computer (Washington, D.C.: Brookings, 1988); T. R. Reid, in *The Chip*, (New York: Simon & Schuster, 1984); Robert Sobel, in *IBM, Colossus in Transition* (New York: Times Books, 1981); and John Hendry, in *Innovating for Failure* (Cambridge, Mass.: MIT Press, 1989). They are not, of course, responsible for my oversimplifications of their work.

2. Flamm, *Creating the Computer*, p. 78.

3. Sobel, *IBM: Colossus in Transition*, p. 128.

Chapter 9

1. Sobel, *IBM: Colossus in Transition*, p. 224.

Chapter 10

1. Intel ad accompanying "The IK-bit DRAM," *IEEE Spectrum*, 25th Anniversary Issue, November 1988.

2. Quoted by Brian Santo in "The IK-bit DRAM," *IEEE Spectrum*, 25th Anniversary Issue, November 1988.

3. Peter H. Lewis, "Chips for the Year 2000," *New York Times*, June 19, 1990, p. C 8.

4. *Science*, June 8, 1990.

5. Interview with DARPA official who requested anonymity, September 1989.

6. Jack Kuehler, testimony before the Subcommittee on Economic and Commercial Law, House Judiciary Committee, September 28, 1989.

7. "A Strategic Industry at Risk, a Report to the President and Congress for the National Advisory Committee on Semiconductors," November 1989.

8. Perkin-Elmer financial meeting text, April 21, 1989.

9. Interview, September 1989.

10. Larry Armstrong, "Designer Chips While You Wait," *Business Week*, August 28, 1989, p. 848.

Chapter 11

1. M. L. Lepselter & S. M. Sze, "DRAM Pricing Trends—The Pi Rule," *IEEE Circuits and Devices Magazine*, January 1985, p. 53.

Chapter 12

1. "The Japanese Success Formula: Quality Equals the Competitive Edge," in Quality Control: Japan's Key to High Productivity, a seminar conducted by the Electronic Industries Assn. of Japan, Washington DC, March 25, 1980.

2. Ibid., p. 20, also Jacques Gansler, "The Changing Emphasis on Manufacturing," a speech to the Society of Manufacturing Engineers, November 1, 1988.

3. Deming, quoted in Reid, *The Chip*.

4. EIAJ Quality Control Seminar, p. 7.

5. EIAJ Seminar, p. 9.

6. OTA, *Making Things Better*.

7. Ibid.

8. Ibid.

9. Interview, February 1987.

Chapter 13

1. Michiyuki Uenohara, Takuo Sugano, John G. Linvill, and Franklin B. Weinstein, "Background," in *Competitive Edge: The Semiconductor Industry in the U.S. and Japan*, ed. Daniel I. Okimoto, Takuo Sugano, and Franklin B. Weinstein (Stanford, Calif.: Stanford University Press, 1984), p. 31.

2. Dempa, October 14, 1975, quoted in "Japanese Market Barriers in Microelectronics," a report published by the Semiconductor Industry Assn., June 14, 1985.

3. Okimoto, Sugano, and Weinstein, *Competitive Edge*, p. 211.

4. House Ways & Means Committee, *Overview and Compilation of U.S. Trade Statutes*, 1989 edition, (Washington, DC: GPO, September 1989).

5. In Okimoto, Sugano, and Weinstein, *Competitive Edge*, p. 223.

6. Howard Gruenspecht, letter to the editor, *The Wall Street Journal*, June 8, 1989.

7. Gruenspecht, letter to the editor.

8. *Washington Post*, March 1, 1988, p. A-19.

9. Interview; the official asked for anonymity.

10. Many Japanese articles are cited in Kenneth Flamm, "Policy and Politics in the International Semiconductor Industry," presented to the SEMI ISS Seminar, Newport Beach, Calif., January 16, 1989, pp. 9–16.

11. Interview, May 1990.

12. Flamm, "Policy and Politics," p. 19.

Chapter 14

1. Interview, February 1990.

2. Interview, February 1990.

3. The three quotations are from a Semiconductor Industry Assn. press release dated June 21, 1989.

4. *The Wall Street Journal,* June 22, 1989, p. 1.

5. Flamm, "Policy and Politics," p. 23–24.

6. *Electronic News,* January 22, 1990, p. 1.

7. Ibid.

8. Ibid.

9. *Electronic News,* July 31, 1989, p. 1.

10. *Electronic News,* January 22, 1990, p. 1.

11. *New York Times,* January 18, 1990, p. D1.

12. *Economist,* February 3, 1990, p. 66.

13. *The Wall Street Journal,* January 12, 1990.

14. Interview, June 1990.

Chapter 15

1. William D. Metz, "Midwest Computer Architect Struggles with Speed of Light," *Science,* January 27, 1978, pp. 404–9.

2. "Computer Model Flagged Problem," *Washington Post,* May 23, 1990, p. A-18.

3. "Money Is the Means, Not the End," *Forbes,* November 15, 1975, p. 30.

4. Ibid.

5. Metz, "Midwest Computer Architect," p. 404.

6. "Knowing a Good Thing," *Forbes,* June 26, 1978, p. 101.

7. "Cray, King of the Giant Processors," *Business Week,* October 29, 1979, p. 156.

8. Cray 8-K filing with SEC, November 1, 1989.

9. Interview, February 1990.

Chapter 16

1. U.S. Congress, Office of Technology Assessment, *High Performance Computing and Networking for Science* (Washington: GPO, September 1989), OTA-BP-CIT-59.

2. SDSC Annual Report for 1988.

3. Science Highlights 1988, a report of the National Center for Supercomputing Applications, University of Illinois, Urbana.

4. SDSC report derived from *Supercomputing Review* 1, 38, 1988.

5. SDSC Annual Report for 1988.

6. *Esprit,* a publication of the Commission of the European Community, cited in OTA's *High Performance Computing and Networking.*

Chapter 17

1. Michael B. Smith, letter to the editor, *Washington Post*, April 25, 1989, p. A 14.

2. Interview, February 1990.

3. Nobuyuki Oishi, "Computer Makers Shut Out of U.S.," *Japan Economic Journal*, October 6, 1990, p. 14.

4. "Cray to Deliver Super Computer to Tohuku University," Jiji Press Ticker Service, October 18, 1990.

5. Oishi, "Computer Makers."

6. Jeffrey Bairstow, "Redefine Desktop Computing," *High Technology Magazine*, March 1987, p. 18.

Chapter 18

1. These Hillis quotes are drawn from a presentation to an IEEE Briefing on Supercomputers, October 1989.

2. Harry E. Plumblee, Jr., "Massively Parallel Computing," *Horizons*, Lockheed Co. #28, January 1990, p. 33.

3. Irving Wladawsky-Berger and Marjory S. Blumenthal, *Issues in Science and Technology*, Spring 1989, p. 48.

Chapter 19

1. Interview, January 1990.

2. D. Allan Bromley, testimony before the House Subcommittee on Science, Research, and Technology, October 3, 1989.

3. Randolph B. Smith, "Future Shock," *The Wall Street Journal*, March 15, 1990, p. 1.

Chapter 20

1. Interview, March 1987.

2. Interview, August 1989.

3. "Keeping the Computer Industry Competitive," a colloquium report by the Computer Science and Technology Board, Commission on Physical Sciences, Mathematics, and Resources, National Research Council, National Academy Press, Washington, D.C., 1990.

Chapter 21

1. "The UNIX System Oral History Project," by Michael S. Mahoney, a historian of science at Princeton University, obtained from Bell Labs.

2. W. Russell Neuman, testimony before the House Telecommunications Subcommittee, October 4, 1989.

3. D. Allan Bromley, testimony before the House Subcommittee on Science, Research, and Technology, Oct. 3, 1989.

4. Senate Subcommittee on Science, Technology, and Space, June 21, 1989.

5. Robert W. Lucky, testimony before the House Telecommunications Subcommittee, Oct. 4, 1989.

6. David C. Walden, testimony before the House Telecommunications Subcommittee, Oct. 4, 1989.

7. Hearing of Senate Science Subcommittee, May 17, 1990.

8. Ibid.

Chapter 22

1. White House Office of Science and Technology Policy, *The Federal High Performance Computing Program*, September 8, 1989.

2. Robert W. Lucky, testimony before the House Telecommunications Subcommittee, Oct. 4, 1989.

3. Alan Chynoweth, testimony, Oct. 4, 1989.

4. Lucky testimony, October 4, 1989.

Chapter 23

1. Stewart Brand, *The Media Lab: Inventing the Future at MIT* (New York: Penguin Books, 1988), p. 19.

2. W. Russell Neuman, testimony before the House Telecommunications Subcommittee, October 1989.

3. Ithiel de Sola Pool, *Technologies of Freedom* (Cambridge: the Belknap Press of Harvard University, 1986), p. 226.

4. See several articles in *Byte*, July 1, 1990, including "Reach Out and Touch Your Data," by Howard Eglowstein, and "Computing without Keyboards" by Paul McAvinney.

5. G. Pascal Zachary, "Artificial Reality," *The Wall Street Journal*, January 23, 1990, p. A-1.

6. Ibid.

7. David Sheff, "The Virtual Realities of Timothy Leary," *Upside Magazine*, April 1990, p. 30.

8. Sherrie van Tyle, "The Promise and the Power of Hypertext," *Electronics Magazine*, Feburary 1, 1990, p. 104.

9. See for example, "The CD-ROM Connection," by Tim Oren of Apple in *Byte*, December 1988.

Chapter 24

1. "A Nation At Risk," report of the National Commission on Excellence in Education, 1983.

2. Michael J. McLaughlin, "High School Dropouts: How Much of a Crisis?" *Backgrounder*, No. 781, Heritage Foundation, Washington, D.C.

3. "Foreign and Foreign-Born Engineers in the United States: Infusing Talent, Raising Issues," National Reasearch Council, National Academy Press, 1988.

4. "Meeting the Needs of a Growing Economy: The CORETECH Agenda for the Scientific and Technical Workforce." Council on Research and Technology, Washington, 1989.

5. Press conference, December 1989.

6. Bill Emmott, *The Sun Also Sets* (New York: Random House, 1989), p. 70.

7. "Keeping the U.S. Computer Industry Competitive: Defining the Agenda." A Colloquium Report. National Academy Press, Washington, 1990.

8. Ibid.

9. "Keeping the U.S. Computer Industry Competitive: Defining the Agenda." A Colloquium Report. National Academy Press, 1990.

10. Lewis Branscomb, testimony at a Hearing of Senate Subcommittee on Science, Technology, and Space, September 28, 1989.

11. Donald N. Langenberg, testimony. Hearing, September 28, 1989.

Index

/ 27829